The Low Countries

Cover:
Lynne Leegte, *Untitled* (detail), 2015
Piezographic print on paper, 81 x 37.5 cm
© Lynne Leegte

TLC

2016 The Low Countries

ARTS AND SOCIETY IN FLANDERS AND THE NETHERLANDS

VTOPIAE INSVLAE FIGVRA

24

Published by
the Flemish-Dutch
cultural institution
Ons Erfdeel vzw

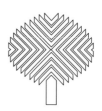

Contents

'**Read it: it doesn't say what it says.**'

Chronicle

Next page:
Lynne Leegte, *Flight*, 2012.
Treated paper, each page is 30 x 40 cm
Collection Doopsgezinde Singelkerk, Amsterdam © Lynne Leegte

On page 112-113:
Lynne Leegte, *Torn*, 2015.
Ultra chrome print / diasec, 90 x 140 cm
© Lynne Leegte

Black Pudding and Cheese?

'Read it: it doesn't say what it says.'

'In the soaring, soberly furnished hidden church (1639) of the Mennonite congregation on the Singel in Amsterdam a book lies open on the pulpit. Pages flutter as if playfully caught up by the wind to be suspended frozen in the air. Time seems to stand still.'

You'll find this quote on Lynne Leegte's website, beneath the first of the three works comprising the project titled *Flight*, which you can see opposite. The book lying open can only be the Dutch Authorized Bible, the cornerstone of the culture of words in the young Republic of the seventeenth century. In the North people read God's Word and even interpreted it; the Word emancipated them. In the Catholic South the Book usually remained closed; people tiptoed around it.

Timeo hominem unius libri is an ambiguous warning. Beware those who swear by one book. Or is it just the opposite? A person with a thorough knowledge of one book, one author is the one to fear because of the depth of his knowledge.

In 1993 Dutch literature was, for the first time, the guest of honour at the *Frankfurter Buchmesse*, the biggest book fair in the world. This year it will again be the guest of honour, which is unique. It is not a nation state but a language that links this literature, written in Flanders, the Netherlands and the 'warmer parts of the kingdom' such as Suriname and the Antilles.

Blessed are a language that is spoken and a literature that is written in different countries. They can only be enriched by it.

There are many clichés doing the rounds about the different characteristics of Dutch language and literature in the North and the South. Apparently minimalism is prized in the North. Writing there is sober and accurate. In the South, on the other hand, extravagance - linguistic diversity and impurity, mannerism - is said to be rife. The critic Kees Fens once used the metaphor of black pudding and cheese to characterise the literature of Flanders and the Netherlands.

But the truth is more nuanced.

In five substantial essays in this yearbook we take stock of the most important literary genres in the Low Countries today: poetry, prose, essays and non-fiction, children's and young adult literature, the art of illustration, comics and graphic novels.

We sing the praises of language, the raw material of all the writers who use it. We give a platform to translators, the ultimate carriers, for they journey back and forth not only between languages but between cultures. What a paradox that the more successful their work, the more they disappear behind the text, the more we forget them. After all, as Umberto Eco once remarked, the language of Europe is translation.

To round it all off we suggest a canon, a clear choice of the books that matter in Dutch literature, from an amorous eleventh-century lament to Harry Mulisch and Hugo Claus. It is a canon that is intended as an invitation not as an imposition. A canon is, after all, always the conversation, the discussion about the canon.

In this book you will also find illustrations of people reading, in all forms, attitudes and formats, caught in all sorts of places. Those who read withdraw, absorbed into a parallel universe, to emerge again changed.

Finally, I am delighted to announce that at the opening of the 68th *Frankfurter Buchmesse* on 19 October 2016 we shall make all the articles about Dutch literature, the oeuvre sections, book reviews and translations of prose fragments and poetry that have appeared in the 23 editions of *The Low Countries* yearbook available via open access for interested readers (see www.onserfdeel.be/en).

Tolle et lege. Take and read. For this is a treasure trove.

LUC DEVOLDERE | *Chief Editor*

The STATE of the UNION

Poetry
Prose
Essays
Children's Books
Comic Strips and Graphic Novels

How Free Is Dutch-Language Poetry?

[PIET GERBRANDY]

The word is free. Like Gezelle's swift it soars through the immeasurable space of the mind, lifted up or blown along by cool or sultry winds from distant parts, by 'Luft von anderem Planeten', as Stefan George has it. Nothing and no one can thwart its vitality and urge to freedom, however much social institutions, small-minded moralism, money or terror try to subjugate it. The poet's soul is linked to an origin that no church or chancellery will ever domesticate.

I know, this is romantic enthusiasm in which I only half believe myself. Perhaps it is more an ideal to strive for, a benchmark to hold on to desperately, because without faith in the possibility and sense of creativity we might just as well shut up shop. And why should poetry have the best papers to claim the domain of total freedom for its own, rather than music, theatre, film or sculpture? Because it needs nothing but a thinking brain and a hand that can hold a pencil? No money is involved with poetry, the poet needs no studio, he doesn't need to hire an orchestra or acquire a camera. And because he knows from the outset that 'little profit' is to be expected from poetry, as the poet of Beatrijs puts it, he doesn't put his energy into marketing strategies. In short, even if you approach poetry from an economic perspective, it should able to move among people unimpeded, like breath, light or pheromones.

Yet this vision is also too romantic. Behoud de Begeerte, the Poet Laureate, Poetry International, the VSB Poetry Prize, Perdu, Nooit meer slapen, the School der Poëzie, *De Standaard*, the Herman de Coninck Prize, the *Poëziekrant*, De Bezige Bij, the Tuinfeest in Deventer, Uitgeverij P., De Wintertuin, the Poet Laureate of Antwerp, the Writers' Professional School, *De Morgen*, The Netherlands Poetry Centre, *De Gids*, the World Slampionship, *Menander*, the Turing Prize, the Foundation for Literature – I could continue this list effortlessly for at least another page, there are so many agencies that concern themselves intensively or even exclusively with poetry. For about the past ten years every self-respecting town or city has had a Poet Laureate, poems grace walls in Leiden and pavements in Leeuwarden, scores of Dutch and Flemish publishing houses bring out at least two metres of poetry collections a year, every month there is a festival somewhere, no exhibition is complete without an obligatory poet. Although I suspect that the total sum circulating in the sector would make

any bank manager or consultant chuckle, it is also clear that poets also form part of the commercial circuit – and at a time that, so they say, is plagued with financial crises. Do they actually still exist, the poets who retreat into their hut or garret to devote themselves exclusively to words? More than that, have there ever been such poets?

Untitled, 2001,
Acrylic, acrylmedium on paper,
31.7 x 42.2 cm

No centre anymore

Anyone reviewing the landscape of the Dutch-language poetry of the last few years is bound to note that it is flourishing, that it is characterised by an enormously multifaceted structure and that, considering its negligible economic importance, its virtually complete disappearance from education and the low level of social relevance usually attributed to it, it is extraordinarily visible. Of course, there are different circuits and one poet is more successful than another, but a thousand voices can be heard, and they are well looked after. What does this mean for what all those poets have got to say? Does *anything goes* imply that unknown vistas are actually being explored? To what extent are people aware that they are imbedded in social and economic structures? And are globalisation, ecological disasters, Islamist barbarity and unsustainable migration making their influence felt on an art form that could afford to be as free as the ancient song of the thrush?

Untitled, 2001,
Acrylic, acrylmedium on paper,
22.2 x 29.9 cm

True freedom is an illusion. Moreover, resistance and limitations force one to be inventive and creative. Where everything is possible and permissible there is no point to anything. Goethe rightly observes: 'In der Beschränkung zeigt sich erst der Meister, / Und das Gesetz nur kann uns Freiheit geben.' If I look at the Dutch poets who really count at the moment, I see that they are struggling with the limiting frameworks imposed on them by human nature, by socio-economic factors and by the supposed laws of literature itself. In this respect their situation is not basically different from that of all other poets in world literature, but they do look for new forms for it.

However, it is not that easy to establish which poets can at this moment be included among the grandmasters. In recent years a number of undisputed leading lights have been lost to us: Hugo Claus (1929-2008), Rutger Kopland (1934-2012), Gerrit Kouwenaar (1923-2014), Leo Vroman (1915-2014) and H.H. ter Balkt (1938-2015). Of living poets who have won the major prizes, none has the stature to hold a candle to the aforementioned icons. Leonard Nolens (1947), Anneke Brassinga (1948), Tonnus Oosterhoff (1953) and Nachoem M. Wijnberg (1961), for example, are regarded as good poets, but do not really stand out from the scores of others by whom a collection occasionally appears. Probably that has less to do with quality than with the fact that poetry no longer has a centre. We no longer think in hierarchical patterns and, apart from that, poetry criticism has gradually shifted from its fixed place in authoritative dailies to the diffuse world of the web. Consequently I don't think Claus and Kouwenaar will have successors, and perhaps that is just as well. If I mention a few names below that I consider of importance, it is a fairly arbitrary selection from an overwhelming choice.

In the shadow of tradition

Tonnus Oosterhoff is known as an innovator. He was the first poet of repute to begin experimenting with the possibilities of digital poetry. On his website poems appear that change shape as one reads them, as if to stress the provisional nature of every statement. In some of his collections he disturbed the typography of his poems by adding notes in his own handwriting, as if the reader had only a rough version in his hands. However revolutionary these formal procedures may be, they cannot hide the fact that Oosterhoff's themes are overwhelmingly traditional, because he writes about loss, transience and futility. The final poem of *Wij zagen ons in een kleine groep mensen veranderen* (We Saw Ourselves Change into a Small Group of People, 2002), in itself a title that evokes the omnipresence of death, seems to achieve a harsh departure from both language and life. 'Go on,' he says, 'demolish this house / Use my pneumatic hammer'. If in the second stanza there is still talk of a summer barbecue, a little later it is already autumn and a storm is brewing. The text is presented as a still fragmentary whole to which a few suggestions have been added by hand. For example, the third stanza ends with the printed letters 'ades', preceded by three possible words to fill in, two of which are legible enough to give 'galoppades' and 'Hades'. When at the bottom of the poem a deeply religious song is quoted three times, 'Ach wie nichtig, ach wie flüchtig' ('Ah how insubstantial, ah how fleeting') it is as clear as day that in terms of content Oosterhoff has little to add to Sappho, Horace and J.C. Bloem. He is aware of the limited scope of the mayflies that we are.

Runa Svetlikova (1982), who was awarded the Herman de Coninck Prize for the best debut in Flanders, also produced a collection, *This Soft White Room*, in which the fragility of both the world and human existence is central. The book is structured in an idiosyncratic way, referring to recent scientific research, and here and there cultivates a certain casualness in style, but what she is speaking about is located in the all-too-familiar terrain of love and death. In one of the best poems a child is born: 'Every birth is an infectious wound / so I don't hold it right up against me,' reads the opening. Then the 'thing materialised in my arms' is regarded with disbelief, when the young parents realise that something has been produced 'with at least as great a capacity / for horror as we have'. Once they get home 'we lay it carefully between us: as if this child / could detonate at any moment'. It is a feeling that many mothers and fathers will recognize: that you have brought something into the world that on the one hand is a part of yourself, but on the other hand an alien being that you will never be able to fathom.

Svetlikova allows herself the freedom to create her own universe, but the elementary building blocks have been established for thousands of years – or actually since the Big Bang. The first poem in the collection is called 'A Big Bang' and begins with the sober observation:

> Nothing more is needed than distance to see us as we are
> the growth and dying off of temporary structures, light
> in the darkness in the light we grow in all directions, proliferate

In the last poem, 'The Big Rewind – Revisited', the cycle of expansion and contraction is complete, perhaps ready to start again: 'we all fall back into the same bang. There is only beginning – '. Not only these themes, but also the fact that the duration of the universe coincides with the course of the collection itself, so that the cosmological layer acquires a metapoetical layer, are traditional through and through.

Refugee camps should preferably be on the horizon

Other poets focus on the way in which mankind has ordered the world. It is not only scientific laws that determine our scope, we are also governed by structures and concepts that we have produced ourselves. Political activism may be rare in Dutch-language poetry, but that by no means implies that the alarming reality of racism, terror and environmental devastation do not appear as themes. In 'Wwwwwhoooooshh', the last poem in *The Herald of Something Great* (2006), Dirk van Bastelaere sketches a modern dystopia which he constantly interrupts with quotes from a German work on political systems: *'Der Faschismus an der Macht ist / die äußerste Systemsicherung in äußersten Krisenlagen / des monopolbestimmten Kapitalismus.'*
Then he writes:

> Begin again with the sun, which is sailing to nowhere, a pure event, a catastrophe with no quarter given or 'powerful voice'. No religion is involved. No anthropomorphism. 'In four billion years' time your phenomenology and utopian politics will be dead and there will be no one to sound or hear the death knell.' Nature ignores our existence, that much is clear. The only remaining question is whether here and now you have a sore throat, stroke her shaved mons Veneris, smell petrol vapour, feed the cats or like Harrison Ford in Blade Runner are uncertain about your 'life'.

So even in the poetry of Van Bastelaere, heavily charged with political theory, the cosmological perspective is not missing.

That also applies to the work of Mustafa Stitou (1974). In *Pig-Pink Postcards* (2003) he depicts a soulless new estate, where, despite the cheerful ideology of progress and financial security, suspicion and petty-mindedness rule:

Here pioneers are little shits or criminals

and those who can't be categorised go
in a separate box – parlours teem
with rumours about a paedophile neighbour

and refugee camps should preferably
be seen on the horizon, in that way one can tell
the good from the black.

The series in which these lines occur, has an epistemological as well as an anthropological tenor, since the poet speaks several times of 'underlying what shows itself, / what shows itself what shows itself'. How knowable is the world? That is not exactly a new question. The fact that Stitou is fond of his classics also emerges when we see that this series is made up of tercets. Suburbia is hell, that much is clear.

Familiar rhythms

For a third group of poets it is precisely those ancient literary conventions that limit the freedom of poetry. With a degree of self-mockery Leonard Nolens looks back at his period of *Sturm und Drang*, which has produced depressingly little new. That can indeed be seen from the form of his poems, on which a well-tried rhetorical order has been imposed:

> *We rewrote Athens, Schubert and Rembrandt*
> *In the tongue of our vanished home region.*
> *We wrote theses on our personal pathos.*
> *We gave our heart a degree.*
> *We gained doctorates in lyricism.*
> *We set our sights on many forward positions*
> *Without status. We couldn't find our feet.*

Our feet, says Nolens, searched for a point of attachment in 'the thread of old traditions'. No wonder that Nolens' poetry is so popular: readers feel at home in familiar rhythms.

Mirrorbook, 2006,
Acrylic, acrylmedium on paper,
16.9 x 24.2 cm

However, there are also a few young poets who are actually campaigning to ditch literary tradition. The most interesting of them is undoubtedly Maarten van der Graaff (1987), who in 2014 won the Buddingh' Prize for the best Dutch-language debut. In *Getaway Car Poems* he cheerfully dispatches his predecessors.

> *I saw Rutger Kopland hunting in blind panic for that and that*
> *poem. Tonnus Oosterhoff may die amazingly early,*
> *or he'll die on the motorway with a dog in the boot.*
> *Jules Deelder must die on the platform.*
> *H.H. ter Balkt will be standing weeing by the side of the road*
> *and then it will happen. Not like he has lived, because dying that way*
> *is sentimental and besides that a lie.*
> *Duinker doesn't get anything and grows old.*
> *Whistling he receives the Dutch Literature Prize.*

Van der Graaff sees the traditional forms as passé, and enjoys sowing confusion, but his personal commitment is great. He could grow into a poet of great stature.

Yet not even Van der Graaff rejects the possibility of assigning meaning. He is sharp and rebellious, but his world is ours. With Marc Kregting (1965), even meaning and coherence sometimes go out of the window. In *Our Nietzsche. Catechisms* (2014) he appears to juxtapose separate sentences haphazardly. True, the text is constructed in such a way that after a while you start to discover leitmotivs, but the whole radically resists interpretation. Surprisingly enough this chaos is not only highly amusing, but even has a conjuring effect. That comes from the rhythmic effect of the separate sentences and the sound repetitions with which they are linked together, which ensure that the text does not disintegrate at the auditory level. This is an arbitrary fragment:

> *Apart from that our Nietzsche has nothing to complain about after going bankrupt. The clocks can be restarted with relief. Where is the inspector? You mustn't cycle without a G-string. The almighty cannot bear that. That will cost her a reprimand from behind. Does that smell like an extra round of Paris Camembert? And are you coming in? 'Tolerance is conditional, elaborate, anxious hospitality,' says Jacques.*

Despite destroying most aspects which have made poetry poetry for the last few centuries, Kregting maintains precisely the principal element that underlies the poetic experience, and that is its physical manifestation. Language without semantic coherence continues to fascinate, as long as it is supported by sound and rhythm.

Untitled, 2006,
Acrylic, acrylmedium on paper,
18.5 x 28.6 cm

The age of one-sided movements has gone

Dutch-language poetry, in short, is multifaceted, alive and well. Its social im-beddedness may have changed, the advent of the internet has created new op-portunities for publication, old forms are adapted or rejected, 'the age of one-sided movements has gone', to quote Lucebert. But ultimately poets are still doing what they have always done, with the freedom and the limitations which also characterise the flight of the swift and the song of the thrush. That is a hopeful thought. ■

Translated by Paul Vincent

Dutch and Flemish Prose of the Early Twenty-First Century

[MATTHIJS DE RIDDER]

When the twin towers came crashing down on 11 September 2001, so did the post-modern belief in the end of the 'grand narratives', which had all but dominated Dutch and Flemish literature in the 1990s. Or so it seemed. The era-changing event certainly brought about a new sense of historical awareness, provoking novels that grappled with the hubris of the preceding decade. Set in the 1990s, Marja Brouwers's *Casino* (2004), for instance, tells the story of a critical, albeit suggestive journalist who enjoys a summer of carefree joy in the Mediterranean on a friend's expensive yacht. Each time the protagonist's moral compass starts to tilt a little (shouldn't they come to the rescue of a sinking refugee boat heading for Lampedusa?) his conscience is soothed by the promise of sex, luxury and a free mansion in Amsterdam. A couple of years later, the journalist slowly awakens from the dream in which he has been living. While researching an undercover operation, in which the Dutch government tried to bust drug organizations by itself acting as a drug dealer (the so-called IRT affair), he discovers that his own life has been funded with dirty money all along. He wants to be outraged, he even wishes to re-instate the old categories of right and wrong, but he knows he is complicit in the crime.

After 9/11 it was clear to many people that a new era had begun, yet it proved very difficult to start with a clean slate. Though a lot of writers felt the need to descend from their ivory towers, so to speak, and shed their light on recent events, it still seemed impossible to go back to the time of all-encompassing philosophies. Awoken by the disenchanting incidents in recent times and in dire need of clarity or even 'truth', many a protagonist became tangled up in ever more complex fictions. This is the surprising plot of Désanne van Brederode's novel *Mensen met een hobby* (People with Hobbies, 2001). Its protagonist Lilly finds the fact that grand narratives have lost their validity has not led to a society that felt uprooted or in any way insecure. People simply focus on their own small narratives, or 'hobbies' as Lilly's boyfriend Tom calls them. While she wittily bemoans the *Cosmopolitan* etiquettes and homegrown philosophies that structure the lives of her acquaintances and artist friends, Lilly gradually embraces the philosophy of an obscure Danish thinker, planning her every move according to his moral system. When this philosopher turns out to be invented,

Reading causes ageing of the skin

gone is her refreshing opinionated self-confidence. Her whole endeavour has proven to be nothing but a hobby.

Not all hobbies or small narratives turned out to be so devastatingly futile. The beginning of the twenty-first century saw the birth of various small-time heroes, who tackled their marginal existences in their wee narratives, gradually turning them into tales of grand(er) proportions. In Annelies Verbeke's *Slaap!* (*Sleep!* 2003), the sleepless protagonist goes through a rough period. When she finally comes to her senses, she finds herself on the beach, where she is reborn, rapidly reliving all stages of human evolution. Dimitri Verhulst's *De helaasheid der dingen* (*The Misfortunates*, 2006) introduces the reader to a cast of colourful people, who, while living a life of liquor and licentiousness, imagine they are on top of the world. Likewise, the brawling and bantering heroes of P.F. Thomése's *J. Kessels, The Novel* (2009) manage to turn their absurd quest into a return to the Garden of Eden, or in their case the 'Snack Bar of Yore'. And even the story of a rival band of school buddies in Tommy Wieringa's picaresque novel *Joe Speedboot* (*Joe Speedboat*, 2005), on second glance turns out to be a clever retelling of the Apocalypse.

Whereas most of these extrapolations of the characters' misfortunes are fairly harmless for society at large, in his quest for a better understanding of things, Jörgen Hofmeester, the protagonist of Arnon Grunberg's novel *Tirza* (2006), constructs a fantasy that proves to be as delusional as it is dangerous. Hofmeester has never been very successful in life, but a combination of a frugal attitude and a high-risk hedge fund keep him afloat during the nineties.

Reading is highly addictive, don't start

A couple of weeks after 9/11, however, his carefully constructed *Dutch dream* goes up in smoke. Desperately trying to find an explanation, he soon identifies the perpetrator:

> History, he feared, was getting personal now. The anonymous world economy had gotten a face, a body, a name. Mohammed Atta, he was the one who stole Hofmeester's money, his financial independence, his children's freedom, which was almost within reach, almost within reach. Mohammed Atta was to blame, Atta had decapitated Hofmeester's hedge fund.

A couple of weeks later, his precious daughter Tirza introduces Hofmeester to her Moroccan boyfriend, Choukri. Hofmeester, at this point completely delusional, is sure he recognizes Choukri as his nemesis: 'Mohammed Atta is in my home. Atta has arisen.' He then vows to rid the earth of the man he holds to be the infamous terrorist.

Atta is but a figment of Hofmeester's imagination. Gradually, however, his ever more crippling fantasy becomes exemplary for the way in which the western world reacted to the 9/11 attacks. With his deceptive tale, Grunberg shows that the world had not become more dangerous because of the sudden rise of a ruthless agitator, but because of the fact that the West itself got stuck in a blinding narrative in which Evil had to be met with even bigger Evil, allegedly for the sake of civilisation.

In search of a new grand narrative, more than one fictional character discovered that the theorists of post-modernism might have had a point when they stated that reality was unknowable. Despite claims to the contrary, at the turn of the century writers didn't simply turn their backs on post-modern principles – in many cases they merely employed them differently. Instead of representing the world as an endless patchwork of tales and images, writers often subjected 'reality' to apparent 'truths', which had a tendency to complicate matters even further.

Whereas novels tended to be more straightforward in terms of story line and structure than in preceding years, in many cases they explicitly challenged history. In *De heldeninspecteur* (*The Hero Inspector*, 2010), Atte Jongstra tells the story of a Dutch officer during the Belgian revolution of 1830 and the subsequent Ten Days' Campaign of 1831. This man has the daunting task of assessing the exploits of his fellow soldiers. Impressionable as well as near-sighted, he re-writes history as it happens. In his *Canada Trilogy* (1999-2006) Pol Hoste delves into the confusion of tongues known as world history. The main character of Koen Peeters's *Grote Europese roman* (Great European Novel, 2007), meanwhile, tries to capture the essence of the abstract concept of Europe. He travels to all the political, financial and administrative hubs of the continent. Along the way, however, he finds that the heart of Europe isn't to be found in Brussels or Strasbourg, but in Auschwitz and Mauthausen. These are the places where history speaks of terrifying, but real human emotions. Set in the Cold War's heyday, Marc Reugebrink's *Het grote uitstel* (The Great Delay, 2007) features a band of characters that also have a hard time reducing their political disputes to more human proportions. Political theories are flying high, but in the end the heated discussions aren't really satisfying. They are going to change the world, the characters say, and they are going to make love, that as well, but their climaxes – politically as well as sexually – are endlessly postponed, until, in the end, nothing really appears to have happened. And finally, in Jeroen Olyslaegers's diabolical novel *Wij* (We, 2009), 1970s' Flemish nationalism

Books contain
ideas, insults,
opinions and
provocations

is portrayed as an ideology awakening to the fact that it cannot reside in the realm of ideas forever. The choice is a daunting one: either realize the long-standing demands by force, or commercialize the main ideas in light entertainment and popular song form.

The limits of literary fiction

Telling disrupting tales – one could say this is one of literature's more exciting tasks. But is it all literature can do? This question is the starting point of Charlotte Mutsaers's novel *Koetsier Herfst* (Coachman Autumn, 2008). Its protagonist is writer Maurice Maillot, who has had a huge success in the past, but hasn't been able to write a sentence since the decease of his cat Grappa, eight years before. The death of his beloved pet, and the indifferent reactions of his fellow human beings to its death, has made him renounce fiction. Now he longs for 'factuality not virtuality'.

Maillot meets Do, a militant animal rights activist. She is a big fan of one of his earlier books, which she claims is written 'in the spirit of Bin Laden's masterful statement: *under which doctrine is your blood, blood and our blood water?*' Maillot reacts in surprise, but Do is dead serious, both in her reading of Maillot's work, and in her assessment of Osama bin Laden. In her view Bin

Laden is not a reprehensible terrorist, but a poet who doesn't tolerate any form of domination. Furthermore, in Do's mind, literature and terrorism are interchangeable. Gradually Maillot begins to warm to the idea. Maybe this is the key to the kind of factual literature he craves. He follows Do to Ostend where she is to join the Lobster Liberation Front. When Do dies and the stigmata on her body suggest that she might have been the Messiah, Maillot turns out to be a somewhat reluctant apostle. Suddenly he is not so sure literature should be a poetic form of terrorism, or that he is a dedicated enough fighter for the cause. At the same time, however, the quirky novel *Koetsier Herfst* is presented as his; as the Gospel of Maurice.

Needless to say, *Koetsier Herfst* did not start a wave of terrorist fiction, nor did the book aspire to such a thing one-dimensionally. Mutsaers takes the idea of veracity to the extreme, yet it remains perfectly possible to read the novel as a tale of universal human endeavour. The same goes for other books of the same period that have taken their cue from the zeitgeist or even real-life events, such as Peter Verhelst's *Zwerm* (Swarm, 2005), Yves Petry's *De Maagd Marino* (Virgin Marino, 2010), Peter Terrin's *Post Mortem* (2012), and the contemporary family epics *Pier en oceaan* (Pier and Ocean, 2012) by Oek de Jong, *De omwegen* (Detours, 2013) by Jeroen Theunissen, and *Ik en wij* (I and We, 2014) by Saskia De Coster.

Yet, the sheer number of novels devoted to the pressing issues of the time is remarkable, especially the issue of migration. Ranging from problems concerning multicultural society to mass immigration, the subject has been tackled in near documentary style, as in Dimitri Verhulst's *Problemski hotel* (2003) and Tom Naegels's *Los* (Loose, 2005); in symbolic tales like Arnon Grunberg's *De asielzoeker* (The Asylum Seeker, 2003), Tom Lanoye's *Het derde huwelijk* (The Third Marriage, 2006) and Tommy Wieringa's *Dit zijn de namen* (*These Are the Names*, 2012); and in confrontational narratives including Elvis Peeters's *De ontelbaren* (The Uncountables, 2005), Koen Peeters's *Duizend heuvels* (A Thousand Hills, 2012), and Annelies Verbeke's *Dertig dagen* (Thirty Days, 2015).

The most successful migration novel of recent years is arguably *La Superba* (2013) by Ilja Leonard Pfeijffer, in which the narrator, also named Ilja, guides his readers through Genoa, a city that is as real as it is an integral part of this dreamer's imagination. 'In a way, the city also exists without me,' he admits at some point, 'at least, I'm willing to assume this much.' Imagining a life in the city with its picturesque alleys and theatrical inhabitants, Ilja discovers there is a limit to the world of make-believe that he, as a writer, tries to comprehend. He then meets Djiby, a Senegalese refugee. At first Ilja is eager to hear his story, as it would benefit the novel he is working on, in which 'the discrimination against immigrants will be a major theme'. Ilja writes down Djiby's story of false hope and deception, but when Djiby returns a couple of weeks later, to tell Ilja his subsequent experiences, the story turns out to be too much to handle for this writer of fiction. Djiby has been beaten up and his papers taken, which effectively renders him an outlaw. Suspicious of his motives Ilja says that he doesn't believe Djiby. But the Senegalese assures Ilja he is not after his money or anything like that. 'I want you to tell my story to the people in the North. That's the only thing I ask of you. Will you promise me that, Ilja?' Ilja remains speechless. The bitter reality of migration has caught up with his fictitious ideas.

Readers
die younger

War and dreams

If one ventured to come up with an over-arching theme for a decade and a half worth of literary fiction, it would probably be the dramatic attempt to bridge the gap between the harsh reality and our creative, yet inadequate imagination.

This theme was perhaps most prominent in the war novel genre. In the past sixty-plus years the Second World War has been a persistent subject in Flemish and Dutch prose. The war never really wanted to become history. Even quite recently plenty of novels set in the war period were published, both by writers who witnessed it first-hand, like Hans Croiset with *Lucifer onder de linden* (Lucifer Underneath the Linden, 2010) and *Lente in Praag* (Spring in Prague, 2013), and by second or third generation writers, such as Johan de Boose in *Bloedgetuigen* (Blood Witnesses, 2011), Nico Dros in *Oorlogsparadijs* (War Paradise, 2012), and Jan Brokken in *De vergelding* (Retribution, 2013).

With its centennial in sight, even the previously often neglected First World War became a popular topic. In the Netherlands (neutral during WWI) greatly divergent novels such as *Dünya* (2007) by Tomas Lieske, *De Nederlandse maagd* (The Dutch Maiden, 2010) by Marente de Moor, *Het grote zwijgen* (The

Great Silence, 2011) by Erik Menkveld and Martin Michael Driessen's novella *Een ware held* (A True Hero, 2013) were at least partly set in 1914-1918. In Flanders (where much of the fighting took place) the shift towards WWI stories was even bigger. *Post voor mevrouw Bromley* (Mail for Mrs. Bromley, 2011) by Stefan Brijs, *Woesten* (2013) by Kris Van Steenberge, *Meester Mitraillette* (Schoolmaster SMG, 2014) by Jan Vantoortelboom (2014) and *Godenslaap* (*While the Gods Were Sleeping*, 2008) and *De spiegelingen* (Reflections, 2014) by Erwin Mortier all transported the readers to the horrors of the Great War.

In the case of Stefan Hertmans's *Oorlog en terpentijn* (*War and Turpentine*, 2013), the situation is almost inverted. This novel does not create an image of the First World War through literary means, here the war presents itself to the writer, in the form of a number of notebooks the author's grandfather, WWI veteran Urbain Martien, left his grandson. While recounting his grandfather's exploits before, during and after the war, Hertmans attempts to bridge the gap between the twenty-first century and the absolutely incomprehensible era in which Martien lived. He paints a portrait of a pensive young man and art student, who saw his world shattered to pieces in a devastating nightmare of violence.

Although he holds his grandfather in high esteem, the writer never really succeeds in bridging the abyss that lies between them. It is only when he trades the political for the artistic realm that Hertmans really begins to understand his grandfather. Throughout his life Martien had been a keen amateur painter, specializing in copying the great classics. But it turns out he did more than just copy. In his rendering of Vélazquez's *Venus*, instead of copying the face of Vélazquez's model, he painted in the likeness of his one true love, a girl that succumbed to the Spanish flu, months after Martien returned from the trenches. Through his grandfather's diaries, Hertmans gets to know him as a courageous man, yet only in his paintings, in which Martien tried to alter history by briefly imagining his long lost love in the flesh. The writer does meet a kindred spirit here.

Longing is literature's lasting liability. ■

Prometheus Unbound

Essays as an Orphic Counterforce

[CYRILLE OFFERMANS]

The Dutch – or rather Hollanders, Frisians and Zeelanders – are coastal dwellers, and traditionally their eyes were focused more on the sea than on dry land. As long ago as the early and high Middle Ages, long before the rise of the Hanseatic towns in the East of the country, they earned their living from fishing and trade. By the end of the sixteenth century, thanks to the nautical knowledge and know-how it had acquired over the centuries, the Republic of the Seven Provinces, tiny as it was in surface area, became the richest and most powerful nation on earth – a fact which astonishes historians to this day.

The Dutch had by far the largest fleet among the seafaring nations, discovered in every remote corner of the world opportunities for conducting trade – often not distinguishable from plunder and piracy – and at an early date, in 1600, founded the first multinational, the United East India Company, known as the VOC for short after its Dutch initials. That left a decisive mark on the Dutch national character. Roughly until the industrial revolution of the nineteenth century – in literary terms, until Jules Verne's *Around the World in Eighty Days* (which makes particular fun of the allegedly adventurous modern, organised travel) – navigation was a highly risky undertaking. Crews were decimated by disease, privation and violence, and the lucky ones who survived all that were away from home for years.

Conditions at sea and abroad were unpredictable and often required immediate and spontaneous action. Besides physical strength and courage, seamen needed a good deal of improvisational ability. Relying on rigid command structures and rehearsed routines was often undesirable, and potentially fatal. However much discipline prevailed on board, without a certain degree of anarchy (*an-archè* = without ground), survival, both individual and collective, was impossible.

That made many seafaring Dutchmen unsuitable for life in strongly hierarchical structures and also explains their constitutional predisposition towards the Reformation, which championed individual responsibility of the believer towards God, as well as their eventually successful resistance to the feudal Catholic Church, which had become one with the Spanish empire. From the outset they showed little attachment to their own soil and history, indeed, to anything that is understood today by a national or otherwise geographically de-

"YECH .... MACHO!"

fined identity, including language. The other side of this lack of interest is also typical of Dutch power, for that matter. Unlike the Spanish and Portuguese, French and British colonialists, the Dutch were scarcely if at all interested in territorial expansion, or in exporting their culture or language. Cultural imperialism was alien to them, all that mattered was trade, yield, profit.

America

All this also explains why Dutch culture, especially after the Second World War, is so strongly Anglo-Saxon in orientation. English, after all, is the lingua franca of international capitalism and hence also of scholarship, cosmopolitanism and the associated culture. 'Everyone' speaks English, or something that passes for it. English is the common language at Dutch universities. No language has as many modish English loanwords and expressions as Dutch. The literary supplements keep the reader closely in touch with new British and American publications, which have long set the norm for the bulk of reviewers. No less than seventy percent of all literary translations relate to English-language books. Many authors, particularly younger ones, are consequently influenced by Anglo-Saxon writers.

The Americanisation – read also commercialisation – of Dutch literature seems more dramatic than in other European countries. True, plenty of good books still appear. Perhaps more than ever, but for fewer and fewer readers. The Republic of Letters is a seriously ageing and contracting area.

Symptomatic of the almost axiomatic Anglo-Saxon dominance is the reception of the translation of a book by the British historian Michael Pye, *The Edge of the World* (2014), the subtitle of which, *How the North Sea Made Us Who We Are*, must have particularly caught the attention of Dutch readers. Pye tries to show that the Middle Ages were by no means a patch of darkness between Antiquity and the Renaissance but, at least for the peoples on the coasts of the North Sea, a time of lively navigation, trade and still relevant discoveries in a variety of different areas. Unfortunately he gets no farther than mainly disjointed, often unproven stories. The book is, in all respects, messy, incoherent and unconvincing. Yet it was virtually unanimously enthusiastically praised by Dutch critics and was on the bestseller lists for months.

That is all the more remarkable because a thematically somewhat related book by a Dutch author went completely unnoticed: *Water, een geofilosofische geschiedenis* (Water, a geophilosophical history, 2014) by René ten Bos. Like Pye, but in a considerably more structured, clearer and more convincing way, Ten Bos ventures the thesis that there is a link between general forms of consciousness and the geographical environment in which they arise. He concentrates on the Greek archipelago, where eyes were focused almost automatically on the sea – like centuries later on the Dutch coast, as I have just argued. But Plato hated the harbour, sailors and the sea. They had no clearly circumscribed identity, no stalwart character, no firm backbone. His whole philosophy was opposed to the ominous power of the intangible – with immeasurable consequences for European culture.

Europe

This example immediately indicates the downside of Anglo-Saxon dominance: it often goes hand in hand with a rapidly growing blind spot for continental European culture. Ten Bos's book draws philosophically not only on Greek sources, but also on Dante, Grotius, Kant, Carl Schmitt (critically of course), Peter Sloterdijk, Michel Serres and, of course, on *Moby Dick*, Herman Melville's encyclopaedic novel. And these are names, perhaps apart from the last-mentioned, which, like all other 'historical' names, are becoming blurred in the collective consciousness of Dutch literature until they become just names. The orientation towards America goes hand in hand with a lack of interest in what is not topical or potentially useful. Hence also – for example – the demolishing of

"SO YOU'RE GOING TO DEDICATE
YOUR BOOK TO ME?"

"MAKE YOUR MAIN CHARACTERS DO SOMETHING
ONCE IN A WHILE, HERBERT."

historical humanities departments, which is being conducted with considerably fewer scruples in the Netherlands than in other European countries.

All of this applies mainly to 'Holland', or the North Sea agglomeration. In the rest of the Netherlands and in Flanders the dominance of Anglo-Saxon culture seems less great and the isolation with regard to the various continental cultures is consequently less serious. Unlike in the Netherlands, where the knowledge of French and German is crumbling, Flemish essayists and prose writers like Paul de Wispelaere (1928), Paul Claes (1943), Stefan Hertmans (1951) and Luc Devoldere (1956) have never lost touch with France and French culture in particular. It is not improbable that for that reason literary experiment has always enjoyed more enthusiasm in Flanders than in the sober Netherlands.

Whatever the case, quality essay-writing resists the advance of the one-sided, American-orientated, memory-less culture. That motive unites all the authors discussed here, even Jacq Vogelaar and Kees Fens, though at first sight they seem very divergent. The former became famous – or rather infamous – mainly as an experimental author in the tradition of Kafka, Joyce and Beckett, while the latter, coming from a conservative Catholic background, was interested above all in early Christian culture, medieval monastic life, St Augustine and Dante.

But both were readers with an open mind and a strong sense of what in a more general sense is at stake, a culture of reading and practice as the basis of civilisation. Both focused with unbridled energy on the revitalisation of unknown or forgotten but interesting authors and traditions; Fens, the post-Catholic, mainly on the rapid disappearance of Christian culture.

Accomplice

Vogelaar (1944-2013) is the most important literary essayist of his generation. After, as a very young critic, he had wiped the floor very harshly and, it should be said, not always in a nuanced way, with 'Dutch realism', he switched his interest abroad, in particular to modernist, experimental, critical authors like Robert Musil, Virginia Woolf, Andrey Platonov, Unica Zürn, Carl Einstein, Claude Simon, Julio Cortázar, Thomas Bernhard, Maurice Blanchot, Wolfgang

"HAVE A DRINK ON ME LOVE... TODAY I'M CELEBRATING I'VE BEEN A VERY PROMISING WRITER FOR THE LAST TWENTY FIVE YEARS"

Koeppen and Danilo Kis. With the meticulous commitment of an 'accomplice' he introduced them into Dutch literature in long, well-crafted essays.

Vogelaar's most important essay is perhaps that on concentration camp literature, *Over kampliteratuur* (2006), a colossal book in all respects, not comparable with anything in Dutch or any other language, and probably partly for that reason scarcely noticed by the critics. In 700 closely-printed pages he assembles everything written in whatever corner of the world in a primary and secondary sense on the German and Soviet-Russian concentration and extermination camps, by well-known but also completely unknown authors, all genres mixed up.

Somewhat related in intention is the work of the Flemish historian Gie van den Berghe (1945), especially his monumental *De mens voorbij* (Beyond Man, 2008), an ambitious, wide-ranging study of the theory and practice of the perfectable, 'transhuman' human being. The book begins with Malthus and his fight against the poor laws and utopian Enlightenment optimism and then concentrates on Darwin, Gobineau, Houston Chamberlain and Nazi eugenics. In the topical concluding section Van den Berghe argues that eugenics, popular since the late-nineteenth century, especially in America, after the War has quietly merged with genetics. There is still a drive to 'perfect' man, now via molecular biology.

Unlimited

Although I count Kees Fens (1929-2008) among our best and most productive literary essayists – his bibliography contains over forty titles – he did not write a single book in the strict sense of the word. The vast majority of his books are collections of columns, a genre that is particularly popular in the Netherlands. That may be connected with an obviously highly developed language talent for irony, cynicism, absurdism, playfulness or awkwardness, for which there is little use elsewhere outside the newspaper, but also with the circumstance that many writers, given the relatively small language area, can only live by their pen by writing for the papers. In the case of Fens it must also be connected with a sharp ideal in terms of style and his unlimited, capricious interest – he writes just as easily about the spaces in a complex modernist poem as about vanished smells, the letters of Erasmus, a winter painting by Hendrick Avercamp or the bend in Regent Street.

Fens is one of the exceptional generation of columnists born in the 1920s and 1930s, of whom only the poet Remco Campert (1929) and the versatile journalist Henk Hofland (1927) are still alive and active. Campert is striking for his almost weightless, melancholic reflections, Hofland for sharp political and cultural analyses. The most original, polemical and high-profile columnists of this generation are Rudy Kousbroek (1929-2010) and Hugo Brandt Corstius (1935-2014), who published under countless pseudonyms. The influence exercised by this generation of newspaper article writers over many decades on Dutch public opinion is difficult to overestimate.

Originating as they did from the world of literature in a narrow sense, a highly developed sense of style and form was axiomatic for all these authors. That made it possible for the emancipation of political and cultural commentary in the newspaper to become a difficult to define but fully-fledged literary genre – a sub-genre of the essay – comparable with the way in which German-language commentators in the pre- and early-Fascist era (Kraus, Tucholsky, Walser, Kracauer, Benjamin) gave the short prose piece literary respectability and at the same time political relevance.

Guardians

Brandt Corstius, trained as a linguist and a mathematician, with a special interest in translation machines, was for a long time the fiercest and hence the most controversial columnist in the Netherlands. His philippics – his favourite genre along with satire and pastiche – were feared. His favourite stylistic device was hyperbole; he liked to compare politicians to high-ranking Nazis like Eichmann or Mengele. The unique power of his columns lies in his refusal to spare anything or anybody, a mercilessness reminiscent of Kraus, and an inexhaustible formal-literary wealth of ideas. Brandt Corstius even turned the tiny columns that he published daily on the front page of *de Volkskrant* into stylistically surprising, hilarious, mysterious miniature works of art requiring decoding.

In addition, under the pseudonym Battus he wrote countless pieces on the potential of language where the primacy of form is absolute. Since meaning, use or usage, in short everything that binds language to obligations and hence limitations, no longer matters, he speaks in his magnum opus *Opperlans! Taal-en letterkunde* (2002) of 'Dutch on holiday'. This unpaged and very long book offers a marathon programme of superior language acrobatics, inventory description and amazing demonstration, and is as (un)translatable as, say, *Finnegans wake*.

Rudy Kousbroek began as a poet in the experimental group the *Vijftigers*, or Men of the Fifties, but from the 1960s developed into a critic, as feared as he was witty, of all dogmatism, modishness, secret language and humbug in spiritual philosophy, including religion, and in academic, philosophical, literary and pedagogical discourse. At an early stage he raised the question of where the lack of manners of Dutch children came from. His answer: it must be connected with 'a broken continuity, a vanished interest in what we were yesterday, in how we thought and felt then.' The Dutch have 'a lack of resistance to short-lived fashions and unrealisable figments of the imagination; hence the attempts at renewal without retaining the good, that constant throwing out of the baby with the bathwater.'

In his melancholy reflections on (old) photos, collected in *Opgespoorde wonderen* (Unearthed Wonders, 2010), he vies with Roland Barthes. Using well-chosen examples, he once again expresses his contempt for our 'world', in which everything that is beautiful, precious and vulnerable is strangled by commerce. It stands to reason then that Kousbroek is very unimpressed by such an ahistorical and moreover so religious and prudish country as America. The only city he praises unreservedly is New Orleans, 'but, after all, that is a Southern French provincial town in which not very much has changed since the eighteenth century.'

Nicolaas Matsier (1945) is not a columnist, but his work, even the novel *Gesloten Huis* (Closed House, 1994) and his autobiographical *Compositieportret* (Composite Portrait, 2015), has the features of column writing. It seems like a single large, loosely linked collection of short prose, in which the author shows himself above all as the careful guardian of simple, everyday things and the corresponding words, which are rapidly disappearing from life and hence from the collective memory. From his pen come no helpless jeremiads but unvarnished, precise, loving and witty observations, in the hope perhaps that at least something of that *attitude* will survive.

In this way Matsier also contributes to a theme that implicitly or explicitly runs right through contemporary Dutch literature in the broadest sense of the word, the marginalisation of a humanist culture of patience, attention and responsibility for what is close to hand by a post-human, commercial, mass culture focused on immediate profit, to which it no longer means anything.

Travellers

The popular books of Geert Mak link thematically to this, although they are nothing like collections of columns. They are rather detailed, sometimes even long-winded stories about what has changed in the Netherlands, Europe and America since the nineteenth century. His first popular success was *Jorwerd: The Death of the Village in Late 20th Century Europe* (2000, *Hoe God verdween uit Jorwerd*, 1996), on the changes in traditional village life as a result of industrialisation, the move to the towns and the decline in church culture. Later there followed, among others, *De eeuw van mijn vader* (My Father's Century, 1999), a personally tinged history of the twentieth century; *In Europe: Travels through the Twentieth Century* (2007, *In Europa*, 2004), a monumental, two-fold travelogue, about Europe and the history of the continent, which was also successful in several foreign countries; and *In America: Travels with John Steinbeck* (2014, *Reizen zonder John*, 2012) a similar travelogue about a trip through the US in the footsteps of John Steinbeck, which paints a shocking picture of the once so promising New World.

Of the many excellent travel writers one should mention at any rate Lieve Joris, Chris de Stoop, Jan Brokken, Adriaan van Dis, Frank Westerman and the extremely productive Cees Nooteboom, who is particularly popular in Germany. Westerman, like Mak, began as an engaged journalist, and was one of the first to write about the Battle of Srebrenica (*De slag om Srebrenica*, of which an expanded version appeared in 2015). He also impressed with *De graanrepubliek* (The Republic of Grain, 2003), on the vagaries of Groningen farmers, and with *Engineers of the Soul* (2011, *Ingenieurs van de ziel*, 2002), in which guided by the brave anti-Stalinist Konstantin Paustovsky he shows how Soviet writers celebrate the forcible industrialisation of agrarian Russia.

Nooteboom also writes on important political events, such as the fall of the Berlin Wall, but is mainly interested in cultural-historical and philosophical matters. He must be the most widely travelled Dutchman. There is probably no corner of the world where he has not searched for transient traces of an intransient poetry. I must limit myself to mentioning a few titles: *De roeiers van Port Dauphin. Alle Afrikaanse reizen* (2011), about his African journeys; *Eilanden, rif en regenwoud. Alle Australische reizen* (2013), about his Australian trips; and *Continent in beweging. Alle Zuid- en Midden-Amerikaanse reizen* (2013), about his South and Central American journeys.

Resistance

One finds a philosophical dimension in practically all the above-mentioned books, yet philosophical and anthropological essays are not widely developed in the Low Countries. Exceptions to this are Hans Achterhuis (1942), Ton Lemaire (1941) and David van Reybrouck (1971).

In his most recent book, *De utopie van de vrije markt* (The Utopia of the Free Market, 2013), Achterhuis tries to fathom neo-Liberalism as the ideology of global capitalism and in particular its excrescences, the much-decried grab and bonus culture. To this end he looks extensively, not always with equal stylistic refinement, at the reactionary kitsch novels of Ayn Rand, which had a

"DON'T HAROLD, I ADMIRE YOU ONLY AS A WRITER"

considerable influence in the US on important free-market ideologues. In this context the successful book of Joris Luyendijk (1971), *Swimming with Sharks: My Journey into the World of the Bankers* (2015, *Dit kan niet waar zijn*, 2015), in snatches a shattering anthropological investigation into the life, work and ideas of bankers in the City of London, must not go unmentioned.

Lemaire was already the author of *Filosofie van het landschap* (Philosophy of Landscape, 1970) and various other books on the downside of progress when, in 1991, he gave up his lectureship at the University of Nijmegen to settle in the Dordogne, where he combined his cultural-anthropological and natural philosophical insights with a better life, not fatally harming the planet as a part-time eco farmer and writer. In seclusion his committed and multifaceted oeuvre grew steadily. In 2007, for example, he excelled with a book on the traces birds have left in the human imagination of myths and legends. That Lemaire, as far as I know, was the only Dutchman to honour Claude-Lévi-Strauss with a book on the occasion of the latter's hundredth birthday, in 2008, came as no surprise.

In 2013 followed *De val van Prometheus* (The Fall of Prometheus), in which he reminds us that, for the Greeks, Prometheus was not only a symbol of the greatness, ingenuity and cunning of mankind, but also of the overconfidence, the hubris, which was punished by the gods. That aspect retreated into the background for Europeans from the eighteenth century onwards. No hubris could restrain him, 'modernity recognises itself only in an unchained Prometheus.' An interesting aspect is Lemaire's reappraisal of Herbert Marcuse who, particularly in *Eros and Civilisation* (1955) shows himself to be an anti-Promethean thinker. With Marcuse he sees more in Orpheus, as a singer and poet, the symbol of the reconciliation of man and nature, and in countless, mostly small-scale 'Orphic' counter-practices.

David van Reybrouck, finally, is a cultural historian, archaeologist and philosopher. In 2010 he published one of the best books of the last decade, *Congo*, about the vast African country that was regarded by Leopold II as his private domain, after which, until 1960, it was colonised by Belgium and subsequently disintegrated dramatically over a long period of dictatorship in an endless series of bloody civil wars. The book is a perfect synthesis of travelogue, cultural anthropology and political history, written in a supple, graphic style.

It is also literally polyphonic: during his journeys Van Reybrouck spoke to people from all layers of society and smoothly blended the stories he obtained with the chronology of the great events. In this way knowledge acquired in the library was, as it were, verified and personally coloured by the experiences of those directly involved. A hopeful sign is the improbable number of copies (approximately 200,000) sold of just the Dutch version of what is, after all, a highly ambitious and voluminous book.

Finally, a handful of important names and titles that would have found a place in a longer version of this article, without commentary or context: the work of Benno Barnard, Patricia de Martelaere, Piet Meeuse and Willem Jan Otten. Douwe Draaisma, *Why Life Speeds Up As You Get Older. How Memory Shapes Our Past* (2004); Trudy Dehue, *De depressie-epidemie: over de plicht het lot in eigen handen te nemen* (The Depression Epidemic: On the Duty to Take One's Fate in One's Own Hands, 2008); Luuk van Middelaar, *The Passage to Europe. History of a Beginning* (2009); Siep Stuurman, *De uitvinding van de mensheid. Korte wereldgeschiedenis van het denken over gelijkheid en cultuurverschil* (The Invention of Humanity. A Short World History of Thinking about Equality and Cultural Difference, 2009); Rens Bod, *A New History of the Humanities* (2013, *De vergeten wetenschappen*, 2010); Paul Verhaeghe, *What About Me? The Struggle for Identity in a Market-Based Society* (2014, *Identiteit*, 2012); Wouter Kusters, *Filosofie van de waanzin* (Philosophy of Madness, 2014).

These books also testify to mental resistance. The fact that they are there at all is nothing short of a miracle. They embody an ambition which runs counter to the cynical neo-Liberalism that has the world in its devastating grip. Promethean forces, which were constrained in the decades after the Second World War, have over the last quarter of a century been given free rein once again even in old Europe, which follows the US like a faithful dog – with disastrous results for the welfare state and the "state of the Culture". The essays discussed here form – in the sense of Lemaire – part of a pluriform Orphic counterforce. ■

All cartoons © Peter van Straaten.
www.petervanstraaten.nl

Translated by Paul Vincent

A Gaze Trained on the Horizon

Children's Books in the Low Countries

[MIRJAM NOORDUIJN]

A country by the sea is boundless, or perhaps it would be better to say, it seems boundless. The open water with the distant, intangible horizon urges exploration and adventure, but close by the undulating power of the salt sea and the constant wind cause continual commotion. Inevitably this is coupled with a battle for space. What is the most sensible solution? Contain it with dams and polders? Or let the water flow freely?

The cultural landscape of the Low Countries as a battleground for freethinkers and those who would draw boundaries is a tempting metaphor for the conflict which once again flared up at the start of the twenty-first century in the land of children's writing, where child-oriented people and literary figures tussle over the notion of the children's book.

This battle really springs directly from the question of what children's literature is. Does it actually exist? And if it exists, how does it relate to adult literature? Is a children's book just meant for children and, if so, should it be written specifically for the target group and judged as such? Or is a good children's book one written with literary devices to be criticised according to text and image and only considered a success if adults, too, can appreciate it? Under the motto that pedagogical principles and target groups are foreign to the nature of literature?

By the end of the twentieth century this battle seemed to have been settled in favour of the literature camp. Children's literature had grown up, or so it appeared. Imme Dros, Wim Hofman, Joke van Leeuwen, Bart Moeyaert, Anne Provoost, Toon Tellegen, the writers of children's books who allowed their language and imagination to flow freely, were applauded, as were illustrators such as Kristien Aertssen, Carll Cneut, Gerda Dendooven and Klaas Verplancke, who have elevated the art of illustration in Flanders through their courage to colour outside the lines. Until the turn of the millennium these now established linguistic and visual artists lived happily in a boundless country by the sea, where the artistic quality of their work was highly regarded. In the end everyone agreed that children are not half people. That children are familiar with all the emotions adults are familiar with. And that therefore children's books are not half books and children's authors are not half authors. They try, just like writers for adults, to imagine 'the space of life in its entirety', to quote Lucebert (1924-1994), each in their own poetic manner.

Kaatje Vermeire in *De vrouw en het jongetje* (The Woman and the Boy)
by Geert de Kockere and Kaatje Vermeire (De Eenhoorn, 2007)

'The sky sewn onto the world'

What makes their books unique and distinguishes them from adult books is the fact that they are 'written from the bottom up', as creative all-rounder Joke van Leeuwen puts it. With a subversive, childish gaze, which often guarantees a fare dose of absurd logic – certainly in the case of Van Leeuwen's stories – they force us to see the world through other eyes, or new ones, for a while. Sjoerd Kuyper, whose work won him the triennial Theo Thijssen Prize in the Netherlands in 2012, along with his younger, much-praised colleague Edward van de Vendel, supports Van Leeuwen's vision. A good children's book, said Kuyper, in 2009, in his Annie M.G. Schmidt Lecture – one of the few platforms in the Low Countries offering respected children's authors the opportunity to express their views on developments in their profession since the start of the new century – is 'written with the heart of a child and the hand of an adult'. Or, to put it in Van de Vendel's words, there should be 'a child's breath blowing through the book' (from his Annie M.G. Schmidt Lecture, 2006). The aim of these children's authors, however, is the same as that of adult writers: they seek to create amazement and confusion through words. Great life issues, such as death, are therefore excellent subject matter, as long as the author gets the child's perspective right and treats it with respect.

Van de Vendel himself does this very well. The poetry collection *Superguppie* (2003) – with lively illustrations by Fleur van der Weel created with pen and ink – offers children's poems whose deceptive simplicity goes straight to the heart. 'Merel' ('Blackbird') for example: 'A blackbird lay dead / fallen, folded / on the platform before me. / I didn't know such a thing could be. / People dashing everywhere, / leaving him uncovered there. / I didn't know such a thing could be. / Everything in vain. / Mummy rushing in a hushed voice called, / We're going to miss our train.' Kuyper, too, knows how to describe the emotional world of a young child cleverly from the inside. His imagery always fits perfectly into the referential frame of a young child, leading to clever dialogues and reflections which are telling in their simplicity. There is a particularly beautiful scene in *O rode papaver, boem pats, knal!* (Oh red poppy, boom bang, crash! 2011) Kuyper's ninth and last book featuring the disarming little Robin, charmingly illustrated in dreamy colours by Marije Tolman. Here, on the edge of the village where Robin lives, Kuyper captures in words the immensity of the world as a child might experience it: there – where the village ends – 'there you come to the meadows. They're so big – from your toes to the horizon. On the horizon are trees. They look small and thin as threads - the thread mummy uses to sew buttons onto Robin's trousers. It's as if the sky were sewn onto the world there.'

Carll Cneut in *Het geheim van de keel van de nachtegaal* (The Secret of the Nightingale's Throat) by Peter Verhelst and Carll Cneut (De Eenhoorn, 2009)

The masses dictate

Since the start of the twenty-first century, however, the world has changed rapidly. Life has come under great pressure from web 2.0 and the rise of new media. The entire world is on a digital drip: constantly online, we are now so stupefied that we systematically confuse the continual bellowing which washes over us each day with freedom of expression. The consequence is that the taste of the masses dictates and literature barely retains any status.

Obviously these developments have their repercussions on the world of children's books in the Low Countries. The old guard notes that 'the golden age of children's literature is gone forever' and speaks of 'a restorative tendency, which looks to return to safe times of yore, when an undisputed difference existed between children's books and adult literature'.

These critics are not altogether wrong. Seeing a children's book as a form of literature is immediately considered suspicious and child-unfriendly these days. The 'dictatorship of the literary norm' is feared by teachers, parents, librarians, reviewers and yes, even writers themselves. Publishers opt less and less for literary books, for children or adults, afraid that they will not sell. Bestsellers and formulaic series full of WhatsApp, Snapchat and navel-gazing, a clear example being Francine Oomen's contemporary series *Hoe overleef ik* (How to Survive), simply stand to make more money than exceptional literature such as Bart Moeyaert and Gerda Dendooven's *De gans en zijn broer* (The Goose and His Brother, 2014), or *De Noordenwindheks* (The Witch of the North Wind, 2004) by double talent Daan Remmerts de Vries. *De gans en zijn broer* is a small collection of beautiful short stories and equally appealing illustrations of two brother geese, who unintentionally go in search of the meaning of their existence. *De Noordenwindheks* is a disturbing reversible book in which two terminally ill eleven-year-olds sharing a hospital room tell their stories, meanwhile making up the myth of the dangerous 'witch of the north wind' against whom they are engaged in a life and death battle.

Against the tide

However, despite the fact that 'the space of life in its entirety' has been contained with dams due to commercialisation and fear, there are still children's authors and illustrators who set out to sea – following Paul Biegel's famous little captain – 'feet firmly planted, eyes on the skyline' against the tide, on their way to the horizon and preferably beyond, with a new, boundless generation of children's book makers in their wake.

What this new, boundless generation has in common with the old is its vision of authorship. They are all happy to be called *children's* authors, but feel they are first and foremost authors. Just because a book is prefaced with *children's* does not mean it is not worth adults reading it, they say. Young, valued and highly praised writers such as Gideon Samson and Simon van der Geest believe that literature for children and adults comes from the same source. In several interviews Samson has stated that he is not concerned with his readership when he writes: to him writing children's books is a way of expressing himself artistically. Similarly Kaatje Vermeire, currently one of Flanders' great illustrators, does not think of her viewers when she draws and, she admits, never started out with the intention of illustrating for children. In search of the core of life, she aims to cross boundaries freely. In short, she seeks to create art. The same goes for poet and visual artist Ted van Lieshout. When he won the Woutertje Pieterse Prize in 2012 for *Driedelig Paard* (Three-Part Horse) – an intriguing and unique combination of word, image and form, and a highlight in his oeuvre, for which he was also awarded the Theo Thijssen Prize in 2009 – he said frankly in an interview that for him every book had to be a work of art.

Beautiful border traffic

Remarkably enough, works of art in the form of children's books have been steadily gaining ground in recent years. Flemish writers Peter Verhelst and Carll Cneut, for example, have received a great deal of praise for their brilliant picture book *Het geheim van de keel van de nachtegaal* (The Secret of the Nightingale's Throat, 2009). This book is an altogether enchanting retelling of Hans Christian Andersen's fairy tale *The Nightingale* (1843), in which adult writer Verhelst and master illustrator Cneut follow one another perfectly in movement and rhythm, as if performing an intricate dance, to create a new story with unprecedented panoramas. Similarly, spurred on by the drive to experiment, Bette Westera (the new Annie M.G. Schmidt of the Low Countries) and Sylvia Weve (originally a graphic designer) have pushed one another to great artistic heights in recent years. In two poetry collections, *Aan de kant, ik ben je oma niet!* (Scram! I'm Not Your Gran! 2012) - which can best be described as 'a paper care home' demonstrating that the elderly were once young too - and the taboo-breaking, highly praised collection *Dood-Gewoon* (Dead Normal, 2014), they show how skill and imagination result in extremely original, creative books, in which ethics and aesthetics, poignancy and humour go hand in hand with bold social criticism. A recent non-fiction highlight and delight for the eyes is *Het Raadsel van alles dat leeft* (The Mystery of Life, 2013), a surprisingly imaginative and at the same time clear representation of the story of evolution by Jan-Paul Schutten and new Dutch illustration talent Floor Rieder. It is, by the way, remarkable and delightful to note that this subgenre of children's literature has reached full maturity as a literary art form in recent years and that so many books are succeeding in making the invisible visible to children through a subtle interplay of fact, image and imagination.

Certainly the publishers of these eye-catching books deserve our compliments. Who dares stick their neck out these days, when we all know times are tough for the book industry? Who still dares to put children's poetry onto the market? Or books with cloth spines, ribbon bookmarks and gilt edging? Those who do are few and far between. Unfortunately. As the publishers who have taken the risk over the last decade are just the ones who have shown that there clearly is a market for less obvious books, and that creativity, quirkiness and quality still sell in our digitalised age. You can be sure that without a publisher such as De Eenhoorn, the Flemish art of illustration would never have grown to become the best of what is currently made in the genre. In her book *Buiten de lijntjes gekleurd* (Colouring Outside the Lines, 2006) children's literature expert and Eenhoorn publisher Marita Vermeulen discusses as many as twenty-one

Klaas Verplancke in *Confidenties aan een ezelsoor* (Confidences with a Donkey's Ear)
by Frank Adam (Davidsfonds, 2005)

talents who are exploring the fascinating boundary between illustration and autonomous art, with references to art history's old masters. The naïve approach is represented among others by Kristien Aertssen, Guido Van Genechten and Ingrid Godon, whose portrait book *Ik denk* (I Think, 2014) with texts by Toon Tellegen, sets her unexpectedly among the ranks of pure autonomous artists. The style of Klaas Verplancke seems inspired by the Flemish primitives and Hieronymus Bosch. While Tom Schamp's wonderful 'look and find' books about Otto contain many a nod to surrealism.

The innocent child is dead

Boundlessness: that is what the new twenty-first century producers of children's books have in common. In the knowledge that everything and everyone is constantly connected these days, they see the entire world as their playground. And why not? Why would you want to build walls? It's pointless. It does not make the world any safer. Children race down the electronic highway even faster than adults, with no need for a driver's licence. They go wherever they want to go. They stop wherever they want to stop. And they share whatever they want to share, with friend and foe alike. The innocent child no longer exists. That myth has been thoroughly debunked. The adult world has definitively permeated the world of children, and with it children's books.

Gerda Dendooven in *De gans en zijn broer* (The Goose and His Brother)
by Bart Moeyaert and Gerda Dendooven (Querido, 2014)

Kristien Aertssen in *Tikken tegen de maan*
(Tapping Against the Moon)
(Ons Erfdeel vzw, 2010)

For example, Marjolijn Hof writes masterful stories of children confronted with complicated adult issues they can barely influence. What can you do, for instance, if you are ten years old and fear for your father's fate when he is sent to a dangerous warzone as an army doctor, as happens to Kiek, the girl in Hof's much praised debut *Een kleine kans* (Small Chance, 2006)? Wait until he returns safely? Or give fate a helping hand, perhaps against your better judgement?

The violence of war, domestic suffering, incest, bullying resulting in death, a teenager's planned suicide, homosexuality: there is no subject nowadays that is not addressed in books for children and teenagers. The writers are ruthless, but stylistically they are strong, with a powerful view of the child's psyche.

The most uncompromising writer is Floortje Zwigtman, who first caused a furore with the multifaceted, wide-ranging *Wolfsroedel* (Wolfpack, 2002), followed by her *Green Flower Trilogy* (2005-2010), three weighty tomes about the homosexual seventeen-year-old Adrian Mayfield who has to survive in the Victorian London of Oscar Wilde, the most famous homosexual figure in literature, and who finds himself in an existential battle on the edge of the abyss. Violence and bloodlust in *Wolfsroedel*, blackmail, explicit gay sex scenes and prostitution in the trilogy. Zwigtman is ruthless. The unpleasant side of existence need not be corrected in her view, just because it is a book for children or young people. In several interviews she emphasises that she is allergic to people who still think children and young people live in 'a lovely world' in which everything works out fine in the end, with a moral to the story.

The same boundless development can be observed in the children's novels on the First and Second World Wars, which continue to appear in large numbers. These novels hinge less on their historical plot, than on the inner growth of the young protagonists and the impossible dilemmas of life and death, loyalty and betrayal, with which they are confronted. A prime example is *Allemaal willen we de hemel* (We All Want Heaven, 2008). In this sweeping, cleverly constructed narrative, set against the background of the Second World War, Els Beerten unfolds the life stories of four Flemish youngsters who, balancing on the thin line between good and evil, come to the painful conclusion that the heaven which everyone on earth longs for is in fact extremely ugly. And there are more of these strong psychological war stories about human shortcomings and human suffering. Equally impressive is *De Hondeneters* (The Dog Eaters, 2009), which is set during the First World War. Here Marita de Sterck paints a picture of the Flemish countryside in wartime through the eyes of an epileptic young man, revealing bitter poverty, deep hunger and sordid betrayal turning people into animals. Less grim but just as painful to read is *Bajaar* (2011), Martha Heesen's intriguing Brabant family history drawn over two world wars, dealing with waiting and hoping against all the odds, where 'someday' turns into 'never'. And anyone who believes that the story of the Second World War has been told and every war novel written, has not yet come across *De hemel van*

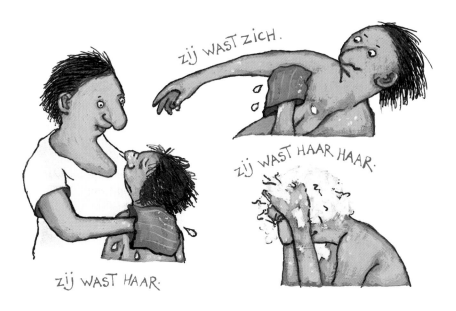

Joke van Leeuwen in *Waarom een buitenboordmotor eenzaam is*
(Why an Outboard Motor Is Lonely) (Ons Erfdeel vzw, 2015)

Translated by Anna Asbury

Heivisj (Heivisj's Heaven, 2010), by Benny Lindelauf. A closely composed novel about choosing and not choosing and losing all the same, rich in storylines, characters and powerful images, sparkling dialogue, humour and tragedy: in the Netherlands, the war claimed the highest percentage of Jewish victims in Sittard (Limburg). 'On a rainy afternoon I had to go to Heaven,' Lindelauf's opening sentence states hopefully. In the end, only one percent survived hell. *De hemel van Heivisj* may be the most complete children's novel of the past ten years, showing that children's literature has finally become adult.

Alive and kicking

However the Low Countries' battle for children's literature develops, and however sombre some old guard critics may be about the future of the artistic children's book, evidently each decade brings enough literally and figuratively magnificent, authentic, high quality books to prove that the genre is still alive and kicking. That freethinkers are more powerful than those who would draw boundaries. That you cannot – and never will – dam the flow of creativity. That 'the space of life in its entirety' is infinite and unpredictable. For everyone. And that all of us – children and adults alike – need our boundless imagination and the stories which spring from it in the twenty-first century, in order to stand up to the uncertainties of fate and live our lives freely and fearlessly with our gaze trained on the horizon. ▪

Farewell to the Serial

About Comic Strips and Graphic Novels

[TOON HORSTEN]

Comic strips first appeared in Dutch-language newspapers and magazines in the run-up to the Second World War, although these were still chiefly (with a few notable exceptions) American imports. Editorial boards found that translations of *Mickey Mouse* or *Flash Gordon* were considerably cheaper than new, commissioned works. Only when German troops occupied Belgium and the Netherlands, and the supply of American comics was cut off, were they forced to look for alternatives. Many illustrators grasped the opportunity to start their own series. For instance, the classic Dutch comic strip *Tom Poes / Tom Puss*, illustrated and written by Marten Toonder, made its debut on the pages of the Dutch daily newspaper *De Telegraaf* in 1941.

Domestic comic strip production received a second boost immediately following the war. The populace was hungry for information, and newspaper sales skyrocketed. Most papers also wanted to include a serial of some sort, and the comic strip proved to be the ideal formula, as it was hugely accessible and popular among all age groups. The strips were, by and large, adventure stories laden with humour, drawn mainly in a caricatural style, with realistic elements reserved for the backdrop. *Suske en Wiske* (known in Great Britain as *Spike and Suzy* and in America as *Willy and Wanda*), conceived by the Flemish cartoonist Willy Vandersteen and introduced in 1945, was immensely popular from the outset. After completing several stories, the author decided to switch newspapers, taking some 20,000 subscribers with him. The newspaper he left behind, seeking to fill the gap, invited Marc Sleen to introduce a new series. This became Nero, the second Flemish post-war comic strip series that became very popular.

Newspaper comics in the Netherlands differed fundamentally from those in Flanders. In the Netherlands they took on the form of a single strip containing three or four panels, with captions underneath describing the action. Flemish dailies resolutely opted for the two-strip format with speech balloons. Dutch comics were thus far more text-oriented than their Flemish counterparts. Marten Toonder is still regarded as an influential man of letters: he invented countless expressions that have made their way into everyday language. Not coincidentally, well-known authors such as the immensely popular Godfried Bomans and C. Buddingh' also wrote comic strips.

Lucky Luke by Morris on the cover of *Robbedoes* Magazine

Many newspaper strips were later collected into magazine format albums, giving the stories a second life. In Flanders, these albums were often issued by the publisher that produced the newspaper where the comics first appeared, and sales quickly reached astronomical heights. Not so, however, in the Netherlands. Marten Toonder's bookshop sales only truly took off after they were brought out by the literary publisher De Bezige Bij.

Eppo

There were also youth-oriented comic magazines. In Flanders, translations of the French weekly magazines *Tintin* and *Spirou* (in Dutch, *Kuifje* and *Robbedoes*) were the most popular. *Kuifje* also hired Flemish illustrators, including Willy Vandersteen and Bob de Moor, who would serve as Hergé's (the creator of Tintin) right-hand man for thirty-five years. The best-known Flemish *Robbedoes* associate was Morris (Maurice De Bevere), whose 'Lucky Luke' would become an international sensation. Later, in the 1980s, the weekly magazine *Robbedoes* would play a key role in the growth of the Flemish and Dutch comic strip. Marc Legendre (*Biebel*), Luc Cromheecke (*Tom Carbon*) and Gerrit de Jager (*Roel en zijn Beestenboel*) were among the magazine's contributors.

In the Netherlands, *Donald Duck* became one of the country's most popular weekly comic books. Much of its content consisted of translations, but today it also includes original Dutch work. Another important comic strip weekly that frequently changed both its name and logo was known, in its most familiar guises, as *Pep* and *Eppo*. The magazine published many French comics in translation, but it was also instrumental in the emergence of a specifically Dutch comic strip scene. Illustrators like Peter de Smet, Henk Kuijpers, Dick Matena, Martin Lodewijk, Daan Jippes, Hanco Kolk and Peter de Wit made a name for themselves with their contributions. Additionally, popular news journals and even women's magazines included comic strips: the news weekly *Nieuwe Revue* brought Gerrit de Jager fame with his *De familie Doorzon*, and the women's weekly *Libelle* treated its readers to a full-page *Jan, Jans en de kinderen / Jack, Jacky and the Juniors* by Jan Kruis.

Today many comic strips produced in Flanders and the Netherlands still adhere to the traditional newspaper or magazine format. In Flanders these are known as 'family comics', as they appeal to young and old alike. They still boast impressive sales: *De Kiekeboes* by the cartoonist Merho is good for some half a million albums annually, closely followed by *FC De Kampioenen* by Hec Leemans, a spin-off of a popular television series. Even *Suske en Wiske* – some twenty-five years after its creator Willy Vandersteen's death – sees four new albums per year. *Suske en Wiske* is still the only classic Flemish comic to get a foot in the door in Holland, with sales in Dutch-language regions reaching 440,000 copies per title in the 1990s. Since then the numbers have dropped sharply, in part because the newspaper serialisations have largely been discontinued. And the publications where it does still appear have a much reduced impact on overall sales of the albums. Since *De Kiekeboes* in the late 1970s, no Flemish comic strips aimed at the general public have managed to break

Cover of *Eppo* Magazine by Hanco Kolk

Kraut by Peter Pontiac

through via newspapers alone. The 'serial' aspect has consequently become less important over the past three decades. Likewise, family comics are to-day produced mainly with album publication in mind, which in turn opens new doors and offers new possibilities, as the violent but popular *Suske and Wiske* spin-off *Amoras* by Charel Cambré and Marc Legendre proves.

What does continue to thrive in newspapers, especially those in the Nether-lands, is the daily 'gag strip': single-strip jokes, comparable to the internation-ally-syndicated *Peanuts* or *Calvin and Hobbes*. Peter de Wit draws *Sigmund* and joins up with Hanco Kolk for *S1ngle*, Mark Retera pushes the boundaries of goofi-ness with *Dirk Jan*, Gerrit de Jager's *Zusje* is a longtime favourite, and Aimée de Jongh contributes *Snippers* to the free commuter daily *Metro*. These are just a few examples. Humorous Flemish comics appear for the most part in weeklies, usually with a single full-page comic per week – *Boerke* by Pieter De Poortere, *Esther Verkest* by Kim Duchateau, and *Kinky & Cosy* by Nix – while alternative cartoonists Brecht Vandenbroucke and Jeroom Snelders tend to follow in the absurdist footsteps of Kamagurka and Herr Seele, who made it onto the pages of Art Spiegelman's international underground magazine *Raw* in the 1980s.

Columns

Another observation: many illustrators explore the overlap between political cartoon, comic strip and editorial column. Erik Meynen, for instance, provides a political current events comic strip for *Het Laatste Nieuws*, Belgium's most

28

The Jewish Brigade
by Marvano

read daily newspaper, depicting the Belgian politicians as cartoon characters. And for the Dutch daily newspaper *Trouw* and the monthly news magazine *Vrij Nederland*, Pieter Geenen produces madcap comics that lean toward the column or editorial.

Illustrators of realistic comic strips have always faced an uphill battle, as these are labour intensive and the market is limited. Many illustrators therefore set their sights abroad. Some specifically turned, in the 1980s and '90s, to the French market. The Dutch illustrator Paul Teng, for instance, worked at the French comics monthly *A Suivre*, and in 2009 he published a comic strip based on a scenario by the Brussels-born top scenarist Jean Van Hamme (*Thorgal*, *XIII* and *Largo Winch*). Van Hamme also wrote scenarios for Griffo, the pseudonym of the illustrator Werner Goelen, who in the early 1970s was part of the

Antwerp underground collective Ercola but later chose for a career with the large French publishers. Since then he has worked with numerous scenarists, from Jean Van Hamme to Stephen Desberg and Jean Dufaux, all heavyweights in the French comic strip market.

Another fascinating oeuvre is that of Marvano. He was the editor of *Kuifje* in the early 1980s before focusing on his own career as an illustrator. At first he produced mainly science fiction *(De eeuwige oorlog / The Forever War, Dallas Barr)*, but more recently he has turned to historical trilogies *(Berlin, Grand Prix, The Jewish Brigade)*. Marvano's work can be considered a turning point in the evolution of the comic strip in the Low Countries over the past few decades. It is still in the tradition of the classic adventure comic of the French-Belgian school, but it also differs from it. Marvano's stories lack 'heroes' as they are generally portrayed in the Adventure comics. Good and evil do not exist; nothing is cut-and-dried. He allows himself a great degree of freedom, and expects his (adult) readers to follow his lead.

Younger Flemish and Dutch cartoonists have embraced that freedom in the past fifteen years. Series with recurring characters have taken a back seat to the graphic novel, nowadays usually a self-contained story of unspecified length using a wide variety of techniques. And, not unimportantly, they are intended primarily for adults. On the international stage, Marjane Satrapi *(Persepolis)* and in particular Art Spiegelman *(Maus)* have set the tone.

Tante Leny

Alternative or literary comics are, of course, hardly new: in the 1970s some twenty issues of the magazine *Tante Leny presenteert!/Aunt Leny presents!* appeared in the Netherlands, and included work by Joost Swarte, Marc Smeets, Aart Clerckx and later Peter Pontiac. In Flanders, a few issues of *Spruit* by the Antwerp-based collective Ercola appeared during that same period. But the abundance of illustrators outside the mainstream is a recent development, and for them the serial comic strip is dead and buried.

Currently popular Flemish illustrators include Judith Vanistendael *(Toen David zijn stem verloor/When David Lost His Voice)*, Brecht Evens *(Panther, Ergens waar je niet wil zijn/The Wrong Place)*, Randall.C *(Slaapkoppen/Sleepyheads)* and the imaginative Olivier Schrauwen *(Arsène Schrauwen)*. Some have been nominated for an Eisner Award (USA) and for the Best Album prize at the Angoulême International Comics Festival. Willy Linthout, the author of the long-running and folksy 'Urbanus' comic (based on the eponymous singer and comedian, popular in Flanders) has many nominations to his name, and achieved worldwide recognition with *Jaren van de olifant*, a graphic novel drawn entirely in pencil in which he attempts to come to terms with his son's suicide.

Other illustrators making local and international headway with highly diverse projects include Stedho, Conz, Ken Broeders, Steve Michiels, Philip Paquet, Simon Spruyt, Wauter Mannaert, Jeroen Janssen, Joris Vermassen, Ephameron, Serge Baeken, Ivan Adriaensens, Michael Olbrechts, Wide Vercnocke and Ben Gijsemans. Gijsemans's *Hubert* was sold to leading British and French comics publishers the very day it was released.

It is worth noting the current underrepresentation of women. But here, too,

Sleepyheads
by Randall Casaer

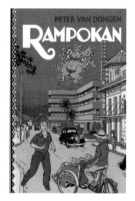

change is in the air. Recent graduates of Sint-Lukas in Brussels (part of LUCA School of Arts) include Charlotte Dumortier, Inne Haine, Shamisa Debroey, and Delphine Frantzen, all of whom have published promising graphic novels. The academy's comic strip faculty – Judith Vanistendael, Ephameron and Ilah (who creates tranches de vie for several newspapers) – is, incidentally, entirely female.

In the Netherlands, Peter Pontiac's *Kraut*, a graphic novel dealing with his father's wartime past, indicates a thematic shift. The illustrated autobiography is a form embraced by Jean-Marc Van Tol *(Opkomst en ondergang van Fokke en Sukke)*, Gerrit de Jager *(Door zonder familie)*, Michiel van de Pol *(Terug naar Johan)*, Gerard Leever *(Gleevers dagboek)*, Barbara Stok and Maaike Hartjes. Others who have garnered attention as author-illustrators of graphic novels include Guido Van Driel *(Om mekaar in Dokkum)*, Peter Van Dongen *(Rampokan)*, Floor de Goede *(Dansen op de vulcaan / Dancing on the Volcano)*, Mark Hendriks *(Tibet)*, Aimée de Jongh *(De terugkeer van De wespendief)*, and Hanco Kolk, whose at times awe-inspiring Meccano is his artistic masterpiece. Tim Enthoven's prizewinning *Binnenskamers / Within Four Walls* is perhaps the most remarkable illustrated book in recent years, as it attempts to bridge an autistic perception of the world with design and styling.

Compared with Flemish counterparts, today's Dutch illustrators are clearly still drawn to literature and the visual arts. In the past fifteen years, Dick Matena has transformed literary classics by Jan Wolkers, Willem Elsschot and Gerard Reve (retaining the complete text!), Milan Hulsing successfully adapted *De Aanslag / The Assault* by Harry Mulisch, and Nanne Meulendijks produced a graphic novel from Ronald Giphart's *De wake*. Other illustrators have created 'graphic biographies': *Rembrandt* by Typex, *Vincent Van Gogh* by Barbara Stok plus *Jheronimus* by Marcel Ruijters.

Amoras is a spin off, aiming at an adult audience,
of *Spike and Suzy/Willy and Wanda*

The Mad Maiden by Joris Vermassen
(notice the eponymous sculpture by Rik Wouters)

Short Stories by H.P. Lovecraft
made into strips by Eric Kriek

Schooling

The paradigm shift from serials to freer, more artistic work is largely due to changes in the comic strip market, but also to the training available to illustrators today. In the old days, an aspiring cartoonist had to put in his or her time as an apprentice in the studio of an old hand, and pick up the tricks of the trade there. No other schooling was to be had. At present, however, arts academies in Brussels, Ghent and Zwolle offer distinct studies in comics, while elsewhere departments of animation, design and graphic design also devote attention to the graphic novel. The illustrators' artistic vision and development is now considered far more important than market norms.

Thanks in part to these developments, the artistic diversity of comic strips in the Low Countries is greater than ever. Yet it is becoming increasingly difficult to earn a living wage. There is still a market for illustrators. But for the makers of comic strips, the possibilities are few and far between. Newspapers and magazines have become limited as a platform, and album production is feeling the squeeze as well. Audiences are shrinking (the entertainment market being constantly in flux) and the deluge of titles means albums are published in ever-smaller editions. According to statistics provided by Stripspeciaalzaak.be, in

2014 some 1270 Dutch-language albums were published. Most of them were translations, but Flemish and Dutch illustrators nonetheless have to compete with these titles in the marketplace. The average edition of albums has been steadily declining for years. Most graphic novels appear in printings of between 500 and 1000 copies, and within a matter of weeks they have to make way for the next batch of new titles. And the shift to a digital income-generating model has yet to take place.

Governments in both Flanders and the Netherlands support comic strip authors as well as publishers of graphic novels through their respective literature funds. A more-than-welcome helping hand, but in order for the medium to remain viable, its makers must creatively confront the genre's challenges, problems and possibilities. Subsidies alone will not keep the ship afloat. ◾

Kinky & Cosy by Nix

Translated by Jonathan Reeder

The Language
of Europe
Is Translation

UMBERTO ECO

HIDDEN TREASURES

New Roads to Paradise

In Praise of Hans Boland

In search of the most beautiful untranslated book from Dutch literature I am re-reading the novel *De zachte held* (The Tender Hero) by my colleague-translator Hans Boland, published in 2014, favourably reviewed in the newspapers, but subsequently relegated to the background until Boland was heard from again in early 2015 when he refused the renowned Pushkin Prize that had been awarded to him for his translations from the Russian. The prize was welcome, but to receive it from Putin's hands was unthinkable. Boland wouldn't let himself be used as a cultural sop for politics that he abhorred. Luckily he wasn't punished for it but was awarded the Martinus Nijhoff Prize for his complete translation oeuvre shortly afterwards. Because I was receiving the same prize for my translations into German we were interviewed together, on a wintry day, at the Translators' House in Amsterdam, where Boland was temporarily residing, since he had not long ago moved permanently to Indonesia.

Shortly before we met I had read *De zachte held* and I was very impressed by it. This was a book I wanted to translate into German. But what a job! And what a book! Nearly twenty years earlier, by translating the autobiographical novel *Het lied en de waarheid* (1997) by Helga Ruebsamen (translated into English by Paul Vincent as *The Song and the Truth*, Knopf, 2000), I had for the first time come into contact with a side of Dutch culture/society that was unknown to me, a kind of undertow in fact, coming from writers who were born and/or had grown up in Indonesia, which was then still a Dutch colony, the Dutch East Indies, authors to whom that land with its tropical climate, its people and its nature had come to look like a paradise, not in the least perhaps because they had had to leave it at a young age. In her famous debut novel *Oeroeg* (translated into English by Ina Rilke as *The Black Lake*, Portobello Books, 2012) Hella Haasse recreates the atmosphere in which the friendship between a Dutch and a Javanese boy, on the borderline between the colonial era and Indonesia's independence, is in fact doomed to failure; the social differences between the two families and the political tension during the War of Independence are simply too great.

Besides such authors, who are forever thinking back nostalgically to their youth in the Dutch Indies, there are also those who articulate different experiences. Thus Jeroen Brouwers with his *Bezonken Rood* (translated into English

by Adrienne Dixon as *Sunken Red*, Peter Owen, 1995, New Amsterdam Books, 1998) reminds us of a whole different chapter in the colonial history, that of the Japanese occupation of Indonesia during the Second World War and the fate of the Dutch who were interned by the Japanese in 'Jap Camps'.

Vincent Van Gogh,
The Novel Reader, 1888,
Private Collection

And this is only a small selection from the great number of novels in which the relationship of the Dutch to their former colony is central. Only a fraction of them have been translated into German. And other than in Germany, where the relationship with its past has been a subject of heated public debate for over thirty years, the crimes committed by the Dutch army during Indonesia's War of Independence are only rarely discussed in the Netherlands. It's unlikely that the German public has developed a feeling for the complexity, range and contradictions of all those memories from that colonial past. Hans Boland's recent book could change this. *De zachte held* is a successful mixture of fiction and travelogue, of a love story and essayistic, critical reflections about the historical development of Indonesia from colony to independent republic.

Boland, in contrast to most others with an Indonesian background, was only born on Java in 1951 and therefore after the Second World War and the War of Independence. His father worked there 'as a missionary' although, according

Rogier van der Weyden, *Mary Magdalene reading*,
fragment from a Sacra Conversazione, c. 1445,
National Gallery, London

to the narrator, he didn't much believe in God and had chosen this route mainly because the Missionary School offered him the chance to receive a higher
education and to realize a boyhood dream: to go 'to Insulinde'. But despite the
fact that the father sympathized with the 'freedom fighters', the situation became more and more intolerable for Dutch people in the new republic. That's
how the narrator, as a nine-year-old boy, landed in the Netherlands, the chilly,
damp country where he would always remain an outsider. Only after a whole
life, when he is sixty-one, does he follow his childhood dream and travel back
to the town where he was born: Jakarta. For three months he explores Java,
Sumatra and a small number of the more than seventeen thousand islands of
the archipelago, and there he meets the love of his life, the Javanese Teguh,
who is thirty years younger than he is.

In the novel there are always two voices; in the first part the perspective jumps back and forth between the boy the narrator once was and the man he is now, between past and present; later in the book there are still two voices, but the voices have changed:

Until halfway through my ninth year Holland was a myth. It rained there, slanting rains. They ate pears and cherries there [...] Java was my country, the country of kantjils and tigers. A kantjil was the most beautiful animal in creation, I myself was a tiger.
But what was supposed to be a temporary visit of nine months became a whole lifetime.
Of course I have to go by sea, in a ship. That's how we left, that's how I want to go back. I have wanted to go back since I left there, fifty-two years ago. I have longed for it for so long that 'going back' has become nearly the same as 'going'. Yet during all that time my decision never wavered, one day I would go back to Java and I would go there by ship.

Part I contains the journey of the tourist, the nostalgic who visits the house where he was born in Jakarta, his parental home and, in vain, his elementary school in Bandung. Details continuously alternate with the main narration. The description of the landscape, the towns and villages, but also of encounters on the train, the street, in hotels and eating places captures the imagination of the reader. Nor does the narrator hesitate to show his other, contradictory, feelings: his homesickness, the confrontation with the changes the country has undergone since his childhood. The cultural differences, the habit of the Javanese to always laugh, evading problems that way, how they never ask questions, the way they still behave subserviently towards Dutch people, the religion, the poverty and their joy of living, the charm of the children. There is no aspect which does not arouse his curiosity. About the Indonesian language he writes a letter to his old friend Ram: 'I never knew that such an enormous quantity of concepts (an estimated five to ten thousand) had been incorporated from the language of the colonizer [...] Once you know the spelling rules you are always encountering Dutchnesian', and that sounds, he shows convincingly with quite a few examples, often very comical to Dutch ears.

Every chapter begins with a memory, a reflection or a glance at the past, a reverie, so that gradually a picture emerges of the first nine years of the main character, to reinforce the impressions of a day or a week during the trip. The reader enjoys accompanying him and seeing things with him, experiencing the downpours, swinging in a hammock on a veranda, climbing a volcano, meeting the new inhabitants of his parental home. You understand that the narrator is in search of his own lost youth. Yet critical thoughts are uttered just as easily as nostalgic ones, he does not mince words and also allows the reader to share in his feelings of hurt or poignancy.

The travelogue never becomes boring, new aspects are brought up continually, humour alternates with quiet reflection or a biting analysis of the narrator's experiences. This traveller is an intellectual, curious, nostalgic and critical at the same time, with a feeling for atmosphere, people's character, while in search of, yes of what exactly? Eventually this turns out to be love.

In Part I of the novel we only meet the Javanese Teguh in passing. He is the errand boy who comes with the little apartment in Jakarta where the narrator spends the first and the last days of his stay. He reminds the narrator of his friend at elementary school in Bandung, 'perhaps because of his smile'. His appearance makes him think of a kantjil, a dwarf deer, so perfectly built he seems, while the way he goes after mosquitoes is more reminiscent of a tjitjak, a gecko. And a little bit later we read: 'His smile is the most beautiful I have ever seen.' Still, this would not give a reader pause, as there are more young

W.B. Tholen, *The Arntzenius Sisters*, 1895,
Photo by Tom Haartsen © Collection Museum Gouda, Gouda

people whose appearance move the narrator or make him enthusiastic. But then, in Part II of the novel, Teguh, whose name means 'steadfast', becomes the centre of his world.

The tone changes from reflective to intimate. The farewell scene at the end of Part I, which already gives the reader a vague though somewhat superficial idea that something is going on between the narrator and his errand boy, is repeated in Part II, now with details that can't be misunderstood.

I will, if necessary, force the stars

Once again the narrator does not mince words. A sixty-year-old intellectual from the Netherlands meets the love of his life: a Javanese who is thirty years younger. The differences couldn't be greater. Is it a holiday fling his Dutch friends ask, concerned, or, as the narrator puts it himself, in his unsparing way: is an older man using a young man from the slums? Is he buying him with his money? Or is the Javanese profiting from him, will he subsequently, once he is totally infatuated, leave him? And if it isn't a holiday fling, isn't it then a post-colonial love relationship?

The answer is in the story itself and can't be summarized in a few sentences. While all those questions whirl continuously through your head, you are swept along into a love between two people who are, for very different reasons, each other's last chance. It's make or break, for both of them. The difference in age and socio-cultural background leads to many nearly intolerable situations and regularly drives the narrator (and most likely his lover as well, but that we can only guess) to despair. Whether it is about dealing with money –Teguh lives from hand to mouth and, for example, spends 450 euros from the communal kitty in one go on pills from a 'quack' – or about the handling of time or appointments. On top of that 'the boy' often disappears for days on end, without giving any sign of life and just stops speaking when there is something he doesn't like - those are only a few examples that seem to make it obvious that any relationship between these two is a complete illusion. And that's exactly why it is both fascinating and moving to follow them on the trajectory they travel together. The narrator, overly conscious of the unevenness in the relationship, does his utmost to learn the 'language' of his beloved: 'He sees images, I see words.' He makes every effort to adjust and to put himself in the world of the other and so you breathlessly read how time after time a reconciliation becomes possible that is also a real coming together, how the 'rich Westerner' lets go of his ideas about relationships, lets go of his 'norms and values', yes, even of his pride, his anger, his fear to become the victim of his own yearning for love. While we read, we partake in a struggle that demands unconditional surrender, a struggle of life and death, no more and no less. And at the end both lovers have grown and the road to a common future seems to lie open. Even the turn the novel takes on the last pages doesn't alter that: while the narrator flies back for, as he believes, a last visit to the Netherlands before he settles permanently in Indonesia, Teguh dies of the disease he has had for many years, a disease that can't be named in Indonesia. Yes that - but more importantly: he is able to accept it.

A gift from heaven

The intimate tone is ushered in by the story about his cat Roes. This cat, that had been his inseparable companion and had sweetened the preceding four lonely years in Amsterdam, disappears shortly before the narrator leaves for Jakarta, just as unexpectedly as she had once appeared. 'From now on it will always be like this. Roes won't be there to greet me.' The love that he is experiencing now is just as mysterious as the one for Roes. 'Roes belonged to me and I belonged to her' - this tenderness and attachment from both sides is moving and recognizable. Thinking about Roes crosses over into thinking about his love for the Javanese Teguh, for where does all this tenderness come from after thirty years of 'living like a monk'?

'I am trying to answer the question whether I fell for this boy because of who he is, or because he happened to be the first Javanese I met.' And just as Roes appears and disappears, to return again one day, Teguh, in his behaviour, is also more like a wild cat than a person. And while the narrator looks back on his life, which during his youth had been rich in sex but had been lacking in love during the last decades, his amazement grows about what is now happening to him: 'Unexpectedly love has once more taken root'. And although the encounter has also on the sexual level reached unknown heights, he concludes: 'And still it isn't the sex that excites me'.

His breath is spicy. Sweet and spicy. The smell of sun on privet leaf. A trace of cow parsley that you smell but can't see when you are cycling through the polder, it's so far away. The smell of dry flowers at dawn.

These words call up associations with the Song of Songs. They form poetic images the narrator uses to bring across something of the intoxicating love that has turned his life upside down. In Part II they introduce each chapter and create the atmosphere that lets you be carried along on a wave of blissful, passionate and tender encounters.

'The infatuation will pass', the narrator muses, 'taking care of the boy can still be done after that.' It is that inner step, long before it has to be taken, that will enable him to endure the tribulations that await him.

'Only now I'm starting to realize what I have missed the most since I no longer have Roes: a living, breathing creature that needs me. "My boy, Guh, you are a gift from heaven", I write to the boy I have automatically started to call Guh. Guh, a sound like a breath in the dark.'

It is the road to this insight, as deep as it is simple, into the secret of love that the author lets the reader traverse in *De zachte held*, and in order to do that you have to be a damn good writer.

Hans Boland, *De zachte held*, Athenaeum-Polak & Van Gennep 2014. ▪

Translated by Pleuke Boyce

Love in the Lost Republic of Amsterdam

In Praise of Doeschka Meijsing

[PHILIPPE NOBLE]

The cultural officer (or ambassador, if you will) that I was for many years, and the reader and translator I still am - and hope to remain for some years to come - are struggling with each other to decide which as yet untranslated book, which as yet untranslated author(s) from the Low Countries I should urgently tell the world about, and why.

For the cultural ambassador, the personal preference for one or more individual literary works is irrelevant. He is concerned with how a foreign readership (French-speaking, for example) can be provided with a reliable corpus of translated highlights from Dutch literature over the centuries. There are three requirements for this: a responsible selection of works, a series of reliable translations, and a willing publisher.

But the civil servant does not raise his head above the parapet; he comes up with no more than an outline for yet another project - for which there is no budget yet. This is talking in a vacuum, and the opposite of a true feeling for literature - the feeling that is based on personal, idiosyncratic choices, far removed from any educational considerations. Both voices fight to be heard but, if I listen to my heart, the voice of the reader is the loudest and strongest. This is the voice that I will allow to speak.

In the past twenty years there have been several novels that I have read with intense pleasure, and afterwards regretted that they had not been brought to the attention of a French-language publisher sooner. The fact that they missed their chance is usually due simply to chance, a lack of information, or to bad timing. But if I had to choose just one title from this series of neglected books, then it would certainly have to be *Over de liefde* (About Love) by Doeschka Meijsing (Querido, Amsterdam, 2008). Meijsing was perhaps not entirely unknown to the French-speaking world; two of her works had already been translated into French, the 'fairy tale' *Beer en jager* (Bear and Hunter, as *L'Ours et le Chasseur* by Xavier Hanotte, Doornik, Estuaire, 2005) and the novel *100 % chemie* (100% chemistry, as *100% chimique. Une chronique familiale* by Charles Franken, Bordeaux/Paris, Le Castor Astral, 'Escales des Lettres', series 2007), but had not made much of an impact. In her own country too, Meijsing's real breakthrough didn't come until the publication of *Over de liefde* (About Love), for which she received the AKO Prize in 2008. Sadly, she was not able to enjoy her success for

long. Less than four years later, in January 2012, she died from complications following major surgery. This largely put paid to her chances of being translated; a deceased author cannot give interviews, sign books or give readings. In the world of publishing, being dead is a deadly sin for an author - unless you've been dead for centuries, of course.

I did not discover Meijsing's work until relatively late, despite the fact that, back in the 1990s when I was living in Amsterdam, I often encountered her in person. She was a friendly, somewhat reserved local resident, a familiar Amsterdam figure who had a drink problem - one that she made no effort to conceal. Perhaps this was why my expectations were not very high when I picked up her last novel. It turned out to be a revelation.

It is difficult to describe the specific charm of *Over de liefde* (About Love), because everything about this novel is paradoxical. The title gives the impression that it is an essay, but there is little about this book that is essayistic; rather, it is a series of stories, anecdotes and recollections, threaded together by a conspicuously present female narrator. Nevertheless, relatively little happens in the course of the narrative, apart from a serious road accident and a fall into the Prinsengracht canal - with the narrator as the victim in both instances. Yet, despite this simple fact, it is almost impossible to summarise the plot (insofar as it exists). There are various storylines that the author/narrator, with great nonchalance, constantly breaks off and takes up again later.

First story line: dealing with heartbreak. The narrator, Philippa ('Pip') van der Steur, an Amsterdam academic, has been deserted by her younger partner Jula, a successful journalist. After an apparently happy relationship that has lasted many years, Jula suddenly falls for a man and soon becomes pregnant. Not long afterwards, Philippa is seriously injured in an accident (a concrete-mixer truck veers out of control and crashes into a café terrace where she is sitting, and just in time she manages to save the lives of two women). Jula has the opportunity to look after her recovering ex-girlfriend. Jula cares for Philippa for many months, and there is a hesitant reconciliation when Philippa agrees to go to the celebration meal that Jula is giving for her birthday. On that same evening, Philippa falls into the canal and is carried away from her former great love - literally and figuratively.

Johannes Vermeer, *Woman in Blue Reading a Letter*,
ca. 1663–64, Oil on canvas, Rijksmuseum, Amsterdam

Second story line: through circumstances that may or may not be coinciden- tal, Philippa is thinking about the first woman she ever loved, her high-school gym teacher, Buri Vermeer, an aloof beauty who grew up in the Dutch East In- dies and, while still a teenager, had been interned in a prison camp during the Japanese occupation. Philippa watches a documentary on DVD about this pe- riod. In the documentary, Buri returns to the place where she was imprisoned. By an incredible coincidence, Buri is one of the two women that Philippa saved in the accident – but Philippa doesn't recall this for a long time because she was in shock after the accident. Eventually she and her former teacher come into contact with each other again. During two emotional visits, Buri confides in Philippa about her secret love for one of the Japanese officers during her imprisonment. Despite their completely different sexual preferences, Philippa discovers a soul mate in Buri and is even able, albeit in a sort of daydream, to satisfy her past longing for this woman.

Third story line: to help her lift her out of her depression, Philippa's three brothers take her on a nostalgic trip to the place where they used to spend their holidays when they were children, a slightly dilapidated house in a village on the border between the Swiss canton of Ticino and Italy. The purpose of the trip is to find a centuries-old painting that is possibly from the studio of Man- tegna and has supposedly lain hidden there for years. This somewhat surreal episode, which would not be out of place among the adventures of Enid Blyton's *Famous Five*, appears to be separate from the rest of the book. It is indeed an intermezzo, intended to introduce a note of Mediterranean levity into an oth- erwise fairly sombre story. But it also has another, more symbolic function: predictably, the search for the alleged Mantegna proves fruitless. The narrator seems to be warning us that the great quest for love and intimacy is doomed to failure too.

So why do readers swallow this rambling story? In the first place, because of the incredible rhetorical talent of the author, whose writing (in the words of critic Jeroen Vullings in *de Volkskrant* newspaper, 12/2/2008) is 'at times beautiful and outrageously witty'. Doeschka Meijsing herself said, half-joking- ly, in an interview: 'I'm just really good at writing beautiful sentences'. There are countless passages that could illustrate this, but I will confine myself to a single example. After her accident, Philippa lands in hospital with a fractured skull. When she comes out of the coma, a doctor tells her that she has to have an operation 'and then, he adds, there is a good chance that you'll be back to your old self again.' The text continues:

For some reason, being back to my old self didn't seem a very attractive pros- pect, and much of what the man said remained gibberish to me, but I knew that when you're in hospital it's best to go along with them, without resisting or want- ing to be smarter than the doctors, so I agreed to everything and soon after, wearing nothing but a short green gown, I was pushed through the corridors of the hospital, and left and right the bags and tubes went too, we moved at a fair pace through a complicated maze, with doors swinging open and shut and people flattening themselves against the wall as we passed, and it was really fun, a bit like being at the fair. And all those lights. Above my head the big wheel started turning and something was put on my face and they forgot to take it off, and then - nothing again.

Michael Sweerts, *Portrait of a Young Man*,
ca. 1656, Oil on canvas, The Hermitage, St. Petersburg

Meijsing is also a master of symbolic detail. A dark patch on the parquet floor of Philippa's new home functions as a tangle of motives developed elsewhere in the novel. By comparing the patch to a Rorschach inkblot test, the author elevates it to a symbol of Philippa's subconscious and the repository of the memory that she has temporarily lost. Yet the book has much more to offer than this sort of sophisticated literary *divertissement*. A sense of tragedy underlies the irony of the narrative. Philippa struggles with the realisation that her love life has been one long failure, and that her desire for happiness may be a mistake. These mostly sombre musings are foreshadowed by death. In a beautifully written night-time scene, Philippa recalls all her past friends from the local bar as she walks home after a birthday gathering. And the fall and swim at the end of the novel, although recounted in optimistic tones, could be interpreted as a veiled, half-hearted suicide attempt.

But there is another aspect to *Over de liefde* (About Love) that moves me on a personal level. It is a brilliant snapshot of a particular place at a particular time: Amsterdam at the *fin de siècle* of the twentieth century. And by Amsterdam I mean, specifically, what Harry Mulisch refers to in *The Discovery of Heaven (De ontdekking van de hemel)* as 'the Republic of Amsterdam', as opposed to the 'Kingdom' – the rest of the Netherlands. It may be that the further one is from the setting, the more sensitive one is to this aspect of the book. The most striking intellectual aspect of this novel is that it makes statements 'about love' - the concept of love in general, that is - based on the protagonist's experiences in a fairly narrow circle of gay women. Apparently this requires no explanation, since it is not mentioned anywhere. There was not a single Dutch reviewer in 2008 who drew attention to this aspect. Despite a few caustic comments by the narrator about gay marriage, the moral equivalence of homosexual and heterosexual love is assumed throughout the book. There are many places in the world - France, for a start - where this equivalence would be highly controversial. For this reason alone, *Over de liefde* (About Love), complete with its Stendhalian title, should be translated into French.

In almost all her novels - for example *Geheel de uwe* (Sincerely Yours) and *Lucifer* - Connie Palmen carefully paints a picture of the world that is sardonically labelled 'the canal belt'. In *Over de liefde* (About Love), this picture emerges in passing. Nowhere is it an explicit theme, merely a secondary effect of the intellectual, aesthetic and emotional milieu in which the narrator and the protagonists live their lives. The book resonates with the libertine spirit of a social group and era in which everything seemed possible, everything was regarded and discussed without prejudice, and everything was considered interesting (or not). Doeschka Meijsing embodied this culture, which has already ceased to exist. It is what gives this idiosyncratic novel a patina of melancholia and nostalgia that touches my heart. ■

Translated by Yvette Mead

Flemish Master of the Small Canvas

In Praise of Willem Elsschot

[PAUL VINCENT]

Willem Elsschot's (1882-1960) eleven novellas, with their irony, sardonic humour and stylistic sophistication, are as vibrant today as when they were written.

Five works have so far been translated into English. In 1963 the great trio of stories, *Soft Soap*, *The Leg* and *Will 'o the Wisp* appeared in one volume translated by Alex Brotherton, introducing us to the recurring figures of the disillusioned idealist Frans Laarmans and the Svengali-like business guru Boorman. Sadly, the impact of the book was muted somewhat by its academic, non-commercial publishing context.

In 1992, I translated Elsschot's brilliant, haunting debut, *Villa des Roses* (republished in 2003). On its reissue the novel benefited from a lively, prize-winning English film version by Frank Van Passel with a largely English cast including Timothy West and Harriet Walter. Press comment on the book was unanimously favourable: 'Absorbing' (Good Book Guide), 'His precise, considered prose... is a joy' (The Tablet), 'Black certainly, but brilliantly comic as well' (Hampstead and Highgate Express).

2002 saw the publication of the most successful Elsschot work in English so far, *Cheese*. Reviewers were quick to appreciate both its literary quality and its contemporary relevance. The book about a disastrous business venture was presented by the publishers as 'Edam's great moment in world literature' and drew such widespread plaudits as: '... a little gem' (Deborah Moggach), 'It has a wonderful Keatonesque pacing which is total bliss. I adored it' (Glen Baxter), '... a surprisingly humane farce of ambition gone haywire and Edam gone bad' (New York Times). Its topical resonance was stressed: 'Pop a dot and a com on the end of Gafpa and the message becomes all too clear' (Daily Telegraph), and 'Perhaps the publishers would also be so kind as to send some copies to the board of Enron?' (The Times). The novel was featured on the prestigious BBC radio series *Book at Bedtime*, where it was read by Richard Griffiths, whose 'absurdly comic élan' was praised. However, although a Dutch film version of *Cheese* appeared under the direction of Orlow Seunke, the chance of a full tie-in was lost when a planned UK production fell through.

In 2016, when the Low Countries will again be in focus as a *Schwerpunkt* at the Frankfurt Book Fair, the time would seem ripe to make the case for a Complete Willem Elsschot in English, either as an omnibus or as separate volumes.

Kik Zeiler, *Fallen asleep*, 1989,
Oil on canvas, 44.5 x 61.5 cm,
Private collection

He is an undisputed classic in the Dutch-speaking world and in my view, given the right exposure, has the potential to become a European and world classic. Elsschot remains a flagship author for the Flemish Foundation for Literature (VFL), the relevant funding body.

Here, as a taster, is a passage from *Soft Soap*, where the zealous Boorman communicates his business creed to his young apostle (the translation is by Alex Brotherton):

'Vanity, that's the cause of it all, de Mattos. Everyone wants to be Number One, or at least wants to make everyone else think so. But there aren't many who get beyond trying to make everyone else think so. And Jesus Christ, who went round spouting as if he had cornered the wisdom of all the ages, didn't change anything. There are more fools in the world than there are grains of sand in a desert and that's what the smart lads reckon on. They pick out a spot, put up a signboard as bright as a rainbow, and then comes the advertising like a gramophone turned full on. Everything is shiny and new, everything is better than anywhere else. Now and then one of them goes under, but he's up again with a flick of his tail, as long as there's a flick left in it. It's these smart lads that I'm after. I drop in on them, one after the other, as the colossal director of the colossal *World Review*. Some of them don't even listen, they're too busy with figures and schemes of their own.

Gerard Dou, *Old Woman Reading*, ca.1631-1632,
Oil on panel, 71 x 55.5 cm,
Rijksmuseum Amsterdam

One or two might even get annoyed, because they're not fooled by the *World Review*. Some of them are short of funds. But you always find some who'll snap at the bait if only you look long enough. We're only doing what they're doing, they get away with it, why shouldn't we? You keep talking and don't listen to anything they say. We're only interested in their order and not in their tales of woe. If they're ready to sign when we've said our piece, then so much the better, and if they're not, it's just too bad, and it's no good wasting any more time. After all, there's no sense in arguing about money, when the other fellow has it and you want it, because you are both in the right. Beggars know this rule. They ask you for money and you ask them how's their family, and then they ask you for money again, and they'll either get some from you or give-up, once they see you're not going to give them a hand-out. They don't waste any more time on you, they try someone else. You do them more of a favour by saying "no" straight out, than by falling round their necks in tears with excuses. You have to be satisfied with what you get, because every deal is a good deal. A business deal is a business deal, it's a game for two players and one of them has to win. Just how much the winner takes is more a matter of chance than anything else. How much a client bites off depends on how big his mouth is. But always start by talking big and let their vanity do the rest. And never give the impression that you think it's a big deal yourself, they'll only laugh at you. If you talk casually about a large sum as if it was a mere trifle, then they'll go one better without a thought of what God's golden guineas are worth, even though it has to come out of their own pockets. When they take up a pen to sign, don't show you're pleased, act as though you didn't want them to sign. Some of them are even likely to give you an order in the hope that all the work it will involve might kill you.

'Try and believe what you tell them is the truth, then your story sounds all the more convincing. You have to sound convincing. If you are, you can talk a hard-hearted miser into an extravagance that he'll probably shudder at the thought of an hour later. Once I had a bank manager properly warmed up, and I didn't realize it. He had one of those stupid faces that stay blank all the time. Suddenly he reached boiling point. He jumped up, he banged on the table, and he ordered a million copies with an article about his bank. Every family in Belgium must have a copy, he was yelling. He looked like a crusader who'd just caught sight of Jerusalem. But when I hesitated, because I didn't think I could risk a million copies with that piddling little printer of mine, he came out of his trance and had me marched to the door.

'Never be discouraged, even if you have weeks of bad luck. Don't trust in God, de Mattos. Be polite to your clients, because they're your enemies, and don't forget it. They'll only give you what you can wring out of them and not a cent more.'

The following is a brief overview of all six hitherto untranslated fictions.

1. Een ontgoocheling (A Disappointment, 1914)

A doting father, the struggling cigar manufacturer De Keizer (whose first name we are never told), becomes increasingly disillusioned with his good-for-nothing son Kareltje. The opening evokes De Keizer's small, claustrophobic world.

2. De verlossing (Salvation, 1921)

In this novella, his only venture into a 'big' theme in Flemish fiction (the power of the Church, especially in rural areas), Elsschot pits the atheist village grocer Pol van Domburg against the doctrinaire local priest, Pastor Kips. The result is mayhem, murder and (possible) redemption. Irony and understatement rub shoulders with melodrama. The priest's answer to Pol's defiance is a boycott of his shop.

Cornelis Brisé, *Documents Concerning the Treasury of the City of Amsterdam*, 1656, 19.4 x 25 cm, Amsterdam Museum

3. **Tsjip** (Cheep, 1934)

4. **De leeuwentemmer** (The Lion Tamer, 1940)
   These two books, which chronicle the writer's daughter's marriage to and subsequent divorce from a Pole and his relationship with his grandson, are at once Elsschot's most directly autobiographical and his most optimistic works. The title 'Cheep' relates to the first sound the grandson produces, which becomes his nickname. 'The Lion Tamer' reverts to the epistolary form first used in 'Cheese'.

5. **Pensioen** (Pension, 1937)

6. **Het tankschip** (The Tanker, 1942)
   In these two novellas Elsschot returns to the murky and occasionally surreal world of finance and business. In the first a parent struggles against the odds to obtain an adequate pension for a missing son, while the second sees the final appearance of the naïve Laarmans and the archetypal dodgy businessman Boorman, this time involved in an offer literally too good to be true: a tanker in good order free to a responsible user. The fantasy bubble is bound to burst…

   If I – reluctantly – had to choose just one work for (re-)publication, it would be *Soft Soap* and its sequel *The Leg*, closely followed by *The Will-o'-the-Wisp*. Hopefully quality will speak for itself and a Complete Elsschot will at long last become a reality. ■

   Samples/complete translations of all works mentioned above can be obtained from paulfrankvincent@gmail.com

Ode to a Bastard Called 'Dutch'

The bastard language is the language of the twenty-first century because we are the children of a crazy, chaotic age in which the individual has to figure things out for himself. Language adapts to who we are. If language has first to conform to the laws of grammar, it must now also conform to the laws of the street, the laws of migration, the laws of liberalisation. The bastard is on the alert. The one you hear is who I am.

The bastard language embraces new words at the speed of light. *Kapsalon* (lit. barbershop) for an abundant meat dish with chips and cheese, *terroroehoe* (lit. terror owl) for the winged creature that terrorises neighbourhoods with its horrific sound, and then there is *aanspoelstrand* (lit. wash-up beach) where the refugees from North Africa are washed ashore. Every day new items come to the language market, like freshly caught fish. Words that have exhausted their usefulness are just as easily thrown back into the language sea.

Dutch is heading along a motorway where vehicles are entering and exiting at high speed. The quicksilver words join the social motorway via the slip roads of the media and street noise. At the end of the year the new words are listed in the press. The lists are a reminder of the world we were living in. This is who we were, this is what preoccupied us, what annoyed us. Those words are the mirror of what we believed in last year, of how we controlled reality and what we thought of it.

Dutch adapts remarkably flexibly to our linguistic wish to name reality accurately; the strength of the bastard language is that it is never lost for words, hence the habit of quickly reaching for an English loanword when the moment requires it. The nigglers are wrong when they say Anglicisms are an admission of weakness. It isn't laziness, it's the powerful, confident way Dutch plays 'word grab'. Like rivers and seas the bastard language knows no bounds.

Our bastard language is a mixture of foreign and local words, of words from the dictionary and words from songs, words from the distant past and up-to-the-minute words, words found in the clouds, low-life words. The bastard language is the thermometer in the bottom. The bastard language is an indicator of the condition of language.

Language is prestige

It was once thought that bastard languages were exotic variants of Dutch. And so they are. They arise when formal language proves inadequate in daily intercourse. It is the secret route to feeling. To understand the origin of the bastard languages we must go abroad.

We'll begin in the former colonies. In the period of slavery Dutch was the language of the master for the Surinamese. Speaking the language was in itself an act of resistance. Anyone who spoke Dutch could see through the machinations of the rulers. On the other hand the language humanised power, and made it vulnerable. Being able to talk back to the rulers in their own language was the first step towards liberation and emancipation. The elite of independent Surinam prided themselves on speaking better Dutch than the Dutch. Language became a matter of prestige. The Surinamese Dutchman Ricardo Pengel, a doctor at the Radboud Hospital in Nijmegen, told me how he learned Dutch geography in Paramaribo: 'I knew all the lakes and rivers and canals off by heart. Only when I arrived in the Netherlands and saw those rivers for the first time, did I realise what I had learned in Paramaribo.'

The Surinamese who came to the Netherlands after Surinamese independence brought their Surinamese Dutch with them, interspersed with words and phrases of the *marons*, runaway slaves, and the Javanese, Chinese and Hindustanis. Under the Dutch surface Sranan Tongo, the language of Surinam, made itself heard like a spitfire. It refused to be forgotten and could never be. The language of the Surinamese was like *moksi metti*, their national dish, in which various types of meat and vegetables are combined. *Moksi metti* means mixed meat. In Surinamese one travels through three cultures in one sentence.

When I grew up in Rotterdam my mother tongue, Berber, was joined by the dominant formal Standard Dutch. At school we learned the correct pronunciation, with every word approved by pedagogues. At home we switched to Berber, but that could not prevent the steady encroachment of Dutch. What began in one language could be finished in the other. Anyone who spoke too correctly was looked down on. Prestige was closely linked to street cred. Outside, a different reality prevailed. In the street raw, stiff Rotterdam dialect danced with the Dutch of the Surinamese. *Wat seggie? Als ie val dan leggie! Ja toch?* (What dya say? If ya fall ya on the floor! Right?)

In the street Dutch freed itself from the tight constraints of formality to be able to sing its polyphonic song freely. It was simply allowed to be. In bastard language liveliness takes precedence over formalism, timing over well-considered periods and humour over seriousness. Bastard language is the currency of the street, which becomes more valuable the more the owner exchanges it. Without the bastard languages Standard Dutch has no right to exist and will die out. The bastard does not give his father and mother a moment's rest in his yearning for recognition.

Secret language

In the street where my father had his butcher's shop, West-Kruiskade, tough Surinamese guys ruled the roost. They stood in front of the shop, the kings of the street. Their Dutch sounded tough. On their heads they wore Panama hats from Venezuela, gold chains hung round their necks and thick silver rings squeezed their fat fingers. Their language was weighed down just as heavily. Their voices growled as low as a chain saw felling a tree, and when they laughed I heard the tree fall. When they laughed, the wires above the tram line vibrated. On hot Wednesday afternoons there was nothing to do in the shop and I eavesdropped on their conversations. At the start it was incomprehensible because it was so far removed from the Dutch I was familiar

with, but little by little I got used to it and actually started to understand it. What happened was that I started to see Dutch as a foreign language, a language that I had to master. And just when I thought I understood everything they turned away from me and never came back, after which other men took their place and the game began again from the beginning. Whenever they had something to discuss in the clan they switched to their secret language, and then the door closed in my face and I again felt like the outsider I had always been. Language could also be a secret language. And I understood that a language that wants to survive has to be reborn each time anew.

I heard the thick 'w's of the tough guys with the chains round their necks again in the Antwerp Flemish of my cousins in Wilrijk, as if they had been to the same pronunciation school. That thick 'w' was suppressed on the news and in formal exchanges – where it had to be as thin as watery soup. My cousins did not stick to grammar, they mixed Moroccan and Berber with Antwerp dialect, a potpourri of Flemish restlessness. The new Belgium. As a favour to me, they toned down their language in my presence, started speaking more correctly and became duller. I didn't care for it at all, but how could I persuade them to be themselves? They were proud of the ability to switch 'languages' so fast within one language. It gave them power.

When a language goes travelling, it assumes the protective colouring of the new environment. Spanish, regional, Antwerp, Portuguese and African words fitted effortlessly into that tropical Dutch and the Dutch of my cousins. Dutch's capacity for absorption was a sign of its vitality. The language's great open-heartedness also met with resistance: a bastard is not yet an adopted child, it is talked of with shame and the outside world must not know about it. 'You have no business here,' Oeroeg barked at his Dutch friend in the novella of the same name by Hella Haasse – this threat that deals a fatal blow to the friendship between Oeroeg and the first-person narrator, is spoken in Dutch, not Indonesian. The last words exchanged between two friends are filled with bitterness. Five words that could not have better summarised the tragic transition from the Netherlands Indies to Indonesia, from a sentiment to a reality. In Hella Haasse Dutch changes from being the language of friendship into the language of the enemy. History dons a new jacket. The Dutch disappeared, leaving behind the plantations, balconies and dusty words. Travelling through Java in search of the roots of the Oerol festival on the Dutch island of Terschelling in the tea plantations around Bogor, I pass shops whose signs refer to past Dutch commercial activity. As if nothing has changed. A pharmacy is an *apotik* (Dutch 'apotheek'). A garage is a *bengkel* (Dutch 'winkel' = shop) and the cemetery (Dutch 'kerkhof'), the place where language finally comes to rest, is a *kerkop*. The Dutch of an elderly Moluccan with whom I strike up a conversation is dusty, formal and far too cultured for the easy-going conversation we are having. That was how it sounded fifty years ago, what I hear is a living fossil.

World language

I shall never forget the man who ran the most famous tango café in Buenos Aires. He had eyes full of fun and a wonderful Latin moustache of the kind that can only be found in those parts. I had taken refuge there with my Argentine

publisher – young dude, ponytail, weak left foot in football – to recover from the interviews I had given. Above us hung a photo of the same table, seated at which were the two sacred monsters of Argentine literature: Borges and Sabato.

'I wonder if the owner has a poster of this?' and I headed for the man behind the bar.

'Do you have a poster of that and if so can I buy one?' I mumbled in English, hoping for the best.

'What country are you from?' he asked in amusement.

'The Netherlands', I replied and to my astonishment he broke into fluent Dutch. 'That photo is not just hanging there for no good reason, they settled a long-standing argument in this café', and he presented me with a poster. For nothing. I had nothing to say about the poster, but I did about his mastery of the language of the Low Countries. 'How come you speak such good Dutch?' His eyes gleamed. 'It's a world language, isn't it?' He had me there. By giving Dutch this predicate, quite apart from the fact whether it was true or not, he had made me a provincial and himself the true citizen of the world. He quickly reassured me. The owner of the café spent a part of the year in Brabant. 'With my love.' So it was another case of love. And the tango danced on. What would Dutch sound like if it were spoken by Argentines? Or Ghanaians? Or Russians?

The future of all languages

A strange sensation, being spoken to in the language of home in unexpected places. In some Berber villages in the Rif they swear in Dutch and count dirhams with a soft 'g'. Seated on the soft sofas of the Moorish palaces of returned emigrants, they watch the Dutch World Service and dream of chips with mayonnaise, a cloudburst and a sprint on the bike. Across the balcony one sister yells at the other to 'Bring back a bottle of coke and a packet of tampons.' No one can understand them. So they thought.

Standard Dutch is a myth propagated every evening anew on national television; the rest of the world prefers to speak in as broad a dialect as possible. You don't hear language, you taste it. On a sandy beach in Al Hoceima there is a cacophony of regional pronunciations, Brabant, Limburg, West Netherlands conurbation, Ghent and Antwerp, all twittering together at thirty degrees in the shade and if I close my eyes and the languages flow into my ears from all sides, they merge into a language I no longer understand, a new language that at some time in the future will assume its fixed form. This must have happened to languages down the ages.

A bastard language diverges from the official language; it is the illegitimate child born of an undesirable courtship between the grand lady and the street urchin, the judge and the whore. In hip hop music the bastard language screams for recognition. In a vital, noisy and fearless mix of street language, pidgin and formal grammatical structures which are played around with to the heart's content of the speaker, the voice of the new, the unpolished, the explosive energy, demands its place. But the raison d'être of the bastard language is that it will never become official; it shrinks from formal recognition as the bat does from the day. It cannot live in that assigned status. All attempts by Standard Dutch to regularise the language will result in its death. Both sides benefit from this uncomfortable relationship, like two lovers who in their quarrels push each other's characters to new heights.

The bastard language is the result of a deep love between language and humankind. It is the future of all languages. ■

All images © Ever Meulen

Translated by Paul Vincent

Olla Vogala (hinase) (All Birds (save))

A Canon of Dutch Literature

I would like to discuss the Dutch literary canon, and already see storm clouds on the horizon. How do you dare to give a ranking to books, to raise the personal preferences of a few self-proclaimed experts to the level of absolute truth, and to solidify living literature into a list set in stone?

And yet I'm doing it. Because the canon is the conversation about the canon, the discussion, even the arguments about books and writers. Because you first have to have something if you want to set yourself against it. Because I would like to be able to answer the woman from Bucharest or the man from Sydney or Osaka when they ask me what Dutch literature they should have read.

In 2015 the Royal Academy of Dutch Language and Literature bent their heads together in Ghent over the canon, and came out with fifty titles, fifty works from between the end of the twelfth century and the 1980s. All the authors on the list are dead. The living need not feel frustrated. The list actually consists of 51 titles. After it was concluded, Jef Geeraerts passed away, so his book *Gangrene 1 (Black Venus)* (1968) was added to the list. Which goes to show that the canon can evolve.

A lament in a margin

Dutch literature begins with an amorous lament in the margins of a manuscript. We decided that unanimously. We are in England, a bit before 1100. The culprit is a monk who most likely came from West Flanders. He tries his pen – *probatio pennae* – bent over a manuscript that he was meant to be copying in a cloister in Kent. The monk first chooses trusted Latin. *Habent omnes uolucres nidos inceptos nisi ego et tu. Quid expectamus nunc.* He hesitates for a moment, then chooses a confession in his own language:

Hebben olla vogola nestas hagunnan hinase hic enda thu wat unbidan we nu.
'All birds are a-nesting / save me and thee / why now do we tarry' (translated by John Irons)

The language is discovering itself: linguists describe it as Old Dutch with an English substrate, or even as Old English - Kentish, to be exact - with a strong Dutch veneer. What does it matter? The language is there. To stay.

The carnival of the bourgeoisie

I, too, would like to begin building a few nests here, but also to limit myself. To books from the twentieth century, roughly speaking. I presume that the woman from Bucharest and the man from Sydney will get more out of a limited number of titles. Even so, I would like to begin with a novel from 1860: *Max Havelaar, or The Coffee Auctions of the Dutch Trading Company*. The author is Eduard Douwes Dekker (1820-1887), alias Multatuli (what a pseudonym! 'I who have borne much'). The importance of this novel can hardly be underestimated: it is the first modern novel in our literature, written in modern Dutch. Even the author said of it, with his provocative irony: 'I set myself to the task of writing living Hollandish. But I went to school.' (Idee 41, in *Ideeën* (1862)).

It is not an accident that in 2002 the book was acclaimed as the best book in the canon of Dutch literature by members of the *Maatschappij der Nederlandse Letterkunde*.

The story, 2015,
Piezographic print on paper,
27 x 39 cm
© Lynne Leegte

In *Max Havelaar*, Douwes Dekker exposes and denounces colonial abuses in the Dutch East-Indies. As a colonial official, he had experienced them first-hand. He had acted against them in vain. Now he chooses the pen as his weapon. And an unusual literary form: a framed story with multiple storylines and various narrators. There are official documents in this book and compelling tales ('Saïdja and Adinda'), and with the figure of coffee broker Batavus Droogstoppel, an immortal caricature of the Dutch-Calvinist entrepreneur takes the stage, upholding the system of repression with his studied and devout self-interest, half naïve and half cunning.

A solid half-century later, Willem Elsschot (1882-1960) would claim of Multatuli: 'This true Prometheus has held aloft the torch of rebelliousness and non-conformism. The whole of modern Dutch literature has flared up from his ashes. His cult is our most sacred duty.' That counts as a salute of honour.

In Elsschot's work, especially on the thematic level, there are also parallels with Multatuli. There is at least *one* noteworthy allusion. In the poem about the confused young Dutchman, Van der Lubbe, who was convicted in 1933 for setting fire to the Berlin Reichstag and subsequently executed, Elsschot writes: 'Let it (Holland and co) suffocate in its money, / in its cheese and in its skinflints' – which most certainly echoes Multatuli's angry jab at Droogstoppel at the end of *Havelaar*: 'Suffocate in coffee and disappear.'

Untitled, 2013,
Ultrachrome print, 48 x 72 cm
© Lynne Leegte

Karel van het Reve (1921-1999), one of the best postwar essayists in the Dutch-speaking world (who, sadly enough, didn't make the canon because the commission decided, with heavy hearts, to leave essayists off the list - for this same reason you won't find Huizinga in the canon. But I will mention van het Reve's *Literatuurwetenschap: het raadsel der onleesbaarheid* (Literary Studies: The Enigma of Unreadability, 1978), the deadliest and wittiest reading on the subject that I know of), Karel van het Reve considered Elsschot the most important Dutch-language writer after Multatuli.

And while we're at it, I'd like in the same breath to mention Nescio (another clever pseudonym: 'I don't know,' alias Jan Hendrik Frederik Grönloh (1882-1961)) who made it into the canon with three short stories.

Multatuli, Nescio, and Elsschot all share a common theme, that of the eternal struggle between the poet and the bourgeoisie, the rebel and the defeated. Multatuli is the man who goes to war against the bourgeoisie with panache. Nescio's characters are young men with artistic aspirations who can't cope with society. They are swallowed up by it, fall prey to insanity, or commit suicide. Elsschot is a full-blooded member of the bourgeoisie who nonetheless dissects it like no other. His scalpel is irony. The result - melancholy.

In *De Avonden* (The Evenings, 1947) Gerard Reve (1923-2006) describes ten dreary days full of loneliness and boredom, in the life of twenty-three-year-old hero/office clerk Frits van Etgers, but really he is the voice of the generation that came out of the war feeling numb and without faith. In this novel the petty bourgeoisie is shot to pieces. The dry, documentary style, in which the smallest details are revealed, contrasts with the hero's solemn style. The grotesque is liberating.

'… the glorious realm of Insulinde that coils yonder round the equator like a girdle of emerald…'

The Dutch East Indies, or the Dutch colony of 'Insulinde', gave us not only *Max Havelaar*, but also *The Hidden Force* (1900) by Louis Couperus (1863-1923) and the gem *Oeroeg* (1948) by Helle S. Haasse (1918-2011).

Couperus, using the narrative sharpness of Maugham, the spiritual depth of Conrad, and the moral compass of Forster, wrote about the decline and fall of a colonial official who remains blind and deaf to the dormant, mysterious powers of the East. 'His insight into the tragedy of European colonialism made Couperus a great writer. And his sympathy for the hybrid, the impure and the ambiguous gave him a peculiarly modern voice. It is extraordinary that this Dutch dandy, writing in the flowery language of fin-de-siècle decadence, should still sound so fresh,' wrote Ian Buruma in *The New York Times Review of Books* about the translation by Paul Vincent in 2012.

Oeroeg tells the story of the friendship between a Dutch and a Javanese boy, and the gap that grows between them because colonial relations simply are what they are. In the War of Independence (1945-1949) the two meet again: now opposed, and only then does the European understand that he never really knew his friend.

'It is a pool, a sea, a chaos'

What does prose of the twentieth century still have to offer? I'll line up a few completely different books.

In the long-winded novella '*Het leven en de dood in den ast*' (Life and Death in the Oast-house, 1926), the autodidact Stijn Streuvels (1871-1969), called the Flemish Tolstoy by David van Reybrouck, describes in an inimitably rich, Flemish idiom, a night in which five seasonal workers do their work in an oasthouse,

a chicory drying factory. Locked up in this *huis clos*, they have to keep the fire going uninterruptedly, night and day. In their moments of rest they daydream by the open hearths. Their conversations turn into dreams; past and future change places. But all the characters remain locked in their own beings. Powerless to understand each other, to change themselves or their lives. A tramp looks in the oasthouse for a place to die. With the arrival of death the dreamers are shaken from their slumber: banal, unavoidable life awaits them.

With a sober 'New Objectivity' style, Ferdinard Bordewijk (1884-1965) in *Character* (1938) tells the baffling story of Katadreuffe, the illegitimate son of Jacoba and the bailiff Dreverhaven, in the hard Rotterdam of the 1930s. These three characters relate to each other like water and fire. They constantly plague each other, but are also irresistibly drawn to each other. Jacoba refuses to marry Dreverhaven. The ruthless bailiff does everything in his power to sabotage the life and career of his son. Despite this, the son becomes a lawyer through superhuman effort. But at the cost of friendship and love. 'What doesn't kill you makes you stronger'? The film of the same name won an Oscar in 1998 for Best Foreign Language Film.

The thoroughbred writer Louis Paul Boon (1912-1979) updated the Dutch-language novel in one stroke, just as Multatuli had done a century earlier. *Chapel Road* is a failed book about a failed world: the ideologies are in fact dead. The author knew it already in 1953 when his book finally appeared, in which the rise and fall of socialism was described. But even individual lives are failures, as well as the novel as a bourgeois epic. An anti-novel then, 'a novel into which you [the author] pour everything higgledy-piggledy, plouf, like a tub of mortar falling from a scaffold'; 'a pool, a sea, a chaos'.

The closing sentence of Boon's *My Little War* (1947) reads: 'Kick people aside until they've obtained a conscience'. In the second edition, from 1960, when the world was irrevocably changed and the West was bracing itself to become rich, the book received a different closing sentence: 'What's the point of anything?' Between the two sentences lies the work itself; the work of a man who was more anarchist than socialist, and no, not a gentle one, a dismal nihilist, who became more and more lonely and melancholy. A dirty old man who kept thousands of pictures of naked women and dreamed of young girls.

W.F. Hermans (1921-1995) described the novel as science without proof. Everything that occurs in a novel and everything described should be, in his eyes, purposeful: no bird should fall from the roof, so to speak, without consequences. In his books he knows how to capture the cruel, ruthless reality that remains after all illusions have evaporated. His obsessive theme is the impossibility of man to really understand the world, let alone communicate with his fellow human-beings.

In *The Darkroom of Damocles* (1958) the protagonist Osewoudt is recruited as a resistance fighter by Dorbeck, who is Osewoudt's doppelganger in appearance, but contrasts with him when it comes to personality. Osewoudt blindly carries out his orders, believing that in doing so he will obtain a personality, but when his doppelganger is nowhere to be found after the war, Osewoudt has no way of proving his actions. Has he been a resistance hero or a traitor? The novel can be read in three ways simultaneously: as a thrilling war adventure, as a psychological story about identity crises, and as a philosophical novel about the inscrutability of the reality of the past. Milan Kundera greeted the French translation of this novel in *Le Monde* in 2007 as a masterpiece. He knew nothing about the author. He didn't know, therefore, that the author was so dissatisfied with the first translation of his book in 1962 that while alive he forbade all translations of his work into French. 'I dive into this book, at first intimidated by its length, then astonished to have read it in one sitting. Because this novel is a thriller, a long chain of events where the suspense doesn't let up. The events (which take place during the war and the year following), are described in a precise and dry style, detailed but quick, they are terribly real and yet at the limit of all probability. This aesthetic captivated me; a novel enamoured of reality and at the same time fascinated by the strange and improbable. Is this a result of the nature of the war which is necessarily rich and unexpected, exorbitant, or is it a sign of the aesthetic intent which wishes to be out of the ordinary, to touch, to use the word dear to the surrealists, what is marvelous?'

But, spoilt for choice, the canon commission chose another of Hermans's novels: *Beyond Sleep* (1966) takes place in the north of Norway. The main character, Alfred Issendorf, undertakes a scientific expedition in search of meteors. Initially Alfred has company as he takes on the inhospitable landscape. In the end he finds himself alone and left to his own devices. *Beyond Sleep* can be read in three ways: as the account of a scientific expedition, as a psychological story about a young adult wishing to step out of his father's shadow, and as a philosophical story in which the search for meteorites functions as a quest for the Holy Grail, which nevertheless results in the conclusion that there can be no deeper insight into unfathomable reality and life.

It was bound to happen that the Second World War, more traumatic for the Netherlands than for Belgium (which had the First World War behind it), would enter this canon in the form of a novel.

Harry Mulisch (1927-2010) threw himself at the task. Didn't he himself say: 'I am the Second World War'? His mother was Jewish and his father a collaborator. The novel could have been *The Stone Bridal Bed* (a novel about the Dresden bombings), but it became *The Assault* (1982).

The Assault is a novel about the enigma of guilt. The book recounts an assault on a collaborator by the resistance during the German occupation. The neighbours set the body in front of the house of Anton Steenwijk. As retribution, Anton's parents are arrested and murdered by the Germans. Throughout the rest of Anton's life, the reader is presented with various perspectives on the assault. In this way it becomes clear that objective guilt doesn't exist, but depends on the situation. Thus *The Assault* reminds us of W.F. Hermans's *Darkroom of Damocles*.

The Sorrow of Belgium is Hugo Claus's (1929-2008) magnum opus. This great Flemish/Belgian novel is seen abroad as the final reading of an incomprehensible country. Claus called his book a family novel. But it is also a mythologized autobiography, a picaresque, a political novel and a *Bildungsroman*. 'It shall be a book about life in Flanders the way I knew it, but which no longer exists', he said. A Flanders in which the Catholic Church still reigned supreme, a Flanders fascinated by the 'New Order' of the Germans, who marched with discipline into Belgium in May, 1940.

Three poets

I must limit myself yet again, but these three poets, 'surprised to find each other together,' belong to, and are quite possibly the best of the first half of the twentieth century (again roughly speaking).

Guido Gezelle (1830-1899) was a priest-poet, with an extreme Catholic ideology best left unexplored, but who, in his poetry, made Dutch, his West-Flanders variety of Dutch, sing as no one else has done. If poetry is 'what gets lost in translation', then the expression certainly applies to Gezelle's verses. In other words: if this poet had written in English with the same ability to manipulate language, he would be world-renowned. You'll just have to believe me, and his translators.

Paul van Ostaijen (1896-1928) casts a great shadow over all Flemish poetry to follow. In the course of barely twelve years he reinvented himself multiple times. He was the pioneer of humanitarian expressionism. Like Apollinaire in France, he introduced wild typography into poetry. The war acquainted him with Dada, and his stay in Berlin after 1918 turned him into a political and artistic radical. In his final years, Van Ostaijen was a proponent of 'simple lyricism': purely phonetic poetry, without ulterior motives. The poem had to be 'de-personalized,' autonomous, separated from reality and from the poet's feelings.

In *Nieuwe gedichten* (New Poems, 1934), a collection that came to light during the great economic world crisis that led to Hitler's rise to power in Germany, Martinus Nijhoff (1894-1953) develops a new, self-confident, and modern poetic form, moving far away from every supernatural or otherworldly ideal, he aims for earthly reality.

In *Awater*, a narrative poem about 270 lines long, someone looks for a travel companion in the desert of the city. The enigmatic clarity of this poem led T.S. Eliot to remark that if *Awater* had been published in English, it would have been world famous, and Joseph Brodsky considered the poem, 'one of the grandest works of poetry in this century'.

Reclining figure, 2015,
Piezographic print on paper,
34.5 x 64.5 cm
© Lynne Leegte

Classics

Every literature has its 'classics.' They say nothing new, discover no new idioms, only perfect existing genres. They deliver the sentences that resonate within a culture and use words common to obituaries and more superior salon conversations. In Dutch literature you encounter J.C. Bloem (1887-1966) and M. Vasalis (1909-1998). Both have left behind a limited oeuvre.

Bloem is the poet of desire, of its fundamentally unfulfilling nature and of, still worse, the absence of desire. He is the poet of resignation in appearance only. In *Dichterschap* (To Be a Poet) he asked the key question for any poetry, any art:

> *Is this enough: a handful of poems*
> *For the justification of an existence,*
> *(...)*

Using timeless words, Bloem mercilessly expresses the failure of every life, the impermanence of everything. The paradox is that these words seem to bring a certain consolation. That has to do with the flawless structural stability of his verses. The wording is inescapable.

I will set Vasalis aside now and look at Ida M. Gerhardt (1905-1997), classic, stately, and robust. She was a 'polder person,' raised with classical discipline; Dutch through and through, a tough cookie, honed in the Greek spirit of 'noble simplicity and quiet grandeur'. The classical, combined with the rustic, was a counterweight to her sombre, at times apocalyptic world view. It made her leaden conception of poetry, the awareness of a task to be completed, bearable. The poetic profession was, for her, a gift from above, a task that the recipient could not refuse. Is loneliness not the fate of the poet, is labour not his daily bread and service not the essence of his being? In this spirit she wrote about the tensions of an unhappy youth, hypocrisy and the demise of Holland's landscape.

Ghent-born Richard Minne (1891-1965), on the other hand, is the greatest of our minor poets. His collection is small. Melancholy fights with bitterness and resignation. His life is that of a loner, impractical and grim. He admired Voltaire, Heine, and Stern, and has elements of all three, though less well developed:

> *Work without plan or measure,*
> *But peep through every curtain;*
> *Despise the solid burgher,*
> *But drink deep of his flagon.*
> (translated by Tanis Guest)

'To express the breadth of life's totality'

In his anthology *Nieuwe griffels schone leien. Van Gorter tot Lucebert van Gezelle tot Hugo Claus* (New Chalk Clean Slates. From Gorter to Lucebert from Gezelle to Hugo Claus, 1954), Paul Rodenko introduced experimental poetry to a large audience. Of the group of poets also known as the 'Vijftigers,' we would like to mention Lucebert (1924-1994) and Hugo Claus.

Lucebert said of 'winsome' poets, who even after the Second World War gladly continued to believe in the traditional values of goodness and beauty, as if these values hadn't been forced to declare bankruptcy by the abominations of that war,

> *I report that the velvet poets*
> *perish shyly and humanistically.*
> *henceforth the hot iron throats*
> *of moved torturers will open musically.*
> (translated by Peter Nijmeijer)

Book, 2012,
Piezographic print on
paper, 22 x 42 cm
© Lynne Leegte

This 'expeditious swindler of love' wanted 'to express / the breadth of life's totality' (Paul Vincent). A new time needed a new poetry, of that Lucebert was convinced. After all, 'in this age what was always called / beauty beauty has burnt its face.' Reason, common sense, good taste, they all had to accept defeat. Taking their place were physicality, intuition, uncensored authenticity. The poet is no longer the master of the language or the form of the poem, on the contrary he must surrender himself to the language and to the mysterious and elusive meanings that emerge from the language.

The Oostakker Poems (1955) by Hugo Claus fell into postwar poetry like a shrapnel shell too. Only Vondel (1587-1679), the Milton of the Low Countries, and the chameleon Claus have two titles in the canon. Because these men were so multifaceted and versatile and used a variety of forms. The critic Paul Claes succinctly described the mystery of Claus's collection: 'A poet on the threshold of adulthood. An attitude towards life that hangs on to the past with every fibre and yet yearns for freedom with all its might. A person that covets animal purity, but is unable to escape society. (...) An experimental poet who writes almost classical verses, and a surrealist who doesn't deny reason. The paradox of a culture that doesn't denigrate nature, but integrates it (...)'.

Send-Off

With these birds - a bird in the hand is worth two in the bush - I send you forth, to your nook with a book. They give a picture of the diversity of literature written in Dutch. Their translators are their best ambassadors. I have full faith in them.

As fodder for the road, these lines by Lucebert:

so that's why I
sought out language in its beauty
heard that there was nothing human left in it
but the speech impediments of shadow
but those of ear-shattering sunlight
(translated by Paul Vincent). ■

(With thanks to my colleagues from the Royal Academy of Dutch Language and Literature in Ghent.)

Translated by Zoe Perot

A Canon
(50+1 Dutch Literary Texts)

Sente Servas
(The Life of Saint Servatius)
Hendrik van Veldeke
> Hagiography (1170/1180)

Walewein
Penninc and Pieter Vostaert
> Arthurian Romance (mid 13TH c.)

Liederen
(Songs)
Hadewijch
> Lyric Poetry (ca. 1240)

Der naturen bloeme
(The Best of Nature)
Jacob van Maerlant
> Nature Encyclopedia (ca. 1260)

Van den vos Reynaerde
(Reynard the Fox)
Willem die Madocke maecte
> Animal Epic (ca. 1270)

Karel ende Elegast
(Charlemagne and the Robber)
Anonymous
> Epic Poem (before 1325)

Die gheestelike brulocht
(The Spiritual Espousals)
Jan van Ruusbroec
> Mystic Treatise (ca. 1343)

Beatrijs
(Beatrice)
Anonymous
> Marian Legend (before 1374)

Lanseloet van Denemerken
(Lancelot of Denmark)
Anonymous
> Theatre (before or ca. 1400)

Gruuthuseliedboek
(Gruuthuse Songbook)
Anonymous
> Songs (ca. 1400)

Elckerlijc
(Everyman)
Anonymous
> Theatre/Morality Play
  (2nd half of the 15TH c.)

Mariken van Nieumeghen
(Mary of Nijmegen)
Anonymous
> Hybrid mixture of prose
  description and verse dialogue
  (beginning 16TH c.)

Refrijnen (I)
(Refrains)
Anna Bijns
> Poetry (1528)

Antwerps liedboek
(Antwerp Songbook)
Anonymous
> Songs (1544)

Geuzenliedboek
(Beggar's Songbook)
Anonymous
> Political Songs (1576-1577)

Spaanschen Brabander
(The Spanish Brabanter)
G.A. Bredero
> Theatre (1617)

**Gedichten van den heere
Pieter C. Hooft**
(Poems of Sir Peter C. Hooft)
P.C. Hooft
> Poetry (1636)

Poëzy of verscheide gedichten
(Poetry or Diverse Poems)
Joost van den Vondel
> Poetry (1650)

Trijntje Cornelis
Constantijn Huygens
> Theatre (1653)

Lucifer
Joost van den Vondel
> Theatre (1654)

De Leeuw van Vlaenderen
(The Lion of Flanders, or The
Battle of the Golden Spurs)
Hendrik Conscience
> Historical Fiction Novel (1838)

Max Havelaar
Multatuli
> Novel (1860)

Verzen
(Verses)
Herman Gorter
> Poetry (1890)

Verzen
(Verses)
Willem Kloos
> Poetry (1894)

Rijmsnoer om en om het jaar
(Rhyme Cord Around and Around
the Year)
Guido Gezelle
> Poetry (1897)

De stille kracht
(The Hidden Force)
Louis Couperus
> Novel (1900)

www.literairecanon.be

Het gezin van Paemel
(The van Paemel Family)
Cyriel Buysse
> Theatre (1903)

Het vader-huis
(My Father's House)
Karel van de Woestijne
> Poetry (1903)

Dichtertje, De Uitvreter, Titaantjes
(Little Poet, The Freeloader, Little Titans)
Nescio
> Novellas (1918)

Het leven en de dood in de ast
(Life and Death in the Oast-House)
Stijn Streuvels
> Novella (1926)

Nagelaten gedichten
(Posthumous Poems)
Paul van Ostaijen
> Poetry (1928)

Nieuwe gedichten
(New Poems)
Martinus Nijhoff
> Poetry (1934)

Elias of het gevecht met de nachtegalen
(Elias, or The Struggle with the Nightingales)
Maurice Gilliams
> Novel (1936)

Karakter
(Character)
Ferdinand Bordewijk
> Novel (1938)

Houtekiet
Gerard Walschap
> Novel (1939)

Eiland der ziel
(Island of the Soul)
Gerrit Achterberg
> Poetry (1939)

Parken en woestijnen
(Parks and Deserts)
M. Vasalis
> Poetry (1940)

Wolfijzers en schietgeweren
(Beartraps and Firearms)
Richard Minne
> Prose and Poetry (1942)

Het dwaallicht
(Will o' the Wisp)
Willem Elsschot
> Novella (1946)

De Avonden
(The Evenings)
Gerard Reve
> Novel (1947)

Oeroeg
(The Black Lake)
Helle Haasse
> Novella (1948)

Apocrief/de analphabetische naam
(Apocryphal/The Analphabetic Name)
Lucebert
> Poetry (1952)

Kapellekensbaan
(Chapel Road)
Louis Paul Boon
> Novel (1953)

Het levend monogram
(The Living Monogram)
Ida M. Gerhardt
> Poetry (1955)

De Oostakkerse gedichten
(The Oostakker Poems)
Hugo Claus
> Poetry (1955)

Het boek alfa
(The Book Alpha)
Ivo Michiels
> Novel (1963)

Verzamelde gedichten
(Collected Poems)
J.C. Bloem
> Poetry (1965)

Nooit meer slapen
(Beyond Sleep)
W.F. Hermans
> Novel (1966)

De aanslag
(The Assault)
Harry Mulisch
> Novel (1982)

Het verdriet van België
(The Sorrow of Belgium)
Hugo Claus
> Novel (1983)

Gangreen 1 (Black Venus)
(Gangrene 1 (Black Venus))
Jef Geeraerts
> Novel (1968)

5 ways
to Start a Canonized Book

"I am a coffee broker, and I live at No. 37 Lauriergracht, Amsterdam. I am not in the habit of writing novels or things of that sort, and so I have been a long time making up my mind to buy a few extra reams of paper and start on the work which you, dear reader, have just taken up, and which you must read if you are a coffee broker, or if you are anything else.

Max Havelaar, *Multatuli*
translated by Roy Edwards

The Hidden Force, *Louis Couperus*
translated by Paul Vincent

The full moon, which that evening had a tragic intensity, had risen early, just before twilight faded, like a huge, bloodred globe. It flared sunset-like low beyond the tamarind trees of Long Avenue and climbed, gradually purging itself of its tragic hue, into an indistinct sky.

The Freeloader, *Nescio*
translated by Damion Searls

"

Except for the man who thought Sarphati Street was the most beautiful place in Europe, I've never met anyone more peculiar than the freeloader.

During the dark days around Christmas, in a Rotterdam maternity ward, Jacob Willem Katadreuffe was assisted into the world by a Caesarean. His mother was an eighteen-year-old servant-girl, Jacoba Katadreuffe, called Joba for short. His father was a bailiff, A. B. Dreverhaven, a man in his late thirties, renowned for his ruthlessness towards any debtor who fell into his hands.

Character, *Ferdinand Bordewijk*
translated by E.M. Prince

Will-o'-the-Wisp, *Willem Elsschot*
translated by A. Brotherton

A dreary November evening, with a soaking drizzle that drove even the bravest of us from the streets, and it was too far to trudge through that icy curtain of rain to the bar I always drank at. So it would be the first time in a long, long while, for the years fly quickly, that I would go straight home. My unexpected arrival would be taken for a step along the road to repentance, and I could hear my wife saying that the beginning is always difficult but better late than never.

5 ways
to Finish it

"Each of them will keep their own experiences hidden, walled up, carried around with them. What they do reveal about them in conversation are merely superficial reflections and meaning-less minutiae; they are incapable of sharing with each other what lies buried in the deeper layers of their subconscious — what they would like, with uneasy words, to blab about, must necessarily sound false, acquire a contrary meaning, be mis-understood; pronounced by an ambiguous heart, these words serve no other purpose than to deceive them and to promote ridicule.

Life and Death in the Oast-House, *Streuvels*
translated by Zoe Perot

The Evenings, *Gerard Reve*
translated by Sam Garrett

"

He breathed in, filling his chest with air, and climbed into bed.
'It has been seen,' he mumbled, 'it has not gone unnoticed.'
He stretched out and fell into a deep sleep.

> " "

I do not pretend to have understood him. I knew him, just as I
knew Telaga Hideung, as a reflecting surface - I never fathomed
the depths. Is it too late? Am I forever to be a stranger to the land
of my birth, to the soil from which I am loath to be uprooted?
Time will tell.

The Black Lake, *Hella Haasse*
translated by Ina Rilke

*You see? That dying woman who was poor but a beautiful girl,
and at her death bed the doctor and the priest who should have
been her husband and son…that would have been a proper book,
but your book won't be a proper book, there'll be nothing in it
about life AS IT REALLY IS.*

Chapel Road, *Louis Paul Boon*
translated by Adrienne Dixon

The Sorrow of Belgium, *Hugo Claus*
translated by Arnold J. Pomerans

"

The nephew walked with me to the little country station.
'It was a fine poem. Bravo.'
'I write three of those a day,' he said.
'That's quick!'
'It's my technique. I take all the clues from a crossword puzzle
and then jumble them together.'
He said nothing more. So I said nothing, either. Together we
sang 'Tout va très bien, ma-da-me la marquise,' the foxtrot by
Ray Ventura and his Collegians. We heard the saxophone and
the beat of the drum. We saw a gull that limped.
We'll see. We'll see. Anyhow.

In Search of Utopia

On the Trail of the Most Influential Book Ever Published in the Low Countries

It was raining as I turned into Eiermarkt. I was looking for a house called De Biecorf, the Beehive, where Pieter Gillis lived in the early sixteenth century. But the street didn't look too promising, with a big car park on one side and the back of a shopping centre on the other. Then I noticed a narrow passage leading into a quiet courtyard surrounded by older houses. High on a wall, hidden from the street, a beehive was carved on a stone.

Here was the evidence I needed. In old books on Antwerp, Pieter Gillis is said to have lived in a tall house on the Grote Markt called De Spiegel. But that is apparently a case of mistaken identity, according to an academic paper published in 1988. Someone else with a similar name lived in De Spiegel, but the Gillis I wanted lived in De Biecorf, on a square then called Oude Veemarkt.

I had hoped there might be a plaque. Or something at least. But there was no mention of Gillis. Nothing to remind people that, some five centuries ago, Thomas More's Utopia was conceived on this spot.

Pieter Gillis was employed as state secretary of Antwerp when he met the English lawyer Thomas More in 1515. More had been sent to Bruges on a diplomatic mission on behalf of King Henry VIII. He spent four months engaged in difficult negotiations on wool imports, like British officials who now take the Eurostar to Brussels to argue over the fine points of EU regulations. During a break in the proceedings, More managed to escape to Antwerp for a few days.

He was put in touch with Pieter Gillis through their mutual friend Desiderius Erasmus. More possibly stayed with Gillis in the house on Eiermarkt. He began Utopia with a warm description of the Antwerp official. 'I do not know if there be anywhere to be found a more learned and a better bred young man,' he wrote. 'There is not perhaps above one or two anywhere to be found that are in all respects so perfect a friend.'

This friendship led to the publication in 1516 of a small book that was to have a huge impact on the history of Western thought. It really deserved a plaque to mark the location.

Thomas Morus, *Libellus de … insula Utopia*, Leuven,
Dirk Martens, 1516, Royal Library of Belgium, Brussels

A work of genius

In December 1516, thanks to help from Erasmus, the first edition of Thomas
More's *Utopia* came off Dirk Martens's presses in the university town of Leuven.
Originally published in Latin, the fable begins in Antwerp, where More bumps
into Gillis on his way from the Cathedral. Gillis introduces More to an old Portuguese seaman called Raphael Hythlodaeus who has recently returned from
a four-year stay on the island of Utopia.

Raphael reveals the existence of an ideal society on an island on the other
side of the world where private property is abolished, men and women are
treated equally and different religions are allowed to exist.

More's *Utopia* was an enormously disruptive book that raised the possibility
of an orderly human society where life could be very different from the brutal
reality of early sixteenth-century century Europe.

The idea of Utopia would change the structure of European thinking for more than 500 years. It was the word that Robert Schuman used in a 1949 speech in Strasbourg when he was launching the idea of a united Europe.

The initial aim of the European Community (as it was then called) was to bring steel and coal production in France and Germany under the control of a single authority, so that the raw materials of war were taken out of the hands of the nation states. But Schuman was already thinking of something much more visionary. 'We are carrying out a great experiment, the fulfillment of the same recurrent dream that for ten centuries has revisited the peoples of Europe: creating between them an end to war and guaranteeing an eternal peace.'

Schuman mentioned some of the past experiments in unification that had failed to work for one reason or another. 'The Roman Church of the Middle Ages failed finally in its attempts that were inspired by humane and human preoccupations.' Then he included a gentle dig at the nation that had recently caused the deaths of millions. 'Another idea, that of a world empire constituted under the auspices of German emperors was less disinterested; it already re-lied on the unacceptable pretentions of a "Fuhrertum" whose "charms" we have all experienced.'

He then referred to some of the great European thinkers such as Dante and Erasmus who had provided the framework for 'systems that were both ingen-ious and generous.' Lastly, he singled out the one system that particularly ap-pealed to him. 'The title of one of these systems became the synonym of all that is impractical: *Utopia*, itself a work of genius, written by Thomas More, the Chancellor of Henry VIII, King of England.'

When the French foreign minister went on to deliver the Schuman Declara-tion in 1950, the word Utopia had vanished from the text. It was perhaps too impractical for the founding fathers of Europe.

Map of Antwerp, detail,
Virgilius Boloniensis, 1565,
Plantin Moretus Museum,
Antwerp

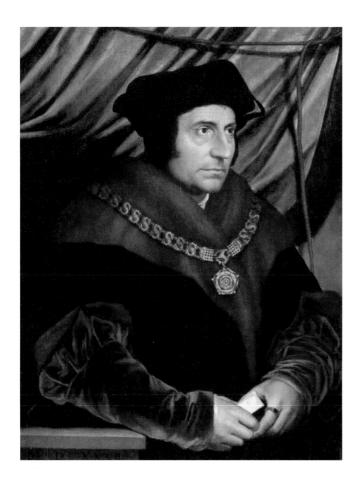

Hans Holbein the Younger (after),
Portrait of Thomas More, 1527
(The Bedford Version), Oil on oak panel,
74.9 x 58.4 cm, National Portrait Gallery, London

The idea of friendship

A few months later, the search for Utopia took me to London. I was looking for the street where Thomas More was living when he completed *Utopia*. A research assistant at the London Museum had responded to my query with a detailed description of More's house.

'More lived in The Barge, in Bucklersbury, in the parish of St Stephen Walbrook', she wrote. 'It is possible that the Bucklersbury garden with pergola, depicted on the Agas map and described by Stow, was part of the More estate. Stow says it was so called because of the sign of the "Olde Barge" hung out there, and that it was a common report that when the Walbrook was open, barges were rowed out of the Thames and towed up here, so that the place has ever since been called the "Olde barge".'

Later that day, I found Bucklersbury buried away among the shiny glass sky-scrapers of London's financial district. But nothing has survived of the manor house that once stood on the banks of the River Walbrook.

Thomas More was living here when he met Erasmus for the first time in the summer of 1499. He invited the Dutch scholar to walk out to Eltham, south of London, where the children of King Henry VII (including the future Henry VIII) were being educated.

Quinten Massys, *Portrait of Erasmus of Rotterdam*, 1517, Oil on panel,
transferred to canvas, 59 x 47 cm, Palazzo Barberini, Rome

This marked the beginning of a deep friendship that lasted more than thirty
years. In a letter to a friend, Erasmus wrote: 'What has nature ever created
more gentle, more sweet, more happy than Thomas More?'

It was while staying in the house on Bucklersbury that Erasmus wrote *En-
comium Moriae, In Praise of Folly*, which was also, as the Latin title hinted at,
In Praise of More. Written in the space of a week, the essay gently mocked the
Catholic Church while raising the possibility of a less corrupt alternative.

More was still living in this house when he returned from Antwerp in 1515 to
complete his own little book. Edited by Erasmus and dedicated to Pieter Gillis,
Utopia was first published in the winter of 1516.

I learned later that the financial company Bloomberg was building its European headquarters on the site of More's Bucklersbury estate. Large panels attached to the barrier illustrated Roman remains found during the construction
work. But there was no mention of Thomas More. Not a word about Erasmus.
Nothing to recall that two of the most important works of northern European
literature were written on this spot.

In praise of friendship

Utopia was a truly European project, the product of deep ties of friendship between three humanists – Dutch, Flemish and English. One year after the book
was published, Erasmus and Gillis decided to send portraits of themselves to

More to remind him of their bonds of friendship. They commissioned the Antwerp artist Quinten Metsys to paint a double portrait as if they were sitting in the same room, with a bookshelf in the background common to both paintings.

The portrait of Erasmus took much longer than expected because the scholar fell ill several times. He wrote to More while Metsys was still working on the portrait. 'My doctor has taken it into his head to get me to swallow pills to purify my spleen and whatever he is foolish enough to prescribe I am foolish enough to do. The portrait has already been begun, but when I went back to the artist after taking the medicine he said that I didn't look the same any more, and so the painting had to be postponed a few days until I looked a little more alive again.'

More finally received the two portraits while he was in Calais. On looking closely at the portrait of Pieter Gillis, he was delighted to discover that his friend was holding a letter in which the handwriting was clearly recognisable as More's own.

The English lawyer later wrote to Gillis asking if he could send back his letter so that he could hang it alongside the painting. 'If it has been lost,' he added, 'I will see whether I in my turn can copy the man who copies my hand so well.'

The two paintings originally hung on the walls of More's mansion in Bucklersbury. Now they have been separated. The portrait of Erasmus hangs in the Royal Collection at Hampton Court in London, while the portrait of Pieter Gillis has ended up on the walls of Longford Castle near Salisbury.

Abraham Ortelius, *Map of Utopia*, c. 1595,

38 x 47.5 cm, Bilthoven, The Netherlands, Collection van den Broecke

The Lost Utopia

In 1623, Thomas More moved from the Old Barge to a new country house near the river in Chelsea. Curious to see what if anything remained of the house, I took the underground to Sloane Square and walked down to the river.

The house has vanished, but a statue of Thomas More stands outside Chelsea Old Church, placed there in 1969. Written on the stone base were the words Statesman, Scholar and Saint. But no one had thought to add that he was the author of *Utopia*.

The church was hit by a bomb in 1941, killing four firemen, but the chapel built by More miraculously survived. Inside is the tomb that More built for his first wife Jane in 1528. He took the opportunity to compose his own epitaph, which he sent to his old friend Erasmus for proofreading before commissioning a London stonemason to carve it on the tomb.

'Thomas More, born a Londoner, of a respectable but not noble family; he engaged to some extent in literary matters,' he began, before listing all the important official posts he had held. He had no idea then that his distinguished career would end up with execution on Tower Hill. His body was buried within the walls of the Tower of London while his head was stuck on a pike.

Then I walked along the King's Road to visit Chelsea public library, where a small bronze statue of Thomas More sits near the entrance. Made by the German sculptor Ludwig Cauer during his stay in London, it shows More slumped in a chair, looking tired and more than a little grumpy.

Quinten Massys,
Portrait of Pieter Gillis, 1517,
Oil on panel, 59 x 46 cm,
Royal Museums of Fine Arts,
Antwerp

'Can I help you?' the librarian asked.

'I'm looking for *Utopia*,' I said.

'Is that by James Joyce?' she asked brightly.

'I think that was *Ulysses*,' I said. '*Utopia* was written by Thomas More, who lived in Chelsea.'

She looked confused, although she must pass the little bronze statue at the entrance every day. She logged on to the library's website and typed 'Utopia' in the search box. The first book listed was Robert Ludlum's *The Utopia Experiment*, clearly more popular with the residents of Chelsea than *Utopia* by Thomas More.

'Unfortunately we don't have it,' she said.

'Thanks anyway,' I said. 'I'll try the bookshop up the road.'

I paused before leaving the library to take another look at the little statue of Thomas More. A small bronze plaque noted that it was bought for the library in 1896 by public subscription, which seems a rather utopian idea.

Then I walked back down King's Road to a bookshop I had passed earlier. It was called *World's End Books*. The owner was sorting some secondhand books as I went in.

'I'm looking for *Utopia* by Thomas More,' I said.

He shook his head. 'No,' he said firmly. 'I don't have anything like that. Sorry, mate. I can't help you.'

Lessius is More

In Quinten Metsys's portrait of Pieter Gillis, the Antwerp official is shown holding a letter from More. I had hoped to look at the original painting, but it is difficult to visit Longford Castle. So I took the train to Antwerp, where there is a good copy, probably painted by Quentin Metsys. It had been moved temporarily from the Fine Arts Museum, which was closed for restoration, to the seventeenth-century Rockox Mansion.

I was the only visitor on a foggy winter morning. The old wooden floors creaked as I moved from room to room, occasionally setting off the alarm when I got too close to a painting. I finally found Pieter Gillis in a large room looking out on the renaissance garden.

I particularly wanted to look at the letter from Thomas More that was so well done. I peered at it as closely as the alarm permitted, but I couldn't see any handwriting at all.

Then I went to meet a friend for coffee. She used to teach at Lessius College in Antwerp, which changed its name in 2012 to Thomas More College. I wanted

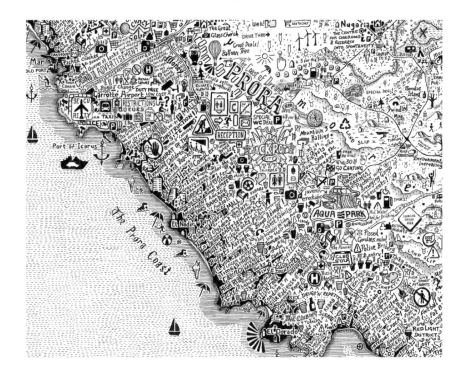

Stephen Walter, *Nova Utopia*, 2013, detail

© Stephen Walter, courtesy of the artist and TAG Fine Arts, London

to know why they had dropped the name of a Flemish theologian in favour of an English lawyer.

It was partly because Thomas More was a famous thinker, I learned. But there was more to the story. It also appealed to the college because it allowed them to play on the English word 'more'.

On its website, the college explained the reason for merging two colleges – Lessius College and the Kempen Catholic College – into Thomas More College. It would, they said, provide 'more education, in more locations, with more cooperation.' And, in case you still didn't get the joke, they promoted the new name with the slogan 'Lessius is More'.

A map of Utopia

I went back to Antwerp again a few weeks later to look at a temporary exhibition in the MAS museum titled 'The World in a Mirror'. The curators had brought together a fascinating range of maps from different historical periods, including a rare map of the island of Utopia made in 1596 by the Antwerp cartographer Abraham Ortelius.

Few people knew of the existence of the map until it surfaced at an auction in 1981. On the map, which is the only copy to have survived, Ortelius indicated many of the places mentioned in Thomas More's book. He also added a Latin inscription at the bottom encouraging the spectator to 'Behold the happy kingdom'.

'The world has no other, which is better or more beautiful!' it goes on. 'This is that Utopia, bulwark of peace, centre of love and justice, best harbour and good shore, praised by other lands, honoured by you who knows why, this, more than any other place, offers a happy life.'

Hanging next to it in the exhibition was a map of Nova Utopia made in 2013 by Stephen Walter. The London map-maker had carefully copied the topography of Ortelius's map, including the fifty-four towns mentioned by More, but added modern details that turned Utopia into an overcrowded tourist resort.

Later that day, I happened to walk past Thomas More College in Antwerp's Sint-Andries district. Only it wasn't called after Thomas More any longer. It had become part of Leuven University in the latest reorganisation of Flemish higher education. The slogan 'Lessius is More' had gone. All that remained was a delivery van with the words 'Expect More Drive' on the back.

I never found out who had come up with the idea of playing around with the name More. But they were repeating a joke that went back more than 500 years, to a friendship that gave the world a description of Utopia. ■

EXHIBITION
In Search of Utopia
20.10.2016 - 17.01.2017
M - Museum Leuven

500 years Utopia is a citywide project in Leuven in 2016.
www.utopialeuven.be

Hieronymus Bosch – Both Trendsetter and Representative of His Time

Reflections on the Significance of His Oeuvre

[MANFRED SELLINK]

It is remarkable that there should be so many similarities in the work and lives of the two artists Hieronymus Bosch (ca. 1450-1516) and Pieter Bruegel the Elder (ca. 1525-30 - 1569), both of whom were so instrumental in forming the visual idiom of the Netherlands in the sixteenth century and, to this day, still determine the artistic image of the period. Extraordinarily little is known about their actual lives and, though highly influential, their oeuvres are small and enigmatic, revealing little or nothing of their intrinsic meaning. This is a combination that has resulted in both cases in a torrent of publications, academic as well as pseudo-academic, expounding the most diverse interpretations, which seem sometimes to say more about the authors in question than about the subject of their study. The singularity and unbridled artistic inventiveness of their visual idiom has resulted in the characterizations 'Boschian' and 'Brueghelian' becoming well established in art literature. That will not diminish in the years to come, either. On the contrary even, for something else that links the two masters is that there are major commemorative years on the horizon. In 2016 it will be 500 years since Bosch died. Three years later, in 2019, it will be Bruegel's turn, when the 450th anniversary of his death is commemorated.

That these days we often and rather too simplistically, for that matter, sum up the sixteenth century in the Netherlands with a title like 'From Bosch to Bruegel' – as in a recent exhibition on the development of the depiction of everyday life in the Boijmans Van Beuningen Museum in Rotterdam – comes as no surprise. That for Bruegel the older master's work must have been an important source of inspiration and posthumous artistic competition was of course just as obvious to his contemporaries as it is to us now. In the earliest literature about Bruegel, published during his lifetime, he was characterised as an artist who had acquired the nickname 'the second Hieronymus Bosch'. This admiring description fits with the enduring popularity of Bosch in the Habsburg Netherlands, and particularly in Antwerp. From his death until the third quarter of the sixteenth century – for longer and more consistently than is usually accepted – the master's oeuvre, or rather what was known of it from copies, variations and pastiches, was *the* benchmark for every artist who wanted, somehow or other, to depict hell; although his influence on Bruegel goes considerably further than this particular theme. The differences, on the

other hand, are considerable too. In contrast to the solo artist Bruegel, who most probably worked completely alone, the Bosch 'label' stands for an active (family) workshop which, as we shall see, makes it extremely difficult for researchers to determine exactly what Bosch himself painted and what was done by possible assistants. The underlying tenor of their two oeuvres – profane and religious – also differs substantially in tone. In contrast to Pieter Bruegel's mild irony, mixed with an essential optimism and zest for life, Bosch's work speaks of a rather sombre and eschatological view of the world that seems to be a search for the (rare) opportunities to achieve redemption from this earthly existence.

After the fall of Antwerp, in 1585, and under the influence of the Counter-Reformation set in motion by the Council of Trent, there was a clear change in the depiction of religious themes in the Southern Netherlands. As a result, Bosch's influence diminished fast – though he would never be forgotten.

However tempting (and correct) it may be to position Hieronymus Bosch primarily as a trendsetter and instigator of artistic developments in the sixteenth century, and to name Bruegel in the same breath as his artistic successor, one should never forget that Bosch was every bit as much a typical representative of his own period, rooted intrinsically in the late-medieval urban intellectual and religious (visual) culture in the Low Countries as it rapidly developed from the end of the fourteenth century. The image of Bosch as a brilliant and idiosyncratic eccentric, disconnected from his environment, has long been proved outmoded and untenable. Yet he was an artist who, with his workshop, developed an oeuvre that was as intriguing as it was innovative in the fascinating transition from the fifteenth to the sixteenth century; an oeuvre that, due to its astonishing ingenuity and its stylistic and technical mastery, will always be counted as one of the pinnacles of art history.

Hieronymus Bosch, *Saint Jerome in Prayer*, c. 1500, Oil on panel, 80.1 x 60.6 cm, Museum voor Schone Kunsten Ghent © www.lukasweb.be – Art in Flanders vzw. Photo by Hugo Maertens or Dominique Provost

After Hieronymus Bosch, *Christ Carrying the Cross*, 1510-1516, Oil on panel, 76.7 x 83.5 cm,
Museum voor Schone Kunsten Ghent © www.lukasweb.be – Art in Flanders vzw.
Photo by Hugo Maertens or Dominique Provost

2016 - Festival and exhibitions in Den Bosch and Madrid

It goes without saying that in the long run-up to the commemorations in 2016 a variety of cities and museums have considered the possibility of putting on a retrospective of the master's work. It is an ambition as challenging as it is complex. The extant oeuvre (paintings and drawings) is not big; the format of the individual works, on the other hand, certainly is; they are painted, without exception, on panels and each of them is one of the most valuable masterpieces and public favourites in the museums concerned. In short, these are often fragile works that are never, or extremely rarely, loaned. Bearing in mind, too, that research into Bosch in recent decades has delivered an extraordinarily fragmented picture with more differences than similarities, it should be obvious that realising a large-scale retrospective is not easy – to put it mildly.

Many people were surprised that 's Hertogenbosch was the first city to take up the gauntlet, with a striking and ambitious initiative. Den Bosch, as the city is affectionately known, is of course the city where the artist lived and worked, but apart from that rather nice starting point it has few assets in museum terms to achieve this type of project. The Noordbrabants Museum is, certainly since its renovation, a valued and active player in the Netherlands, but it does not possess a single work by Bosch himself, nor does it have the sort of collection that would allow it to be an active player in the loan traffic between the major international museums. Den Bosch is not a university city either, and the museum does not have a research tradition relevant to this type of undertaking.

Hieronymus Bosch, *The Garden of Earthly Delights*, c. 1503-1504,
Oil on oak panel, 220 x 389 cm, Museo del Prado, Madrid
Detail from the central panel

Nonetheless, a remarkable and eventually successful strategy was chosen well in advance. With help and (robust) financial support from various other partners, a substantial investment was made in fundamental research into all the materials and techniques used in the artist's entire oeuvre, in preparation for the planned exhibition.

The Bosch Research and Conservation Project (BRCP) was set up in 2010, in collaboration with Radboud University Nijmegen and the Jheronimus Bosch 500 Foundation, in particular. The BRCP's objective is the systematic study of as many of the paintings and drawings attributed to Hieronymus Bosch as possible, with particular attention to scientific examination of the materials and techniques. That means in situ analysis of works using the most modern technology, in order to chart the painting techniques, workshop practices and so on, thereby obtaining structural insight into the production and the methods used by Bosch and his assistants in his 'workshop'. This type of research, which more or less got off the ground in the 1970s, has led in recent years to important innovations in the way anything concerning objects' material properties is charted, thanks to developments in ICT and other technologies, plus the systematic combination of research results with knowledge and insight garnered from 'traditional' art history research and the insight restorers have gained with experience. All of this brings us closer to the crucial question of how an artwork is produced and constructed (www.boschproject.org).

Because Den Bosch financed this research into collections worldwide – regardless of whether a work might be available for an exhibition or not – Den Bosch and the Noordbrabants Museum, in close collaboration with the BRCP, have not only compiled unparalleled knowledge of Bosch's oeuvre, but have also built up the trust and credibility essential to a potential recipient of works on loan. Investments were also made in financing the restoration of works such as the *Four Visions of the Hereafter* in Venice and the triptych of the *Last Judgement* in Bruges. This approach has been so successful that, from 13 Feb-

Hieronymus Bosch, *The Garden of Earthly Delights*, c. 1503-1504,
Oil on oak panel, 220 x 389 cm, Museo del Prado, Madrid
Detail from the central panel

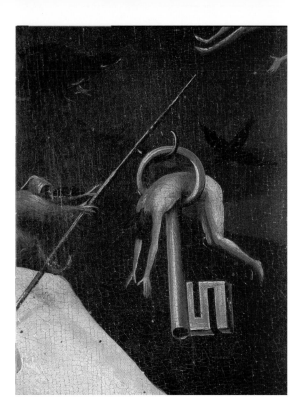

ruary to 8 May 2016, an ensemble of about twenty panels from Bosch's own hand and an equal number of drawings that have never before been together will be on view in Den Bosch with some other works that put the oeuvre in its context. It is quite an achievement! In addition to that, the exhibition will be part of a broadly conceived Bosch year in which the life and work of the artist will form the basis and the source of inspiration for an extremely varied programme of exhibitions, concerts, theatre productions, lectures and public events of all types (www.bosch500.nl).

At a later – actually surprisingly late – stage, the Prado also joined the exhibition initiative in Den Bosch. The Madrid museum is most probably the only institution in the world that could organise a monographic retrospective of Bosch on the strength of its own collections, for it is there that, for historical reasons, several absolutely top works by Bosch himself hang. Moreover, given the strength of its broader collections as well, this museum can obtain additional works on loan, something that is not feasible elsewhere, including Den Bosch (www.museodelprado.es). Real devotees should therefore definitely go to Spain too, where the exhibition will run from 31 May till 11 September 2016.

The importance and need for a commemorative year

It is not unusual for theme years and major exhibitions linked to the anniversaries of the births and deaths of important artists to be frowned upon in museum and cultural circles, with the obvious reproach of pure and simple touristic (city) marketing. Although the programmes of such festivals are sometimes, but by no means always, somewhat unbalanced in terms of content and quality, there is little reason, in my opinion, to criticise the principle. It is a fact, and always will be, that a symbolic year makes it considerably easier to generate resources and public attention, to stir up the enthusiasm of the media and thereby make it possible to realise projects with powerful (and extremely expensive) content, which it would be far more difficult, if not impossible, to do in other years.

In the case of the Bosch anniversary year and the two exhibitions, the great value lies in three indisputable assets. First of all, the systematic study of just about all the works attributed to Hieronymus Bosch, compiled over several

Hieronymus Bosch, *Four Visions of the Hereafter*, Palazzo Grimani, Venice.
Detail from *Ascent into Heaven*, Oil on oak panel, 88.8 x 39.9 cm

Hieronymus Bosch, *The Haywain*, c. 1516,
Oil on panel, 147 x 212 cm,
Museo del Prado, Madrid.
Detail from the central panel

years by one (multidisciplinary) research group has yielded a treasure trove of new information and insights, which will be the basis not only for the various publications that are brought out during the year, but more importantly for further research and interpretation in subsequent years. Added to that, the exhibition, where so many works will hang next or near to each other, will itself evoke more new insights, questions and comparisons in a manner which is absolutely incomparable to working with reproductions in books or on web-sites, whatever the resolution or the number of megapixels. A good exhibition is not an end in itself and certainly not an answer to all the research questions, rather it is a stimulating overview and comparison of artworks where, besides new insights and interpretations, just as many new questions are raised and scientific discussion is provoked, laying the foundations for years of further research. Finally, and not least, every generation of art-lovers has a right to get to know and appreciate the grand masters of art history in the original.

There can be little doubt that the exhibitions in Den Bosch and Madrid in 2016 will attract considerable interest, not least from the media, and will draw large numbers of visitors. It is pretty certain, too, that the results of the *Bosch Research and Conservation Project*, which will be presented simultaneously in vari-ous publications, will also attract plenty of attention from the press, the public and the profession, and get people talking. While this text was being written a press release arrived by way of a teaser, announcing three new attributions in the press: one drawing, in private possession but known from the literature, was apparently done by the master himself, while a couple of well-known works that were always considered to be from his hand, the painted *Tabletop of the Seven Deadly Sins* in the Prado, and *Christ Carrying the Cross* at the MSK in Ghent, were apparently not painted by Bosch after all. That the last two works have been demoted comes as no surprise to specialists; there had already been the necessary discussion about them behind closed doors. Nonetheless, pending the argumentation in the scientific catalogues, the results are highly unlikely to convince everyone. Occasionally Bosch experts find their world is like a can of worms, full of sharp differences of opinion and judgement, both in terms of in-terpretation and of attribution. Moreover, for museum directors demoting works that were previously considered 'original' and from a famous artist's own hand is rather sensitive, although the intrinsic quality of the work in question does not actually change one iota.

In the case of Bosch even more sensitive and high-profile discussion topics press, with the (now open) question of what else the BRCP research has yielded. Those who have had the privilege to study the most famous Bosch triptychs and panels - like those in Lisbon, Madrid and Vienna – under favourable conditions and with the aid of modern research techniques, can hardly believe that just one and the same artist has worked on them; something which has, for that matter, been the subject of fierce discussion in the professional literature and at congresses in recent years. It will be fascinating to hear whether the research into the materials and techniques has brought more clarity or new insights into this and, if so, what that clarity will be. In advance of the exhibition and publications, it looks very much as if what has long been seen as exclusively the work of Bosch must actually have been a 'collaborative effort' by a large workshop - a workshop with an intellectually coherent and artistically clearly recognisable mastermind at its head, where, besides the master himself, a variety of different assistants (family members?) actually carried out the work.

As has already been said and cannot be repeated too often, an exhibition is not an end in itself and certainly not a future canon carved in stone. The changing insights and opinions about artists like Hieronymus Bosch over the last century betray as much about our own time as they teach us about this enigmatic great master. However, the importance of these two exhibitions, in the Netherlands and Spain, cannot and should not be underestimated. They represent a unique (a word that is often misused, but which is absolutely justified in this context) opportunity for every art-lover to see Bosch's oeuvre in its context, diversity, wealth and complexity, all together in one location. So this year is the ideal time to (re) discover his work and to learn to understand it better. Moreover, I am convinced that this oeuvre has much to offer us both in terms of artistic quality and inventiveness, and in intellectual levels and depth. Don't miss it! ∎

Translated by Lindsay Edwards

EXHIBITION
Jheronimus Bosch - Visions of Genius

13.02 - 08.05.2016	31.05 – 11.09.2016.
Het Noordbrabants Museum,	Museo del Prado,
's-Hertogenbosch	Madrid
(www.bosch500.nl)	(www.museodelprado.es)

FURTHER READING

Walter S. Gibson, *Hieronymus Bosch*, London 1973.

Roger Marijnissen and Peter Ruyffelaere, *Hieronymus Bosch; het volledige oeuvre*, Antwerp 1987.

Jos Koldeweij, Paul Vandenbroeck and Bernard Vermet, *Jheronimus Bosch; alle schilderijen en tekeningen*, Rotterdam 2002.

Paul Vandenbroeck, *Jheronimus Bosch; de verlossing van de wereld*, Ghent-Amsterdam 2002.

Matthijs Ilsink, *Bosch en Bruegel als Bosch; kunst over kunst bij Pieter Bruegel (ca. 1528-1569) en Jheronimus Bosch (ca. 1450-1516)*, Nijmegen 2009.

No Sheep

Arno, Teetering Between Emotion and Banality

[DIRK STEENHAUT]

The Americans have Tom Waits, the Flemish have Arno. The singer with the rasping voice is undoubtedly the most colourful and most cosmopolitan rocker that Flanders has ever produced. Arno, né Hintjens (1949), delights in putting listeners off balance. At the same time though he is a master of the art of self-mockery. Regarding himself more as a flop star than a pop star, a clown as much as a singer, he has himself addressed alternately as *Charlatan* and *European Cowboy*.

This Ostend-born resident of Brussels first made himself heard as a singer and harmonica player in the early 1970s, with blues-oriented groups such as Freckleface and Tjens Couter. He would only make history between 1980 and '85 as the front man of the totally unique TC Matic, with whom he performed a blend of new wave and James Brown's funk heritage on countless stages both in Belgium and abroad, and wrote classics like 'O La La La' and 'Putain Putain' (Bloody Whore). From the latter we remember the immortal line, *'k hèn e klintje, moar 't schiet verre'* (I've got a small one, but it shoots a long way).

Inimitable idiom

Arno is the archetypal Belgian who speaks several languages – English, French and his Ostend dialect – but doesn't really master any of them. His inimitable idiom, for which he himself thought up the term *Arnolais*, certainly didn't stand in the way of an international career. Since the singer has been working under his own name, he has collaborated with well-known producers such as Holger Czukay and John Parish, done concerts in both Montreal and Moscow, been heard in the Flemish version of Disney's *Toy Story* and figured as an actor in various films. In between times he disappeared into bands like Charles & Les Lulus, The Subrovnicks and The White Trash European Blues Connection.

Arno makes no secret of the fact that he's not very practical. 'The only thing I can really do is make music', he says. 'And that's all I need to be happy. For me, music is the ultimate refuge; something that makes me forget my worries. Thanks to the path I've chosen I can be a voyeur. I'm not much of an autobiographer, I prefer to observe. I absorb the things I see and spit them out again later. But I am in charge

of my own life, so I don't need to join in any parade. And since I've been making music for over forty years, I'm well aware of all the pitfalls. I'm not worried about losing my recording contract any more. I know I'll be making music till I die.'

TC Matic, Brest, France, 1984
© Danny Willems

Arno's lyrics are the result of automatic writing: they come out in one spontaneous gush. In the singer's opinion, they risk sounding forced if you think about them too much. 'Most of the stuff I record sounds radically different two years later. Your songs make a journey and as an artist you journey with them. Writers, painters or film directors make things they can't change afterwards. Songs, on the other hand, are pliable. They keep developing.'

Jukeboxes were inestimably important for Arno's musical education. 'As a young boy in the '60s, I watched the illuminated glass, fascinated as the records went round and round. You had categories like 'rock', 'slow', 'cha-cha-cha', 'rumba' – perhaps that's why my tastes in music are so eclectic?'

Hintjens's father served in the RAF during the Second World War and brought English-language music culture back home with him. 'I still know all Vera Lynn's songs. Mother, on the other hand, was crazy about Mistinguett. These artists all left their mark on me. And, of course, I grew up in a port city. Twelve packet boats a day called into Ostend, bringing the whole world with them – including a lot of imported records from England and the US.'

Although Arno has lived in Brussels for years now, the queen of seaside resorts still draws him like a magnet. 'The North Sea is the only sea in the world that changes colour, smell and sound every day. It's at its best in autumn and winter. You can see it in paintings by Spilliaert, Ensor and Permeke, too – the light, the brilliance. My songs are a bit like the waters of the North Sea. They never sound the same two days in a row.'

The blues, over and over again

The *Bathroom Singer* thinks of his recordings – a good thirty of them by now – as snapshots: they show exactly who he was at the time he made them. 'When I listen to *Ratata* now, I see a period in which I looked at the world through a haze of alcohol every day. I used to take dope, because it was fashionable and everyone around me was doing it. But it didn't take me long to realize that you don't need drugs to produce good work. I still like to drink, but never at home. I'm a social drinker, ha ha.' Yet he always managed to avoid extreme excesses during his career. 'Fortunately I only really became well-known when I was a bit older. Fame is a trap. As soon as you let it go to your head it becomes dangerous.'

The artist reserves his respect mainly for ordinary people 'with balls'. For badly prepared interviewers and TV talk show hosts, on the other hand, he can be a real scourge. Like Serge Gainsbourg he can sometimes be a bit of a loose cannon. 'In this business people are forever putting on an act. But I'm not a *product*, you know?'

Arno admits that the exuberant singer we know from the stage is actually a rather shy guy at heart, hence a song like 'Dancing Inside My Head'. In the world of the imagination all the inhibitions that get in the way in real life disappear. 'That's why I'm a musician. Music is basically therapy for me. What for? For the bullshit that's all around us. I'm just my own shrink.'

Tjens Couter, 1976 © Danny Willems

During his long career Arno has borrowed from a great number of styles. But whatever he does, it always sounds like the blues. You notice that with his interpretations of other people's work too. 'I do everything in my own tempo and that's always slower than the original. Yeah, the blues, they're my roots. I picked up the genre from The Rolling Stones. But if you go looking for the source you'll usually find better stuff: Willie Dixon, Fred McDowell, Howlin' Wolf, Sonny Boy Williamson... I admire André Hazes just as much though. Blues from the working-class quarters in Amsterdam, let's say. I'm pretty schizophrenic; I listen to all sorts of music. I've never followed trends. You won't just find Captain Beefheart in my collection, there's Abba, Dean Martin and French chansons too. A good song is a good song.'

Apart from pop standards by David Bowie and Nina Simone or chansons by Jacques Brel and Claude Nougaro, Arno regularly flirts with light music. He recorded 'Viva Boema' with TC Matic, and his interpretation of Salvatore Adamo's 'Les filles du bord de mer' never fails to win over the audience.

The singer is always curious to see what will happen when he lets two musical worlds collide. 'I've been lucky enough to write a few classics that are easy to rework. They're ditties that the audience wants to hear night after night, but to keep them interesting for myself I stick in something new every now and then.' Arno once played the TC Matic repertoire with a brass band, for example. He has played with African musicians from the Matongé district in Brussels, and gave his songs an exotic facelift with a group consisting mainly of Turks and Moroccans. 'You can push your limits every day in music. I get a huge kick out of it.'

Solitary by nature

He doesn't have a problem with artists selling illusions, because music is about laughter and tears. People buy a recording for a particular atmosphere and go to concerts to forget their everyday routine. 'Rock, jazz, funk, house - they're all the same, they're all entertainment. But I don't give a *damn* about musicians that behave like businessmen or drivel on about their own problems. When I write a song I'm like a mirror. People buy what they can recognise.'

Many of his songs are conceived as portraits of women, although for Arno the poetic and the prosaic, the moving and the banal always go hand in hand. In 'Les Yeux de ma mère' (My Mother's Eyes) he sings: *'C'est elle qui sait que mes pieds puent / C'est elle quit sait comment j'suis nu / Mais quand je suis malade / Elle est la reine du suppositoire.'* ('She knows my feet stink / She knows what I look like naked / But when I'm ill / She's the suppository queen.')

However, while the *mamsels* and the *madams* play a central role in his work, they embody both heaven and hell for the artist. 'Men are really the weaker sex', he explains. 'You notice that during wars especially. Women make less fuss about pain; they deal with illness and pain much more bravely. Maybe it's because they carry little'uns for nine months?'

There's no lack of humour in Arno's work. But there's a certain amount of darkness in it too. His biggest nightmare, for example, is the life cycle he sums up in one of his songs as *'Have kids / Get bored / Get fat / Split up'*. 'I couldn't live like that myself. But sometimes you have to go through hell to see heaven. I once felt the beginning of what I described in 'From Zero to Hero' and I knew right away that was not for me.'

In his songs he portrays himself alternately as a *Lonesome Zorro* and a *Solo Gigolo*, because Arno is first and foremost an individualist, who would rather stand on the sidelines than participate. 'I'm solitary by nature. One of the things I'm good at is being alone. I like living by myself and I always go out by myself. I definitely don't want to be a sheep in the flock.'

Life in a melting pot

Arno is not the sort of artist that juggles with clever slogans or enlightening political messages. The fact that you can hear exotic musical instruments on his recordings is a statement in itself. 'It's simple. If there'd never been Moroccans living in Brussels I'd never have tasted couscous. And it just so happens I'm nuts about couscous. I don't want sausages and mash on my plate every day, do I? I've learned a lot from Arabic music too. I live in a street where several nationalities and cultures interact and I think that's a huge advantage. The people I meet when I go to, let's say, Poperinge aren't enriching. But if my Moroccan neighbour's daughter gets married and they party and sing for four whole days, that's incredible. The delicious food, the hospitality – you'd think you were in Marrakesh, but it's happening next door to you. You don't even need to travel to experience it all.

'When I walk around in Barbès, an immigrant district in Paris, it's like a feast of smells, sounds and flavours. That's the essence of our existence in my opinion. We live through our senses, don't we? If you were surrounded only by people of your own kind you'd be a poor sod. Apparently Flanders is a country now – with six million inhabitants, for Christ's sake. That's about half the size of a city like New York. A melting pot produces so much creativity. We wouldn't be sitting here talking now without the Germans and the British that I met as a kid in Ostend.

'I admit I still have that underdog feeling that's so typical for Flemings. Perhaps it's because I stutter. When people used to ask me about my job and I answered "rock musician" they would look at me as if I came from Mars. But nowadays it seems alright. The French even knighted me for it ten years ago. OK, so perhaps it's a kind of acknowledgement, but at the same time I wonder: Why me? It's all so relative. Sometimes you go up in the world and sometimes you go down. I've been through it all.'

So why has he increasingly sung in French since *À la française* (1995)? Obviously his popularity in France and Switzerland has got something to do with it. But there's another reason too, he says. 'I've got two children by a French woman, and if you sleep with the dog you get fleas. I just happen to write differently about the things I experience in French. On the other hand, if I dream up a rock number in the tradition of The Faces or Dr Feelgood, I know instinctively I have to sing it in English – because the French can't make that sort of music.'

Arno, 2010 © Danny Willems

Arno and Danielle, 1988
© Danny Willems

Recalcitrant free spirit

One of Arno's key songs is called 'Vive ma liberté'. It portrays him as a recal-
citrant free spirit through and through. 'I constantly come across people, in
music and outside, who try to tell me what I should or shouldn't do. Then I do
the opposite, on principle. They're always trying to screw you. You've got to
fight that. Drop your guard, in art or in music, and you're vulnerable. You've got
to fight every day to be yourself.'

Arno hates anything soulless and artificial, too. In his work he speaks out
against greedy rich people, know-alls and people with 'cobwebs in their heads'.
He can't stand nationalism, corruption, the extreme right, unrestrained consumption, MTV, the degeneration of his city, the dumping of toxic waste, terrorism in holiday resorts, the demise of idealism and women's magazines that
make their readers unhappy with ideals of beauty that no one can live up to.

Those in positions of authority are often on the receiving end on his CDs too:
*'De politiekers zin oan't diskuteren / Ut ulder valsche mond / Komt er niets dan
stront'* ('The politicians are arguing again / From every lying mouth / Comes
nothing but crap'), goes one of his not very flattering songs. 'When I see a politi-
cian on TV, I often wonder: what's he like in bed? Does he mess about as much
there too?' grins the crooner.

He loathes institutionalised thought systems just as much. *'Aucune réligion
peut nous sauver'* ('No religion can save us'), he sings somewhere. And: *'Moi,
j'aime dieu, mais je fais ce que je veux'* ('Me, I love God, but I do what I like'). Arno
does feel attracted to Buddhism though. 'But that's more of a philosophy than
a religion. Buddha isn't really worshipped; you're not expected to follow him,
because he's in you. You have to follow your own path, and are only accountable
to yourself. Everyone knows the difference between good and evil, don't they? If
you think a bit and are honest with yourself, you can get on very well without God.'

Arno, 2010
© Danny Willems

A preference for the stage rather than recordings

Arno may have made an impressive number of albums, yet he insists that he only makes recordings to be able to perform, never the other way round. 'What you've made breathes and evolves on the stage. And feedback from the audience always provides an extra dimension.

'I'm only a mediocre musician myself, so I surround myself with the best in the business to compensate. After all, Arno isn't just me. Arno is all the guys who sit in the studio with me or do the round of festivals in summer – real musicians, who don't just sell their souls to anyone who comes along. I wouldn't exist without them. But I can only work with people I trust. The question of whether they are technically skilled always takes second place. I function best in a family atmosphere. It's important to me not to have to explain anything. After all, music comes from feelings.

'I'm impulsive in everything I do and I'm happy to take the consequences. No regrets. Because although I've been on the road a long time, I don't feel like I'm retracing my steps. I'm always progressing, slowly but surely. What's important is to know what you can and can't do. There's no point in trying something you don't feel. All things considered, I've been blessed, yes. I travel and get paid for it, see the world thanks to my music. I can't say it often enough: I'm a lucky devil.' ■

Translated by Lindsay Edwards

www.arno.be

Extremely Distant, Yet Incredibly Close

Bieke Depoorter's Travel Photography

[KURT DE BOODT]

Things have moved quickly for photographer Bieke Depoorter (1986). With the photos of her graduation project she won the HP Magnum Expression Award. The design for *Ou Menya* (At my place) was as simple as it was adventurous. Without a clear plan, Depoorter set off on the Trans-Siberian Express, found herself in remote little villages and asked if she could stay the night with a family. Since she did not speak any Russian, communication was conducted via a written note: 'I do not wish to stay in a hotel because I have little money and wish to see how people in Russia live.' The feeling of trust had to be mutual. A lot remained unspoken. The pictures do the talking. Together they tell a story about hospitality in large families who do not have a lot to share. They live together in harsh conditions, occupying a few scant square metres. Together they respond to a primitive, almost animal motive: the search for security. The bitter temperature outside, the damp eating away at the walls and the desolate night landscapes contrast with the warmth exhaled by the inhabitants. *Ou Menya* was not a case of beginner's luck. Several series followed revealing intimate travel impressions during stays in the United States, Egypt, the French seaside resort of Sète, and Istanbul. In 2012 Depoorter became a nominee member of Magnum, progressing to associate member in 2014. She came through the prestigious photography agency's test with verve. What was Magnum so quick to see in her? What does Depoorter show us so consistently? What is it about her photos that leaves such a lasting impression?

Shared intimacy

Bieke Depoorter soon found her own voice, carving out a niche for herself, in a time when it seems nothing escapes the camera's lens. Photography has become a form of hysteria, constant and ubiquitous, as if photos were meant to replace experience itself; as if the selfie were more important than the view; as if the greedy photographers seek to immerse themselves completely in the present, showing what is happening in front of the photo (standing completely in the way, in fact). Depoorter does the opposite: she filters herself out of her images, allowing moments to take place undisturbed as far as possible. She

reinvents travel and reportage photography as she goes along. The unusual is concealed in the obvious, not in the spectacular or the extreme. Depoorter shows us everyday moments, scenes which would never have been seen or ratified without her, partly because she physically travelled many kilometres from home to a special place with extraordinary inhabitants, but mainly because she succeeds in travelling within people. As a photographer she dares to step into unknown territory. From an open, vulnerable position a rapport can be established. The host families continue to behave normally in her presence, allowing her into the most intimate places, including bed and bath. No, the photographer is not a voyeur. She does not stare through a keyhole; she shares moments of time. The inhabitants are not exhibitionists either. They do not impose their privacy upon us in a shocking way. A good many conditions have to be fulfilled before a photograph can be taken at all, let alone to be able to return home with lasting images. There is no room for faking or overacting: not in the setting, the lighting or the right moment of time, either by the people pictured or the photographer herself. Together all the preconditions create something miraculous, shared intimacy.

After all, it did begin with a white lie. Depoorter was not just some impetuous student on a world trip looking for accommodation. The question is the pretext, the necessary step over the threshold to come closer to the *I* (At my place) and ultimately to come to a sense of *we*, allowing authenticity to arise. The note a

Untitled, from *I am about to call it a day*

friend wrote out in Russian for her does not state the truth and nothing but the truth. The final goal of her request for hospitality is not about finding a cheap place to sleep on a tourist trip, but about 'taking' (photos) and 'showing'. On closer inspection Bieke invites not only herself inside, but us too, the viewers who see her selected prints after her return home. We stand with her in the moment, looking over her shoulder into those cramped rooms. We see what Depoorter shows us: pieces of habitat she brought back with her. Perhaps it is we, the onlookers, who most resemble voyeurs.

I have to confess, I like seeing inside people's homes. On an evening walk I struggle to stop myself from taking a peek at their lives if they leave their curtains open, a light glowing invitingly at the window. But not for long. I would not go so far as to stand and stare. So I'm very grateful to Depoorter for going in on my behalf and giving me permission to look on shamelessly with her for as long as I want. At the same time her photos make me mildly uncomfortable. They raise all sorts of questions. Should I be seeing all this? How visible is intimacy? What makes a house a home? How globalised has this world become? And would I do that, give a photographer a bed for the night and expose my family life to her in the process? Would nervous Belgian and Dutch citizens, albeit with a higher average standard of living and a good deal more space, show such hospitality? In the end – besides craftsmanship and a practised eye – it comes down to human qualities, mutual trust, good intentions and empathy.

The photographer does not judge with her camera. Life does not pose for her (not too obtrusively, in any case). We feel welcome.

So much for the conditions. In *Ou Menya*, Depoorter inadvertently created a blueprint for her still young, developing oeuvre. The prize-winning project forms a benchmark. A sense of series dominates the Russian photos, which work best in each other's company. On their own, in all their raw vitality, they look somehow unfinished. It's hard to choose one favourite photo. I prefer the entirety, the interplay. In the book Depoorter allows the photos to run on over one or two complete pages. The page composition frames and gives rhythm between portrait format (one page) and landscape (two pages). Some images show part of an empty room, unmanipulated scenes from life presented as if the world is a stage. In others Depoorter really climbs into the skin of the inhabitants who fill the frame. There is no room left to take a distance. Life cannot simply be arranged within a rectangle. Out of sight, outside the book, life continues.

Only twice does she have inhabitants expressly strike a pose. A teenage girl in a see-through white nighty stands somewhat awkwardly in the corner of the room. She stands before us in her underwear, looks straight into the lens and does not smile. She crosses her largely uncovered legs. Her feet are turned in. The attitude she assumes creates distance and makes her in my eyes even more vulnerable. She looks a touch off balance. Behind her the green and yellow wallpaper with sunflower motif and a poster of a kitsch natural landscape maintains a cheerful mood. A sofa with sheets in disarray indicates that bedroom and living room overlap, as in many of the homes visited. On the next page Depoorter zooms in on the corner of the room (without the girl). Details leap out even more: the light switch, the tear in the wallpaper, the item of clothing pressed into the closed doorway. Depoorter needs such resting points. Soon our eyes are again overwhelmed by overfilled rooms.

The other posed photo is also one of a diptych. Again we see girls in their underwear, this time the colourful, innocently childish kind. Two ballerinas proudly show Bieke what they can do, raising one leg straight up in the air (one the left, the other the right). The sisters hold one another in balance. They have practised it for hours. On the preceding double page we see the same girls just passing the time. One leafs through a photo album. We do not see her looking; her head is hidden behind an open cabinet door. The other girl watches. Most of the image is taken up with the pistachio-green wallpaper. A one-person trampoline and a hula hoop await action. This is what the inhabitants are generally doing, killing time. Lying on their beds. Smoking cigarettes. Cutting hair. Removing makeup. Dressing and undressing. Going to bed. Waking up.

Into the twilight zone

In between scenes Depoorter takes us outside. It's night or very early morning; the faint natural light makes the photos grainy. We have to look carefully to distinguish objects and bodies. The inhabitants wash outside, in a shed or in the open with a bucket in the snow. It is bitterly cold but the kindly light on wet skin emanates warmth. How do outside and inside interact? This is a question Depoorter asks herself on every trip. Panoramic views offer perspective on how people live together behind closed doors. In the Trans-Siberian cold of Russia the outdoors bites into the rooms. Clothes, hats and extra blankets lie within reach. Plastic bins and pieces of newspaper catch drips. Heaters top up the warmth. The curtains curl and the linoleum on the floor cracks with damp. The paper not only covers the damp patches and mould but also breaks the closed world open with colourful motifs. On the walls, photos, posters, carpet hangings and growth charts proliferate like promises. Layer on layer, as if the rooms are trying to wrap themselves up too. Then there's the human contact inside. *Ou Menya* reveals little room for physical intimacy. The generations live practically on top of one another. People sleep wherever there is a free surface. Privacy is a utopia or a daily battle. The only embrace is that of a young woman at the breakfast table trembling as she wraps her arms around herself.

Bieke Depoorter shivers too. She merges into family life. The lack of distance determines her point of view. It would be hard for her to remain an outsider in these familial and spatial circumstances. Once we see her taking the photo in a mirror. In the various rooms the same burgundy and blue sleeping bag also crops up, rolled out on the floor or a chair. The visitor merges into the image, ultimately to disappear. What remains is the observation. She must not become too close to the family. She limits herself to one night. Depoorter wants to get to the bottom of transitions: between day and night, light and dark, inside and outside, commotion and peace, clothed and naked, involvement and distance. It is in the interfaces and twilight zones that things become tangible, aged, authentic.

Land of the free and broken lives

Does Bieke Depoorter show us 'how people in Russia live', as she said in her note that she wished to find out? Not primarily. It becomes clearer when we place the later series alongside it. After Russia, Depoorter picked Europe's other brother, America, 'land of the free'. In the United States, instead of taking the train, Depoorter hitchhiked to her indeterminate destination. *I am about to call it a day*, the series is called. Before people go to bed they turn in on themselves in preparation for sleep. The gaze moves inwards. Activity ceases. Here, on the other side of the Atlantic, there is more space for physical contact than in the Trans-Siberian series. The difference between living and sleeping space is more clearly delineated. Depoorter goes to bed with her subject. A grey couple lie cuddling playfully on the bed under a wall crowded with pieces of worldly wisdom. *There's no place like home*. Despite the cuddling, a stronger sense of despair and loneliness permeates the American series. Materially the families are better off. A bored girl sits blowing bubbles with gum in a room strewn with toys. Another difference, here Depoorter is not communicating with body language alone. The English exchanged between photographer and subject slips a narrative element into the photos. For variety, between the family scenes Depoorter pictures not only landscapes (printed on lighter paper in the book) but sometimes also pieces of text, like a title card in a silent film. Particularly hard-hitting are the farewell letter of a father leaving his wife and child for more than three years and the diary page titled 'My Useless Existence': 'To fail as a person, friend, wife, and finally mother is truly the best definition of a useless existence.' The page is dated 2 July 1997. The woman wanted to share this page from her past with the visitor. Depoorter offers insights into broken lives. In America she gets to hear life stories. The photos are also more individualistic, less grainy (with flash and artificial light), more strongly framed and more independent of one another. Some resemble stills from a David Lynch film. In a forest a woman takes a night bath in a rectangular hole in a layer of concrete, bathing in artificial light. This can't be real. A director could not have set the scene better for this ostentatiously solitary moment of joy. Another photo looks like a specimen of sociological research from a Louis Theroux documentary: a family goes out in the car at night to stare at rich people's Christmas lights. So many artificial lights to dream away on, the Stars and Stripes waving over 'the land of the free and the home of the brave'. America, land of contrasts, inequality and unparalleled possibilities.

Untitled, from *I am about to call it a day*

Untitled, from *In Between*

Naked survival

In 2011 – the year of the uprising on Tahrir Square – Depoorter started the series *In Between*. On her website she marks the series as 'in progress'. The light in Cairo is warmer than in Russia. The chiaroscuro stands out as if in a painting. A symmetrically framed, backlit breakfast scene resembles an Orientalist painting by Ingres. A sublime moment in which everything falls into place. In Cairo Depoorter encounters still other living conditions: a different religion, a different relationship between man and woman, a life closer to the ground and houses where indoors and outdoors overlap. Particularly disarming is the photo in which a little girl sits in her bed roaring with laughter as a pigeon flutters around the room. Happiness is losing oneself in the moment. Luck is being present and pressing the button at the right moment. In the meantime a revolution is raging in the streets.

Depoorter does just as well close to home. The series she took in 2011 at the house of Roger Raveel in Machelen-aan-de-Leie is movingly beautiful: the painter ardently embracing his wife, at the coffee table, painting on a step, waving us off from behind a window reflecting the landscape he so often painted. Depoorter captures the intimate environment from which Raveel observed human activity and recorded it in colour on the white canvas. Raveel died in early 2013. Suddenly we speak of him in the past tense. His death seems hard to reconcile with these lively scenes. On the other side of the window we wave back at him.

Depoorter shows us how people live, how they come together to form communities and how they attempt to make the best of things in their own individual ways. The similarities between the series are more prominent than the differences. The individual and intimate touch on something universal. Above all this oeuvre in the making shows us naked survival: clothing, feeding, protecting, warming oneself and making life more pleasant, passing the time. In unguarded moments life comes down to shared space, losing oneself in the moment, light illuminating skin, becoming visible, existing. With her photos Bieke Depoorter kisses people from different continents goodnight. In the morning she says goodbye and goes on her way to share new evening adventures, extremely foreign yet incredibly close. ■

Translated by Anna Asbury

Untitled, from *In Between*

All photos © Bieke Depoorter/ Magnum Photos

Ton Koopman - Conductor, Organist and Harpsichordist

A Seventy-Year-Old with an Overfull Diary

The September 2015 issue of BBC Music, the classical music magazine published by the BBC, included a feature on what the classical world has been listening to in the past month. The forty-five-year-old German pianist Lars Vogt, one of the most accomplished and adventurous musicians of the moment, replied: *'I regularly listen to Bach's cantatas conducted by Ton Koopman - they're simply food for the soul. I love the way that he phrases everything. This is beautiful music-making, clear in its simplicity and clear in its language. I particularly love the final box of CDs in the series, which has the last cantatas that Bach wrote, such as Ich habe genug. I've never performed with Koopman, but would love to – let's hope he reads this!'* This is praise indeed, and a striking concluding statement, particularly since Lars Vogt has no involvement with the world of Baroque and its performance styles.

Ton Koopman, who is so admired by Vogt, celebrated his seventieth birthday on 2 October 2014. Although his hair and beard may look slightly less profuse and luxuriant than a few decades ago, this ever-courteous, untiring and enthusiastic Dutch harpsichordist, organist, conductor and teacher still has a very full diary. Ton Koopman's name is synonymous with more than half a century of music-making - a long period in which the small world of classical music has seen a great deal of change.

Amsterdam Baroque Orchestra & Choir

How did it all begin? Well, when Koopman was very young. He was born in Zwolle into a Catholic family of seven children. His father was a grocer. They were certainly not wealthy, but there was music in the family. In his very limited spare time, Koopman's father was a percussionist in a jazz band. During the band's rehearsals and performances, which often took place at his home, the young Ton saw his father's face light up with pleasure - something that rarely happened at other times. This was when, as a small boy, Ton first came to realise what music can mean to people and how happy it can make them. At the age of six he joined the boys' choir of the Catholic church, where he was fascinated to watch the organist play. This man could play music with his feet! Ton had

Ton Koopman
Photo by Marco Borggreve

never seen anything like it. Several years later, the new conductor of the boys' choir immediately noticed the young Ton's musical ability and encouraged his parents to allow him to study music. So Ton was given piano lessons, despite the fact that he did not like the instrument at all - and still doesn't! He later went to grammar school and attended the Royal Conservatoire in Amsterdam, where he studied his beloved instruments, the harpsichord and organ, while studying musicology at university. He was twice awarded the *Prix d'Excellence* for his superb keyboard skills on the two instruments. As a student, Koopman's fascination for period instruments and a historically authentic performance style led him to focus on Baroque music and, at this early stage, on

Johann Sebastian Bach, a composer whose works he has performed with undiminished enthusiasm throughout his career, and still does today.

1979 was an important year in Ton Koopman's life. It was the year in which he founded his own ensemble: the Amsterdam Baroque Orchestra, a small orchestra whose members play authentic instruments and replicas of authentic instruments. The orchestra's repertoire is drawn, approximately, from the particularly rich period from the Renaissance to the late Classical period. Koopman himself has always defined his musical 'homeland' fairly precisely as the period that begins with the Renaissance and ends with the Requiem by Wolfgang Amadeus Mozart. In recent years, however, mainly in his work as guest conductor of several famous symphony orchestras (including the Cleveland Orchestra, the San Francisco Symphony Orchestra and the Orchestre Philharmonique de Radio France), he has ventured outside this period, conducting works by Felix Mendelssohn, Franz Schubert and Robert Schumann. But as yet, he has been either unwilling or unable to venture into the music of Johannes Brahms, however highly esteemed, and the major works of Anton Bruckner and Gustav Mahler appear to be unattainable for him, in contrast to his fellow musicians and contemporaries Philippe Herreweghe and Sir John Eliot Gardiner. Koopman prefers the perfect harmony that prevails in the world of Ludwig van Beethoven, but here too, as he has often declared with typical Dutch level-headedness in interviews, his credo has been 'every man to his trade' – until December 2014, that is, when Koopman led the Wiener Symphoniker in its performance of Beethoven's famous Ninth Symphony during the orchestra's traditional New Year concert, in the authentic music style - a winning combination! To come back to the Amsterdam Baroque Orchestra, the unique playing techniques and musical styles of the orchestra's chosen repertoire are

Amsterdam Baroque Orchestra & Choir and Lenneke Ruiten

studied and mastered very thoroughly by its members, all specialists in their particular instrument. Usually, Ton Koopman not only conducts his ensemble but also performs, playing the organ or harpsichord, as a 'first among equals'. That is his credo and he keeps to it. In 1992 there was an important addition to the musical family, the Amsterdam Baroque Choir. And then things start to happen quickly. In no time at all, as the Amsterdam Baroque Orchestra & Choir, the newly formed ensemble made an international name for itself in terms of its authentic performance style.

Bach cantatas

The time had now come for a first mammoth project, which was also Ton Koopman's great dream: to perform all the cantatas by Johann Sebastian Bach and record them on CD. In 1994, when discussing the details of his contract renewal with Erato, his record label at the time, Koopman expressed this wish. To his amazement, it did not meet with a negative response. Quite the opposite, in fact: he was given a short period of time to submit a concrete plan, and, if a sponsor could be found, Koopman and his ensembles could embark on their dream project. A Herculean task! The recordings filled 66 CDs and 44 unique concerts were performed; Koopman's second great wish was namely to perform the cantatas on the concert stage. This body of more than 200 sacral works is a musical cosmos in itself and, for Koopman, there is hardly one among them that is less than accomplished. According to Koopman, however, it isn't just a matter of neatly playing the right notes. Anyone who wants to achieve an in-depth understanding of and approach to the music must aim for more than a beautiful harmony. That is why Koopman studied not only the music, but also the period in which Bach lived, his family, his patrons and the religious culture in which he worked. Or, as Koopman puts it: classical music is not something that you can produce and consume like fast food. The publication of a three-volume work, *De wereld van de Bach cantates* (The World of the Bach Cantatas), was timed to coincide with the release of the CD series. The volumes are the work of a team of internationally renowned Bach specialists and are edited by Christoph Wolff, a professor at Harvard University who was also closely involved with the *Neue Bach Ausgabe*. Ton Koopman himself collaborated on the volumes, writing an essay on the performance style in addition to the introduction to the books. This complete recording, now available under Koopman's new label Challenge Classics, has been well-received by audiences and music critics. The latter appreciate the excellent choice of soloists (especially soprano Barbara Schlick, countertenor Andreas Scholl, tenor Christoph Prégardien and bass-baritone Klaus Mertens), the beautiful performances of the choir and orchestra and, above all, the energetic guiding hand of Ton Koopman, who, throughout all the cantatas, keeps the music vibrant and spontaneous. In between all these activities, Koopman still found the time to record Bach's complete organ works, performing them on different organs, including two on which Bach himself played. The excellent recordings fill no less than sixteen CDs. The twenty-second and final CD box of Bach cantatas was released in 2004. It was ten years in the making, but Ton Koopman, an energetic and driven man, is not someone to take it easy.

Meanwhile, plans for the next major project had been hatched: to be the first to record and perform the complete surviving oeuvre of Dietrich Buxtehude, a composer who was such an inspiration to Johann Sebastian Bach that, in 1705, the twenty-year-old Bach walked 400 kilometres to hear him play in Lübeck.

But there was a problem, the market for classical CDs had shrunk considerably, the golden age heralded by the arrival of the CD – everything could be re-recorded, and budgets were more or less unlimited – had been over for some time, record companies were being taken over by large concerns or closing their doors, and there was hardly any interest in ambitious new projects. So what were the options for an entrepreneur like Koopman - since that is how he sees himself? His solution was to found his own record label and give it his own name, with a French twist: Antoine Marchand (now part of the Dutch label Challenge Classics). As his own boss he was able to embark on the *Opera Omnia* project, recording and performing all the works of Dietrich Buxtehude: the vocal works (cantatas, concerts and arias), organ works (played by Koopman himself on period instruments) and chamber music (sonatas and trio sonatas, performed by Koopman together with members of his Amsterdam Baroque Orchestra). As with the Bach project, the Buxtehude project involved much more than recording and releasing CDs. Ton Koopman is also president of the *Internationale Buxtehude Gesellschaft*, and in that capacity he organises many symposia, exhibitions and concerts. This work earned him the Buxtehude-Preis in 2012, presented by the city of Lübeck. Buxtehude occupied a central place in the musical life of Lübeck for almost forty years, and died there in 1707. On 26 October 2014, a few weeks after Ton Koopman's seventieth birthday, the luxurious and immaculately produced CD box set (29 CDs plus 1 DVD) *Dieterich Buxtehude Opera Omnia vol.I-XX* was presented in the same city. This release also received excellent reviews. Regarding the interpretations of the chamber music works, for example, music critics were full of praise for the soloists of the Amsterdam Baroque Orchestra: the precise articulation of violinist Catherine Manson, the exquisite flourishes of Paolo Pandolfo's viola da gamba and the creative continuo playing by lutenist Mike Fentross. The Amsterdam Baroque Choir was also praised for the flair and conviction with which it brought the words of the spiritual vocal works to life. There was admiration for Ton Koopman too, for the energising way in which he keeps the whole balanced and stimulating, and also for his vibrant, free, improvisational interpretations of Buxtehude's organ works.

'The crazy tremolo man'

Incidentally, regarding that last aspect of his musical style, not everyone is enamoured of Ton Koopman's richly embellished, free interpretations on the organ and harpsichord, whether as a soloist or as a driving and guiding force in the continuo section of his Amsterdam Baroque Orchestra. It has even earned him the nickname 'the crazy tremolo man' (*de dolle triller-maker*)! In an interview with the *Neue Zürcher Zeitung*, Koopman counters this criticism by referring to Johann Sebastian Bach's scores for harpsichord. In Washington he dis-

Amsterdam Baroque Orchestra & Choir and Maarten Engeltjes
Photo by Khalid Al Busaidi

covered a source which showed that the composer himself had subsequently added hundreds of embellishments by hand. So Koopman continues this tradition. The harpsichord is an instrument with limitations, he feels, and the only way to enhance its dynamics is to play it freely.

Naturally, Ton Koopman's rich and extensive discography includes many recordings of works by composers other than Bach and Buxtehude. As mentioned above, while still with Erato he was fortunate enough to benefit from the heyday that followed the arrival of the CD in 1983. One of the 'other' composers is Wolfgang Amadeus Mozart. Koopman, together with his Amsterdam Baroque Orchestra, recorded Mozart's late symphonies, his concertos (including the oboe concerto, with the excellent Flemish oboist Marcel Ponseele) and the *Krönungsmesse*, one of Koopman's favourite works, again with soprano Barbara Schlick. Unlike many of his fellow early musicians (among them Nikolaus Harnoncourt, William Christie, Sigiswald Kuijken and Sir John Eliot Gardiner), Koopman has rarely ventured into Mozart's operas, the exception being *Die Zauberflöte*, released by Erato. On the other hand, the symphonies and concertos by Joseph Haydn have been part of his permanent repertoire for many years. He is the soloist in the still-appealing 1997 interpretation of the harpsichord and organ concertos. And who can still remember the earlier Erato release, from 1986, of the Concert Champêtre by Francis Poulenc, with Ton Koopman as soloist on the harpsichord, accompanied by the Rotterdam Philharmonic Orchestra conducted by James Conlon? But Koopman is certainly open to producing more accessible works now and then – wide-ranging and for a broad audience. Examples include the CD set *Simply Baroque vol.1 & 2*,

Amsterdam Baroque Orchestra in Oman. Photo by Khalid Al Busaidi

in which Koopman and his orchestra were joined by the world-famous cel-
list Yo-Yo Ma, or CDs of Christmas songs – still much sought after in the Low
Countries – sung with style by the famous Dutch artist Herman van Veen with
Ton as accompanist. One of his latest and particularly appealing releases is
the two-CD set with music by Carl Philipp Emanuel Bach. Ton Koopman plays
six organ sonatas on the first CD, and the second CD comprises pieces for
harpsichord by the same composer, played by Koopman's wife (and former
student), Tini Mathot. Tini Mathot, herself an accomplished harpsichordist, often performs with her husband. In December 2014, the couple performed, with
great success, another of Bach's masterworks, *Die Kunst der Fuge*, at various
venues in the Netherlands. Incidentally, Ton Koopman will only make recordings if his wife produces them; they have now worked together on hundreds of
recordings.

Monteverdi, Haydn, Bruhns

They share a great deal more, too. In the first place three daughters, the
youngest of whom, Marieke, managed to persuade her seventy-year-old father
– along with the whole Amsterdam Baroque Orchestra – to take part in her
children's show *Oorwurm* (Earworm). She even persuaded Ton to wear pyja-
mas on stage! Ton and his wife also share an interest in teaching. Tini Mathot
teaches harpsichord at the Royal Conservatoire in The Hague. Ton Koopman is
Professor of Musicology at Leiden University, Honorary Member of the Royal
Academy of Music in London and artistic director of the French music festival
Itinéraire Baroque. Koopman, a man of many talents, also publishes regularly.
He edited a new edition of all sixteen organ concertos by Georg Friedrich Hän-
del for Breitkopf & Härtel. More recently, he edited the *Messiah* (also by Hän-
del) and *Das Jüngste Gericht* by Buxtehude, both for Carus Verlag. Apart from

this, or perhaps as a result of this, there is Koopman's passion for old books. He lives in Bussum, twenty minutes by train from Amsterdam. His home, a nineteenth-century mansion that used to be a home for the elderly, is bursting at the seams, not only with several harpsichords and organs but also some 10,000 antique music books and 35,000 other works from after 1800, from all over Europe.

No-one will be surprised to learn that the seventy-year-old Ton Koopman still has many plans for the future. He is keen to perform works by Claudio Monteverdi, and more of Joseph Haydn's works too. He is particularly keen to record the work of Nikolaus Bruhns, a lesser-known German Baroque composer. Bruhns died at the early age of twenty-nine, and composed only fifteen cantatas. Ton Koopman is already looking forward to all the fine music that he – and his grateful listeners with him – will discover. ■

Translated by Yvette Mead

Amsterdam Baroque Orchestra. Photo by Khalid Al Busaidi

On Rembrandtness

The Rembrandt Research Project Revisited

[GARY SCHWARTZ]

The year 2014 saw the appearance of the closing volume, vol. VI, of *A Corpus of Rembrandt Paintings.* The *Corpus* was the main product of the world-famous Rembrandt Research Project (RRP, founded in 1968), which came to a close after forty-six years. The Project has a founding myth. A full sixty years ago, in 1956, a young curatorial assistant at the Rijksmuseum, Bob Haak (1926-2005), was arranging the displays for a major exhibition of Rembrandt paintings commemorating the 350th anniversary of the master's birth in 1606. As the paintings leaned against the wall to be hung, Haak was struck by their diversity. They couldn't possibly all have been painted by the same artist, he thought. In stages, he and his friend Josua Bruyn (1923-2011), professor of Dutch art at the University of Amsterdam, forged plans to launch an investigation that would distinguish between paintings by Rembrandt himself and works wrongly attributed to him.

The programme they set up for this purpose, funded by the Dutch government, was unprecedented in its scope and thoroughness. Two by two, 'in constantly changing combinations', the team members – in addition to Bruyn and Haak, the others were Simon Levie (b. 1925) and Pieter van Thiel (1928-2012) of the Rijksmuseum and Ernst van de Wetering (b. 1938) of the University of Amsterdam – travelled the five continents to study all the Rembrandt paintings in the world. On the spot, they wrote descriptions of the painting 'seen as an object, as fully as possible'. They also set out 'to benefit as much as possible from ... scientific examination in the laboratory ... and from the various photographic techniques.'[1] The RRP set up headquarters in the Central Laboratory for the Study of Works of Art in Amsterdam and assembled a vast archive of information on all aspects of Rembrandt's paintings. All aspects, that is, which the group felt were relevant to distinguishing between an A-group of 'Paintings by Rembrandt' and a C-group of 'Paintings Rembrandt's authorship of which cannot be accepted.' (Between these is a small B-group, to which only five percent of the entries belong: 'Paintings Rembrandt's authorship of which cannot be positively either accepted or rejected.') The aspects considered relevant for this end do not include iconography, provenance or archival references, which are given short shrift by the Project, as are seventeenth-century prints after Rembrandt's paintings. 'Authorship', in the view of the RRP, is a property

Rembrandt, *Saul and David*, ca. 1650-1655,
Oil on canvas, 130 x 164.5 cm
Photo by Ivo Hoekstra
Credits: Mauritshuis, Den Haag

of the painting 'as an object,' a property whose presence or absence can be established only by observation and comparison. The completion of *A Corpus of Rembrandt Paintings*, the monumental six-volume set in which the RRP published its findings, affords an outstanding opportunity – indeed, it demands of us – to evaluate the project in terms of its original intention. At the close of this review we will reveal the results of this stress test.

An unfinished, hybrid product

As work on the first three volumes proceeded, from 1968 to 1989, covering the years 1625 through 1642, Ernst van de Wetering brought an increasing amount of material research and historical reconstruction to bear on the definition of authorship. His dissatisfaction with the overly deterministic way in which the RRP defined Rembrandt's style, with consequently unconvincing de-attributions, led to a break in 1992. Van de Wetering took over the RRP on his own and revamped the format of the *Corpus*. Rather than continuing chronologically, he devoted vol. IV to the self-portraits and vol. V to the small history paintings postdating 1642. Underestimating the extent of the task, he found himself unable to write subsequent volumes on the landscapes, portraits and larger

Rembrandt, *Self-portrait*, 1635,
Oil on panel, 90.5 x 71.8 cm.
Buckland Abbey (National Trust)

history paintings. Instead, he devoted vol. VI, the final one in the *Corpus*, to what he calls a 'complete survey.' The book offers good colour plates of all the paintings and entries on all. This is needed especially for paintings not included in vols. I-V. Unfortunately, the coverage of those paintings as well as others is uneven. Some entries, such as that on *The Jewish Bride* in the Rijksmuseum and *Simeon and the Christ Child* in Stockholm, are too brief. This internal inconsistency, compounded by constant cross-references to vols. I-III, means that vol. VI does not function well as a stand-alone one-volume catalogue of Rembrandt's paintings. It is in fact misleading to speak of 'a' corpus in six volumes. What we have is an unfinished, hybrid product with three distinct constitutions.

Not only was the format of the *Corpus* revised by van de Wetering, he also reversed the tendency to reduce Rembrandt's oeuvre into a spirit of expansionism. From 1982 to 1989, with the publication of vols. I-III, we grew accustomed to stories of this kind in the press and the media:

AMSTERDAM, Dec. 8, 1989 (Reuters, in *The New York Times*): The Rembrandt Research Project, a group of art experts, said today that 39 paintings attributed to Rembrandt are not genuine, including one at the Metropolitan Museum of Art in New York. Among the 39 paintings deemed by the group to be painted by students of Rembrandt are works in the Metropolitan, the Hermitage Museum in Leningrad, the Louvre in Paris and Britain's Wallace Collection.

Then, from 1993 until today, the rejected paintings began coming back into the fold, and we were treated to reports such as this one from *Die Welt*, 15 October 2014:

Braunschweig. Art experts have withdrawn their doubts concerning two Rembrandt portraits in the Herzog-Anton-Ulrich-Museum in Braunschweig. Researchers of the Dutch Rembrandt Research Project concede that the *Portrait of a Man* (1632) and *Portrait of a Woman* (1633) are by the Dutch Baroque painter after all. Twenty-eight years ago the group of experts had still doubted this.

The reversal is apparent for all to see in the six monumental volumes of the *Corpus*. Vols. I-III were heading for an oeuvre of about 260 works. Vol. VI ends up with a list of 348.[2] What are we to make of this self-contradictory project? And now that it has been closed, what assurance does it offer us concerning the authorship of the paintings attributed to Rembrandt van Rijn?

Which volume to believe?

The shift from deletion to expansion is accounted for by Ernst van de Wetering, the director of the RRP since 1993, in a remarkably personal essay in vol. VI. There he sketches an epic methodological and personal drama that took place in the course of the decades. As the RRP rolled on, he became increasingly convinced that the project was on the wrong track. Bruyn and the others, he felt, were concentrating too exclusively on Rembrandt's style in their judgements.

1

2

Saul and David,
1. Before restoration
2. During restoration
3. UV Light
4. After restoration
All photos by Margareta Svensson
Credits: Mauritshuis, Den Haag

Saul and David (Retouch during restoration)

Photos by Margareta Svensson

Credits: Mauritshuis, Den Haag

Any painting that showed excessive divergence from the way they thought Rembrandt painted was eliminated from his oeuvre. Van de Wetering wanted to give more weight to the different functions of the paintings and their techniques, to allow greater latitude for levels of quality and to acknowledge the participation of workshop members in some Rembrandt originals. (Of the 146 A-paintings in vols. I-III – 'Paintings by Rembrandt' – none is said to contain even a single passage by an assistant.)

It is often a matter of choice which volume of the *Corpus* to believe. One example will have to serve for all to demonstrate how confusing this can be.

In vol. III (1989), the RRP devoted a dismissive entry in the C-category to a painting of Rembrandt (see p. 158) that until then nearly all cataloguers of Rembrandt's paintings had considered to be an autograph self-portrait.[3] In vol. III of the *Corpus* they wrote of it in notably disparaging terms.

> At first sight the painting has a certain impact... On closer inspection, however, no. C 92 exhibits a great many jarring features... it is disappointing to see how clumsily the structure of the body relates to the arms hidden beneath the cloak; the depiction of form is so poor that large areas of the painting have a strange emptiness. This extends to the head, where the rather uncertain modelling in the lit and shadow parts produces hardly any effect...; the eye area, in shadow, is not only fairly flat... but is also weak and insensitive in its linear construction. Brushwork and use of paint do lead, seen overall, to rembrandtesque effects, but they differ quite decisively from Rembrandt's own... The remarkably diffuse appearance of the X-ray... in this respect must be termed untypical for Rembrandt.... The signature and date on the painting do not give an impression of authenticity... The painting belongs in the ... category of portraits of Rembrandt done by another hand.

The entry goes on to specify other aspects of the painting that are irreconcilable with the RRP's standards of Rembrandtness, concluding that it is not a self-portrait but a 'Half-length figure of Rembrandt' 'that was probably done in Rembrandt's workshop around 1638.' (The panel is signed and dated 1635.)

Then, in vol. IV (2005), Ernst van de Wetering returned to the painting, which he now calls 'Rembrandt workshop (or Rembrandt?).'

> There are several reasons for once again raising the question of the author-ship of this painting. The visual material that a user of the *Corpus* would have needed to arrive at his or her own judgement over this (long since virtually inaccessible) painting was missing from the relevant entry in vol. III. In ret-rospect, it is regrettable that owners of paintings allegedly by Rembrandt, but whose authenticity we doubted (as, in this case, had others before us), refused us permission to publish the relevant visual material.

In the rest of his remarks, van de Wetering deals only with the X-rays and re-pentirs. He does not comment on the specific weaknesses that are described in detail in vol. III, of which he was co-author. In a remarkable twist, he lays responsibility for what has turned out to be a completely misleading judgement in vol. III at the feet of the painting's owner, while suggesting that the arbiter of authenticity is not the RRP but the 'user of the *Corpus*.' Yet the RRP had been given every opportunity to examine the 'virtually inaccessible' painting and its X-rays. In vol. VI (2015), van de Wetering moves the question mark in his attribution, to 'Rembrandt (and workshop?).' His entry (no. 134) is full of evi-dence corroborating an attribution to Rembrandt. There too, however, he fails to explain when, how and why the pertinent observations and criticisms in vol. III ceased to be valid and why the X-rays are no longer untypical of Rembrandt. The lessons that could be learned from this concerning Rembrandt and the ways of the connoisseur now remain unlearned and the methodological faults perpetuated.

This particular case is more than a little painful, involving as it does a consid-erable loss to a family that deserved better. The private owner of the painting in the 1980s was the wealthy property developer Lord Harold Samuel of Wych Cross (1912-1987), who had the generosity to bequeath his outstanding collec-tion of Dutch and Flemish old masters to the City of London.[4] The Rembrandt was not in the collection, because he had given it during his lifetime to his wife Edna. She too, upon her death in 2008, bequeathed art to a public body, the Na-tional Trust. Under the terms of her will, which was passed in 2010, her daugh-ters were each entitled to keep a painting for themselves. Consulting Sotheby's for an estimate of what the 'half-length of Rembrandt' would fetch at auction, they were told that it would be in the vicinity of 20,000 pounds. This suggests that Sotheby's was basing its estimate on the entry in vol. III of the *Corpus* rath-er than vol. IV or taking the opinion of any other expert than the RRP. Believing that the painting was not worth very much, neither daughter kept it.[5] In 2010 the National Trust deposited it in Buckland Abbey, Devon, which at first treated it as a non-Rembrandt and put it into storage. Apparently, it was only when the new owners became aware of van de Wetering's remarks in vol. IV that a new investigation was launched, including in-depth scientific examination by the outstanding Hamilton Kerr Institute of Cambridge University. On the basis of the positive outcome of the investigation, the painting was treated to a clean-ing. Following this campaign and a re-examination of the painting, Ernst van de Wetering has been quoted as declaring 'I am satisfied it is by Rembrandt', which has also satisfied the National Trust and the media. The painting went

Saul and David (Detail)

on view as an undoubted Rembrandt self-portrait in a special exhibition in June 2014, with an estimated value of 30 million pounds.[6] (One re-reads with some amazement the remarks in vol. IV castigating the Samuel heirs for displaying less than exemplary cooperation in robbing themselves of 30 million pounds).

While Ernst van de Wetering's opinion on attributions is considered to be definitive, it should not be ignored that none of the three long, involved passages in the *Corpus* on the Buckland Abbey painting is an adequate representation of the evidence concerning its attribution. This reflects on the *Corpus* as a whole.

A treasure chest after all

Despite its deficiencies, inconsistencies and incompleteness, *A Corpus of Rembrandt Paintings* is the most extensive catalogue ever published on the master's paintings, with an unequalled, immense wealth of information and opinion. It is indispensable for all and any Rembrandt research and will remain so into the distant future. Discussion will continue on specific attributions and on the nature of connoisseurship, but no serious publications on Rembrandt will ever bypass the entries and judgements in the *Corpus*.

The project also produced some important collateral benefits. It has drawn the attention of scientists in the fields of dendrochronology, molecular research, conservation science and even engineering, who have broadened the scope of art research. In the later volumes there are valuable essays on the Rembrandt documents, costume and material substances. Van de Wetering himself, in illuminating and stimulating ways, has pursued favourite themes such as hitherto unrecognized sets and series among Rembrandt's paintings; patterns in his use of formats, supports, grounds and pigments; the original compositions of cut-down works; the function of particular kinds of paintings; and the relevance for Rembrandt's art of the theoretical writings of Karel van Mander and Samuel van Hoogstraten.

What we are left with is a treasure chest of sorts that did not fulfil its initial promise and never acknowledged that it failed to do so. It is an extended exercise not in science and not in logic – van de Wetering claims incorrectly to be practising the Bayesian variety – but in amplified connoisseurship, in which the amplifications mainly add to the traditional uncertainties of connoisseurship.

Looking forward to a different corpus

What is the RRP's answer to Bob Haak's dilemma? The Rijksmuseum exhibition of 1956 that irritated Bob Haak into initiating the RRP showed no fewer than 101 paintings. Of these, sixty-four are still today accepted unanimously as works by Rembrandt. The input of the RRP, as against the choice of the Rijksmuseum in 1956, lies in the other thirty-seven paintings. However, if we inspect them, we find that the RRP has left out sixteen of these debatable attributions completely. It did so, on its own statement, because Horst Gerson had removed them in 1968 from his own catalogue of Rembrandt paintings. In other words, the *Corpus* is based in significant measure on the judgement of a connoisseur of an older generation whose intuitive style it was out to improve and replace.

Ten more paintings rejected by the RRP were already doubted by Gerson, and one more by Claus Grimm, so they would have been omitted from future Rembrandt catalogues even without the RRP. That leaves nine paintings out of the 101 that the RRP excised on its own authority from the Rembrandt corpus. When, in 1969, the 300th anniversary of Rembrandt's death was marked by another exhibition in the Rijksmuseum, thirty-four paintings were included that all, without exception, are accepted by the RRP. One can therefore say that Rembrandt connoisseurship was already, in the first months of existence of the RRP, moving in a direction that the project would not catch up with until nearly half a century later.

In terms, then, of Bob Haak's discomfort, the contribution of the RRP to Rembrandt attribution lies less in the removal of paintings from the oeuvre in vols. I-III than in van de Wetering's additions to it in vols. IV-VI. These include mainly marginal works which, if they were put on the floor next to the traditional corpus, would undoubtedly lead another young curator – probably even the older Haak himself, who did not support van de Wetering's re-attributions – to wonder whether they could possibly be by the same hand. In fact, most of the de-attributions and many of the new attributions in the *Corpus* have been challenged by others.

At the presentation of vol. VI in the Rijksmuseum on 8 October 2014, Ernst van de Wetering declared that he had put to an end uncertainty concerning the attribution of Rembrandt paintings. This is not his judgement to make. It is to be hoped that the next round, based less on categorical judgements and more on consistency and sound methodology, is at hand. To help things along, allow me to remark that the built-in assumption of the RRP that authorship is a property of the object and the object alone is disputable. If authorship is conceived not as hardened pigment but as a set of dynamic physical but also historical and conceptual criteria, in constant movement, then we can look forward to quite a different corpus of Rembrandt paintings than that of the RRP. ■

A Corpus of Rembrandt Paintings, vols. I-VI, is published by Springer. Vols. I-V are available online at The Rembrandt Database.

NOTES

1   Quotations from the introductory matter in vol. I of the *Corpus*.

2   Van de Wetering made the world press with his statement that in vol. VI he reversed the attributions of seventy paintings rejected in earlier volumes. In a blog of 8 November 2014 Michael Savage criticizes this claim.

3   Disclosure: in my own book on Rembrandt of 1984, which covered all paintings accepted as by Rembrandt by Horst Gerson and the Rembrandt Research Project, I did not include this self-portrait. This was not an independent judgement on my part. As I indicated in a table on p. 380, I did so on the authority of Gerson, who had suggested in 1969 that the panel was by Govert Flinck.

4   See Peter Sutton, *Dutch and Flemish Seventeenth-Century paintings: the Harold Samuel Collection*, Cambridge (Cambridge University Press) 1997.

5   Information kindly provided by a grandson of Harold Samuel.

6   See various pages on www.nationaltrust.org.uk.

Unsentimental Compassion

The Documentaries of Peter and Petra Lataster

[JELLE SCHOT]

Peter Lataster (Amsterdam, 1955) and Petra Lataster-Czisch (Dessau, GDR, 1954) have worked together as documentary filmmakers for the past quarter of a century. A harmonious alliance – 'together we are a single director', they always say – that has already earned them a wide array of Dutch and international film awards, including a Golden Calf for *Tales of a River* (1994) and *Not Without You* (2010). And in 2012 the Netherlands Institute for Sound and Vision spotlighted the team as 'Documentary-makers In Focus', an honour falling previously only to John Appel, Hans Heijnen and Heddy Honigmann.

This confirms the Latasters' status in the Dutch film world, all the more remarkable considering the fact that the couple's repertoire is hardly one of large-scale, sensational stories or of dazzling cinematic flamboyance. Their work consists mainly of intimate, personal documentaries. 'We're not after exoticism or shock value,' they wrote in the introduction to the Sound and Vision booklet *Petra Lataster-Czisch & Peter Lataster In Focus*. 'For us, making a film is an encounter with other people, a journey of discovery to places we've never seen so close up. We believe that by focusing at length on the smaller picture, we can better comprehend the big picture, and are able to communicate something universal.'

Artists and caregivers

The Latasters' oeuvre, developed largely in co-operation with the humanist broadcasting company Human (formerly the Humanistiche Omroep), can be roughly divided into two categories. The first includes films about artists and thinkers whom they admire. In 1991 they made their debut with *De bekoring*, a poetic portrait of Peter's grandfather, the sculptor Frits van Hall, whose participation in the Dutch artists' resistance movement resulted in his deportation in 1944 to Dachau and, later, Auschwitz. And over the years they have produced portraits of other artists and scholars, including the sculptor and illustrator Auke de Vries (*I Like to Touch Everything*, 2006), the mathematician Hendrik Lenstra (*The Things You Don't Understand*, 2010) and the Moroccan-Belgian choreographer and dancer Sidi Larbi Cherkaoui (*The Need to Dance*, 2014).

The other thread in their work is the relationship between society's more vulnerable members and the people who care for them. They documented the life of a group of at-risk women in a domestic violence shelter in *This Will Never Go Away* (2005), the difficult but loving relationship between a severely autistic boy and his ever-patient caregiver in *Jeroen Jeroen* (2012), and paediatricians at the Groningen University Medical Centre wrestling with ethical issues in *If We Knew* (2007).

Peter and Petra Lataster
Photo by Gertjan Miedema

Sometimes the two facets overlap. *Call it Sleep* (1996), for example, is an affectionate portrait of the American author Henry Roth. Peter and Petra Lataster filmed him throughout the last year of his life: a frail, elderly man who relied entirely on his bandana-wearing caregiver. And the much-lauded film about Peter's own parents, *Not Without You*, is in fact an amalgam of the two themes as well – although, in this case, the filmmakers themselves were also the (off-screen) carers.

Demise of grand ideals

It is not difficult to trace the origins of the Latasters' dual fascinations. Peter is the son of the painter Ger Lataster and photographer Hermine van Hall. Their social awareness likewise stems from their youth. For starters there was the untimely death of Petra's mother, which she says 'linked her to the transience of life'. And their parents' political leanings were also influential. 'My father was a devoted communist,' Petra once said in an interview with film journalist Jan Pieter Ekker, 'and Pjotr (her nickname for Peter, ed.) grew up in a communist family too. We had to redefine our world view, and film is an extremely suitable means for doing so.'

The demise of grand ideals played an important role in their early work. They made three films about life in the GDR after the fall of the Berlin Wall: *Tales of a River* (1994), *River of Time* (1999) and *Dreamland GDR* (2003). In the first of these – winner of the Golden Calf for best feature documentary at the Netherlands Film Days (now the Netherlands Film Festival) – they investigated the effect of German reunification on the everyday lives of the inhabitants of Petra's home town of Dessau. *River of Time* is a chronicle of the town of Groß Lüben, situated on the border between East and West Germany. And in the final (and finest) segment of the trilogy, Petra invited her own former schoolmates to share their recollections from before and after the fall of the Wall. 'Cherished memories of a bygone youth in a country that did not truly exist', wrote the Dutch daily *Trouw*.

The GDR trilogy is, in a certain sense, the odd man out in the Latasters' oeuvre, partly due to the dreamy voice-overs that play a conspicuous role, but also because of the degree to which it features the makers themselves. *Dreamland GDR*, for instance, opens with the following quote from Petra: 'I was very young when I fell in love with a cameraman from capitalist Holland. We married and I climbed over the nearly unscalable wall separating two hostile worlds.' She appears on camera often: not only as an interviewer, but also as a participant, visiting her parents' vacant house ('a place of endless dreams'). The viewer watches her peruse her own Stasi dossier and shares her relief in discovering that none of her family or friends had ever betrayed her.

Stills from *Not Without You*, about the parents of Peter Lataster
Photo by Peter Lataster © Lataster&Films 2010

Stills from *Tales of a River*
Photo by Peter Lataster ©
Lataster&Films 1994

The most enduring elements of the trilogy, however, are two figures who openly long for 'the good old days'. In *Tales of a River* there is a man whose entire youth had been spent preparing for his future career as a border guard – until everything he believed in and dreamed of fell to pieces along with the Wall, and he attempted to take his own life. And in *Dreamland GDR* there is Petra's ex-classmate Peter, the son of a former party chief, who out of a sense of nostalgia keeps the East German army's European invasion plans under his sofa.

Dreamland GDR, however, marked the end of the 'grand narratives' in the Latasters' films. Since then they have focused their attention on smaller, closer-to-home dramas – a rather remarkable development, in the light of their shared background. The filmmaker couple met in the mid-1970s at the Hochschule für Film und Fernsehen in Potsdam-Babelsberg, at that time one of the leading film academies behind the Iron Curtain. Peter studied camera technique, having been rejected twice by the Amsterdam Film Academy. And Petra studied scenario-writing and cinematology. She would later recount their first meeting to Jan Pieter Ekker: 'I saw Pjotr in the dormitory kitchen and knew at once: this is Mr. Right. He was a bit slower...'

Direct cinema

It is not only the themes of their films that have changed over the years. The way the Latasters present their stories has undergone a transformation, too, albeit a subtle one. Their style has always been sober and simple – more television than cinema, the acerbic critic might say – with the emphasis on content. But since *Fragile Happiness* (2001) – one of the few lesser works in their oeuvre, a somewhat artificial portrait of ten ordinary residents of The Hague and their day-to-day vicissitudes – the couple no longer makes films on celluloid. Digital

Stills from *River of Time*,
Photo by Peter Lataster
© Lataster&Films 1999

photography, which allows them to film much longer and more cheaply, has clearly freed up their style. And in the tradition of 'direct cinema', their work tends to rely less on interviews: what the viewer sees mainly happens spontaneously in front of the camera.

What has not changed, though, is the meticulousness of their groundwork. In interviews they explain how they often spend weeks discussing a certain camera position or debating to what extent they themselves will be present in the film. And while it is hardly noticeable, there is a specific choice of imagery for each film. Take, for example, *Not Without You*. They agreed beforehand that Peter's parents, Ger and Hermine, would always be shown together in each shot, underscoring their mutual reliance. If this was not physically possible, then the camera would always pan from the one to the other in the course of the shot. And the tempo was to be intentionally slow, forcing the viewer to become a participant in the rhythm of their daily lives.

The result is a poignant portrait of the last year Peter's parents would spend together (his mother passed away during filming). An honest film too, which often confronts the viewer with the decrepitude of old age, the elderly couple's quarrels, and the rare moments of tenderness. 'Intimate without being voyeuristic, and moving without being sentimental,' wrote *Volkskrant* reviewer Pauline Kleijer. And the weekly *De Groene Amsterdammer* had nothing but praise too: 'More and more, documentaries revolve around the maker himself or his immediate surroundings. This requires walking the fine line between closeness and distance, between intimacy and voyeurism. The Latasters – all four of them – have made a masterpiece.'

For the likewise magnificent *Jeroen Jeroen* (2012, nominated for a Golden Calf for Best Short Documentary) the camera was removed from its tripod. The film closely follows the profoundly autistic Jeroen for two days, observing him in good as well as bad moments. One minute he is as happy as a child, the next minute he flails wildly, trying to hurt his caregiver. And the Latasters, albeit out of sight, are right there on top of it all, not affording the viewer a moment's respite, just as Jeroen's parents and coach never get a moment's rest.

Sincerity and integrity

These are just two examples of the Latasters' use of film in the service of dramaturgy. And there are plenty more: perhaps their greatest visual coup is how, in *If We Knew*, they transform a sterile hospital into a cocoon of warmth, love and security. But in the end, that is not their forte *per se*, because what makes the Latasters' films so unique is the integrity and sincerity of their approach, regardless of the subject. As the Dutch newspaper *de Volkskrant* put it: 'The Dutch documentary world probably has no more meticulous and conscientious directors than the Latasters.' Bert Janssens, a former editor at the broadcaster Human and its present director, praised their methods in *Petra Lataster-Czisch & Peter Lataster In Focus*: 'Their talent is that they are not calculating in approaching a subject (...) Averse to cheap effects, they focus above all on the subject itself.'

The Latasters never make a film in order to advocate a certain standpoint, or to draw attention to social injustice. The individual is the focal point, and not what he or she stands for. A good example is *The Things You Don't Understand* (2010), their humorous portrait of mathematician Hendrik Lenstra, who garnered worldwide attention as a twenty-eight-year-old professor at the University of Amsterdam and co-discoverer of the LLL algorithm. But rather than mathematics, the Latasters asked him about issues like love and happiness, and turned the camera on Lenstra's close relationship with his mother, who still calls him up every morning and evening.

Stills from *The Things You Don't Understand*, about the mathematician Hendrik Lenstra
Photo by Peter Lataster © Lataster&Films 2010

Making films *with*, and not only *about* people, is the Latasters' philosophy. And this evidently results in a deep trust between filmmaker and 'subject', because time and time again they are privy to the most intimate, often painful moments. In *If We Knew*, for example, when a premature baby dies in the operating room and they witness the father as he touches his child for the first and last time. Or in *Awake in a Bad Dream* (2013), where a woman with breast cancer is being assisted in the shower, because she is unable to wash herself. In the interview with Jan Pieter Ekker, Petra said of this film: 'It's a terrible situation of course. But at the same time it's deeply moving to see how people bare their souls. They have to, otherwise they wouldn't survive. And sharing this results in a deep feeling of sympathy and solidarity.'

Filmmaking has its price

The Latasters do not airbrush reality: illness, decline, death are presented true-to-life, and as painful and confronting as the situation may be, the camera never turns away. Not even in *Not Without You*, when Peter's own father strips and shuffles into the shower. 'It's normal to present bold, hard, reality in war reports or on other momentous subjects, but as soon as we show an elderly man, naked and in need of assistance, people find it unpalatable and in-your-face,' they said to *de Volkskrant* of this particular scene. 'Because it's so much closer to their own reality.'

Stills from *This Will Never Go Away*
Photo by Peter Lataster © Lataster&Films 2005

Stills from *The Need to Dance*,
about the choreographer Sidi Larbi Cherkaoui
Photo by Peter Lataster © Lataster&Films 2014

Stills from *Awake in a Bad Dream*
Photo by Peter Lataster © Lataster&Films 2013

Witnessing all sorts of misery up close is not always easy. In a variety of interviews, Petra has said how difficult making *Awake in a Bad Dream* was. Its completion felt like a grieving process, although she maintained contact with the women in the film after shooting it.

But, they admit, this is simply the price filmmakers like themselves pay for their *modus operandi*. If you want subjects to bare their souls for a documentary, you have to do the same. They wouldn't and couldn't have it any other way: engagement is second nature to them – albeit somewhat less so for Peter, as he confesses on the Human website. Being the cameraman, he says, creates a certain distance: 'Peering through the lens is in fact the first step in translating reality into an artificial product. I certainly won't say I'm never moved, but it's different.'

And perhaps that is the strength of the Lataster team: the combination of Petra's compassion and Peter's unsentimental eye. The viewer never feels like a voyeur, no matter how personal and intimate the events in their films. ■

Translated by Jonathan Reeder

www.latasterfilms.nl

The Lessons of Medea and La Falstaff

A Tribute to My Theatre Work

In the mid-1990s, when director Luk Perceval invited me to join him in embarking on the twelve-hour marathon production which *Ten Oorlog* (To War) was to become, I did not hesitate. Despite having previously only written a handful of plays and a couple of novels, stories, poems, et cetera, I immediately said yes. Correction: I only hesitated for a couple of days. Not out of an aversion to Shakespeare or Perceval, but because I found so few roles for women in the source material, which consisted of eight of Shakespeare's history plays, beginning with *Richard II* and finishing with *Richard III*, a cycle often referred to as *The Wars of the Roses*.

Only when it dawned on me that the lack of women and their suppression was part and parcel of the universal power cycle we were to stage, and after Perceval promised we would make Falstaff into a subversive transvestite, did I decide to agree. Our Falstaff was even permitted to fall in love with the young Prince Henk, later to become the soldier King Henry V, or *Hendrik de Vijfden* as he would be known in our version. In the end I even gave La Falstaff a couple of adaptations of Shakespeare's love sonnets, as a lament after he/she is dumped by his young love Henk, who unexpectedly chooses to grow up, do the honourable thing and become king after all.

Elsewhere in *Ten Oorlog* I also worked in countless references to famous poems or phrases, songs or speeches, from Dutch-language and world literature, from Flemish poet Paul Snoek to American record label Motown. Sometimes they served as meaningful echoes, sometimes they were purely entertaining parodies. Why would I avoid such interventions, which purists make out to be unnecessary and even sacrilegious? Shakespeare himself was certainly not averse to quotes and pastiches. It was from him that I learnt to do it, and from the many directors and actors educated in his teachings. When he was just twenty-eight he was accused by a competitor, the snob Robert Greene, now barely known, of being an 'upstart crow', showing off with the feathers and treasures of others.

A kleptomaniac crow, a thieving magpie... At fifty-eight I would still consider it a title of honour. In fact it is a vocation, particularly in theatre. Nothing is original, everything is adaptation. The greatest flash of inspiration is a clever appropriation, brilliantly disguised as authenticity. Literary theorists and pur-

ists fail to understand one thing. On stage everything is possible and permissible, as long as it works. Writing drama is a celebration of freedom. Nowhere else do you have freer rein than in a play script. Even film cannot compare, however much it is indebted to theatre. I take my hat off to the scripts of David Mamet or Quentin Tarantino but, as in all scenes for the screen, major monologues are limited to between thirty and forty seconds. You can get away with eight lines, ten maximum.

On stage, dialogues can last four to five minutes, giving you two pages. *Ten Oorlog* ended, after more than eleven hours of theatre, with a monologue of almost half an hour, the morbid swansong of *Risjaar Modderfokker den Derde* (Richard Motherfucker III).

Man should aim to build cathedrals

Before we were ready to go, I had been given twelve hours to jumble up idioms and styles into a 'diachronic language spectacle'. I'm not sure what it means, but that was the way a glowing review put it.

Perceval and I constructed our own storyline based on the historic facts and Shakespeare's interpretation, supplementing them with our imagination and sometimes pulling them brazenly apart, in our desire to sketch a kind of history of power and at the same time all of humanity through the ages. There was no shortage of ambition; we were both under forty, back then. 'Man should aim to build cathedrals,' said one of my other teachers, Gerard Mortier (1943-2014), director of De Munt/La Monnaie in Brussels, the Opéra de la Bastille in Paris and the Teatro Real, Madrid's opera, as well as the very first Ruhrtriennale in Germany, and before that artistic director of the Salzburg Festival for many years. I see him as the Sergei Diaghilev of his time and I would like to mention him here because he enabled us to produce *Ten Oorlog* in German. We premiered at the Salzburg Festival in 1999, in coproduction with the Deutsches Schauspielhaus in Hamburg.

In the German version, again, each of the six kings had his own language. The first, our *Risjaar Deuzième*, spoke in frivolously meandering verse, peppered with archaisms, internal rhymes, enjambment and French flourishes. The second, our *Hendrik Vier*, expressed himself in surly, wooden rhyming couplets. Those who belonged to the court of the newly crowned king subserviently adopted his manner of speech. At the same time the language became progressively more slippery, cynical, grotesque, filthy.

At each transition of power there was therefore a change in idiom and style, while all characters persisted in speaking in iambic pentameters. Even the hunchback monster Richard III and his two brothers – the York brothers – availed themselves of this metrical form, also used by Christopher Marlowe and Shakespeare. But the York brothers' language increasingly consisted of verbal rubbish - swearwords and expletives from bad English-language films and series, mixed with Flemish dialect expressions and vulgar threats from hip hop songs.

Only when we came to the final king, our *Risjaar Modderfokker den Derde*, was the verse form permitted to break down here and there – disintegration of rule became disintegration of language. Risjaar's use of power was based nar-

Hamlet versus Hamlet, Abke Haring as Hamlet
Photo by Kurt Van der Elst

rowly on cynicism, self-pity, narcissism, bloodlust and provocation. At the moments of his greatest abuse of power, such as the murder of his two nephews, whom he also partially consumes in our version – the iambic pentameter falls apart and the monster can only express himself in a kind of linguistic mush composed of shrieks, fragments of slogans, peculiar poetic images and raw cursing. A babbling flood of words reminiscent of T.S. Eliot's *The Waste Land* or Austrian playwright Werner Schwab. From linguistic ingenuity to linguistic vomit, scabies, leprosy, underlining the theme of our tale of deteriorating power, creating a slowly shifting and eventually explosive idiom, far beyond grammar and classic versification.

Becoming a better writer

Ten Oorlog cost me more than two years of my existence, innumerable fits of despair, countless sleepless nights filled with doubt. But given the chance I would do it all over again, and I advise any colleague to set off on a similar journey if the opportunity arises.

In those four years – including all the rehearsals and the German production – I learnt more than in five years at university, and more than in my previous fifteen years' writing. My collaboration with Luk Perceval made me a better writer on every level. The lesson went far beyond creating dialogues and monologues in verse form; it was a crash course in applied psychology and a bachelor's degree in dramaturgy, constructing scenarios, themes, characters, relationships – all that and more. I marched through it all at great speed.

We scrapped a couple of hundred characters and extras, but retained dozens. Under the whip of a demanding director and his team of playwrights and actors, I also learnt how to explore what a crown can do to its wearer in a series of six connected plays. Six monarchs, six personality types, and six painful downfalls, intensified by everything this world can throw at a mortal. Overconfidence, paranoia, jealousy, betrayal, revenge and – very occasionally – love and compassion.

Finally I also received a lesson in applied political science, amounting to the idea that without collective transfer of power there is no authority and consequently no society is possible. However, if power is transferred collectively, the risk of abuse always arises. The crown itself is pure, glittering temptingly, but the prestige and authority it confers can corrupt or crush its wearer. Generally both at once.

Everything I learnt from *Ten Oorlog* was useful to me in subsequent projects. *Mamma Medea*, for example, was a very free adaptation of Euripides's famous play. I went resolutely in search of a counterpart to our sixth and final king from *Ten Oorlog*, *Risjaar Modderfokker den Derde*. After the greatest male monster of world literature it simply seemed natural to me to turn to the female version.

Medea and her beloved Jason differ not only in background and temperament, but also, once again, in language. Medea and her barbaric compatriots all speak in verse and in archaic jargon, while Jason and his supposedly civilised Greek Argonauts speak in dry, sophisticated prose, highlighting the war of love between the two spouses.

Bourla Theatre
Antwerp

Their passionate fight to the death also continues to the bitter end in *Mamma Medea*. In contrast with Euripides's version, they each murder one of their two sons, as if in a fanatical competition between two people perfectly alike. Having started out as Greek and barbarian, in the end they converge with George and Martha from Edward Albee's modern classic *Who's Afraid of Virginia Woolf*.

I was able to apply the lessons of La Falstaff and Risjaar Modderfokker extensively in my own prose when I wrote *Het Goddelijke Monster* (The Divine Monster), a family chronical which was soon dubbed 'a pop art Buddenbrooks', after Thomas Mann's family chronical.

Power versus art

Other projects of mine would have looked very different without the lessons of *Ten Oorlog*. In *Bloed en rozen. Het lied van Jeanne & Gilles* (Blood and Roses. The song of Jeanne & Gilles) I wrote my version of the life of two *monstres sacrés* of French history, the people's heroine Joan of Arc and the noble paedosexual serial killer Gilles de Rais, who together liberated the city of Orléans from the English. Both underwent notorious trials, both were executed, both remain the subject of speculation and discussion today, but what connects them for me is again the chiaroscuro of power and human impotence. Who is the true monster and who is the most human? Neither Jeanne nor Gilles is entirely one or the other.

Under the same motto I also wrote down my vision of another two Shakespearean classics. In *Koningin Lear* (Queen Lear) the elderly monarch is transformed into Elisabeth Lear, the leading lady of a former family contracting firm once started up in Flanders, and nowadays a global multinational. Despite her progressive dementia Elisabeth Lear senses the approach of a colossal, all-encompassing economic crisis, a perfect storm for the financial sector. Despite her earlier business intuition she makes a disastrous decision, dividing her entire empire without preparation between her three sons. The only condition? Like Lear's three daughters in the original play, they must publicly profess their love for their mother.

The youngest refuses to cooperate in what he calls an exhibition of bad taste and insincerity, to the frantic rage of his old, sick mother, who disinherits him on the spot, thereby exacerbating the approaching disaster. Her monstrous narcissism, inflated by her dementia, eventually leads to the unfortunate death of her youngest, the apple of her eye – who happens also to be the child of an extramarital affair, like the 'little red-headed monkey' Jonas, the murdered son of Katrien Deschryver from *Het Goddelijke Monster*, described above.

In *Hamlet versus Hamlet*, as the second adaptation is called, I cut out Hamlet's friend Horatio, making the young Danish prince even lonelier than he already was, but I introduced a brand new character as partial replacement, the spirit of the jester Yorick, who accompanies Hamlet and sometimes challenges him.

In my version the play therefore has two ghosts: that of Hamlet's murdered father on the one hand, demanding that his son take bloody revenge and claim the power due to him as prince by right, and on the other hand the ghost of Yorick. He constantly reminds Hamlet of all things frivolous, artistic and truly worth the effort in life, averse to all Machiavellian intrigues. Power versus art: that is a fundamental choice tearing 'my' Hamlet apart from the first scene. To grow up definitively, or not yet, after all?

Mamma Medea
Els Dottermans as Medea
Photo by Phile Deprez

Minard Theatre
Ghent

Mamma Medea. Gilda De Bal as Mamma Medea (Chalkiope/Kirke)
Photo by Phile Deprez

Director Guy Cassiers shared my analysis. I easily persuaded him to have my prince played by a young, androgynous actress, who would further underline my central interpretation. Note that our Hamlet was not a transvestite like La Falstaff in *Ten Oorlog*. Dutch actress Abke Haring interpreted the part of a young man, just as all women's roles were played by boys in Shakespeare's day.

This Hamlet does not simply live between appearance and reality, between thought and action, between revenge and fear... He inhabits that no-man's land because he himself is 'unformed'. He exists in a space between adolescence and adulthood, between purity and political realism, between feelings of revenge and regret, remaining unformed. He still feels pure, untainted by the machinations of power, and really he would prefer to remain so forever. In order to protect himself he feigns madness, so long and intensely that he really goes mad and condemns himself to eternal inaction.

In my adaptation he ends up the only survivor, on his knees at the front of the stage, apparently finally ready for action. He will throw himself upon his own sword, as his rival in love Laertes did with such conviction before him. But even now Hamlet, the young philosophy student, gets no further than interminably conjugating the verb to be.

'I am. *(weeps)*
I was. *(laughs)*
I was. *(stops, nods)*
I am. *(curtain)*'

A magnificently lying world

Two other fictional novels of mine, like *Het Goddelijke Monster*, are tributes to my theatre work. In *Het Derde Huwelijk* (The Third Marriage) an old, terminally ill homosexual accepts payment to enter a sham marriage with a young African woman, with the aim of helping her gain Belgian nationality. Everyone betrays everyone; not even the social security inspectors and family members of the two main characters are interested in the truth. Everyone fashions their own persona and stages their own innocence, to combat betrayal by others. Nevertheless a bizarre and sincere affection grows between the two false spouses – with dramatic consequences for all involved.

In *Gelukkige Slaven* (Happy Slaves) two near-identical main characters come face to face. They are both called Tony Hanssen and look as alike as two brothers, nor do they differ much in other respects. One Tony fled Belgium a couple of decades previously and has since made a mess of his life, running up enormous debts with a corrupt Chinese communist owner of various casinos in Macau, whose wife he allows to abuse him as a toy boy and unsuspecting money courier. During an intense love-making session in Buenos Aires Mrs Bo Xiang dies in Tony's arms, an ecstatic grin on her face.

The other Tony is a computer expert who has fled a failed Belgian merchant bank. He shoots a corrupt guard and a defenceless rhinoceros in a South African safari park, hoping that the trophy, the double horn of the slaughtered animal, will demonstrate that he should be taken seriously. The murder resembles a rite of passage, reminiscent of the Argonaut Jason's reason for travelling to the land of the witch Medea, to win the Golden Fleece and prove his claim to the throne.

The two Tonys first meet in China, the lap of the future, where each realises that the other wants to trick him, but that they desperately need one another if, perhaps, they are to be delivered from their fate. For that, each must play the other, in the hope of them both improving their lot.

In acting the part of an identical person, they shape the deeper theme of the novel, the loss of identity in a globalising world, which lies so brilliantly that everyone can compose their own identity. As long as they have enough money to purchase the right luxury products with the right brand name and look like the photo-shopped Übermenschen from glossy magazines and TV advertisements. The non-existent new gods of fashion. The dazzlingly designed, eternally young, vapid monsters we all emulate, in horror and delight.

Never again speechless

None of my works, however, brings together the influences mentioned above as much as my autobiographical novel *Speechless* (*Sprakeloos*), painful as it is.

Not that I would want to portray my mother, the central character, as a monster. Far from it, although I do not deny a certain form of emotional tyranny and family dominance in her. It was an illness that struck her and slowly drove her towards death which I was compelled to describe as monstrous; aphasia following a cerebral infarction which destroyed the speech centre of her brain.

Vooruit Theatre, 'Art Ennobles', Ghent

The language I had designed for *Risjaar Modderfokker den Derde* in *Ten Oorlog*, described above as 'linguistic mush composed of shrieks, fragments of slogans and raw curses', and as a 'babbling flood of words' reminiscent of an oral *Waste Land* – the same language now afflicted my poor mother. For Risjaar the linguistic mush reflected the complete decomposition of power. For my mother the gibberish formed a harrowing sign of loss of strength, and of everything she had considered worthwhile, in short her own expressive, powerful language so rich in imagery.

She had made use of that language from morning till night. At the breakfast table she would vividly describe her strange nightmares, adding some equally strange interpretation, while at the same time commenting in detail on what she found in her newspaper, which she had been reading out of the corner of her eye as she spoke.

In the course of the day she talked incessantly at my father's butcher shop, where to be honest she was never particularly enthusiastic about helping. She concealed her revulsion by working doubly hard and showing a disposition of cast-iron cheerfulness. Self-effacing and self-sacrificing, with little sign of irritation, day after day, like most women of her generation.

She succeeded, despite her rebellious temperament, because once in a while there would be an evening in which she had something other to do than just filling in the accounts, darning her large family's socks or preparing the next days' meals in advance in her tiny, cramped kitchen. Those were the evenings in which she indulged her heart's desire as an amateur actress. She declaimed and triumphed in rehearsal rooms behind popular pubs or on stage at the constantly busy theatre of the provincial town from which she and I hailed.

Everything I know about theatre, everything appealing and fascinating about language, everything that has made me devoted to art, begins with her and the unintentional lessons she gave me, long before Medea and La Falstaff, without either of us realising at the time that they were lessons. The scene might look as follows: she would be ironing the washing while I sat on the other side of the table, her script in my hands, *A View from the Bridge*, by Arthur Miller, or *Our Town*, by Thornton Wilder, or sometimes, less to her taste, a slapstick comedy such as *Boeing Boeing*. I would correct her when she made mistakes in her lines and read all the other parts myself, in accordance with her double goal, as 'multitasking mother before her time', of simultaneously improving my reading and memorising her role. And all the while she coolly and calmly did the ironing.

That she of all people should lose her capacity for language: I saw it as a cruel, monstrous punishment for a crime she had not committed. Hearing her version of the language leprosy I had so presumptuously and cheerfully created for Risjaar years before – my interpretation of one of the most popular villains of international theatre – left me in despair, even ashamed. When she even lost that gibberish and was driven silently towards her miserable death, the horror was complete. A hideous, wordless silence which I hated from the bottom of my heart.

Ten Oorlog was my second university, as I wrote above. In *Sprakeloos* I had to learn that lesson again, this time at a bitter university of pain, rage and frustration at so much pointless suffering, so much macabre irony. Never have I found a book so hard to write.

But never have I wanted to write a book so much. As an indictment and screeching curse against the inevitability of the decline which awaits us all. Our suffering and our impotence when we stand eye to eye with it. Above all, however, it had to be a homage. To my mother, of course, but also to the greatest gift I received from her. Her language. My mother tongue.

The intimacy of her deterioration was something I could not shy away from. I needed to bear sharp and honest witness to it, giving a humble yet unveiled account. But the book could only end with a son who, as a writer, still sung of triumph. That of language. *Her* language, and mine, in which I – stubborn and demanding, against all decline – make another vow, to her and to myself, only to believe in *one* thing. The power of language, the fire of literature, on paper and on stage.

Sprakeloos, translated by Paul Vincent as *Speechless*, ends as follows: 'The nurse looks at me again for a moment, in doubt. Then she does her work anyway. She inserts two fingers of one hand carefully between the lower and upper jaw of the patient and wedges them open. With the forefinger of her other hand, she frees, from the place from where the language came that I learnt, just a couple of bits of mucus and wipes them off on a tissue. And then and there I swore to myself that from now on I have one vocation, one aim, one godforsaken self-chosen duty, because I can't do much else, haven't learnt anything else and don't believe in anything else. That I, when I see the chance, will combat the silence with my voice, will try to out-argue silence with my speech, will try to attack all the available paper in the world with my language. Let that be my rebellion, my revolt, against mucus, against rattling. Let me do this at least as a mutiny. Let there no longer be a second, a page, a book, that does not speak in a hundred thousand tongues, that does not testify to vocabulary. Never again silent, always writing, never again speechless.

Begin.' ∎

Translated by Anna Asbury

The Low Countries and the Concert of Nations

Contributions to European Culture

[R.C. VAN CAENEGEM]

The purpose of this article is a panoptic survey of the specific contributions of the Low Countries to European culture in its various manifestations.

The historic Low Countries were a conglomeration of principalities in northern France and western Germany which, in the fifteenth and sixteenth centuries, were welded together by their Burgundian and Habsburg rulers into a new political entity, separated from their original kingdoms and occupying their own distinct place on the European map. They reached their apogee as the Seventeen Provinces of Emperor Charles V. The Revolt of the Netherlands against his son, King Philip II, and the Spanish reconquest of the southern part caused the break-up of the Emperor's creation. The south became a Catholic dependency of the Spanish and later Austrian Habsburgs, and the north the Protestant Republic of the United Netherlands. The two parts were briefly reunited (with the addition of the Prince-Bishopric of Liège) under King William I (1815-30), but separated again by the Belgian Revolution. After the Second World War the Kingdoms of Belgium and the Netherlands and the Grand Duchy of Luxemburg formed a loose alliance called the Benelux.

Appraising the contribution of those lands to European civilization in areas stretching from philosophy and theology to the fine arts and constitutional law, I distinguished three categories of achievement: where they underperformed I call their role 'average', where they contributed significantly without being exceptional I speak of a 'distinguished' role, but where their performance was superior and changed the face of Europe, I call it 'outstanding'.

Philosophy

A quick glance shows that the Low Countries were no fertile soil for philosophy: abstract thought was clearly not their priority. They nevertheless played a modest role in the thirteenth century, when William of Moerbeke († 1286) translated Greek philosophy and science, was sent to Nicea, worked at the papal court and ended as Archbishop of Corinth. Siger of Brabant († 1283) was probably born in Liège and taught philosophy in Paris. He defended certain

Dirck van Delen (?), *Interior of the Great Hall at the Binnenhof in
The Hague During the Great Assembly of the States-General in 1651*
Detail, 1651, Rijksmuseum, Amsterdam.

Aristotelian tenets, which led to the condemnation of thirteen of his theses by
the Archbishop of Paris. He fled to the papal court at Orvieto, where he died.

Modern Times did not mean modern ideas in Leuven, Leiden or Utrecht,
three conservative centres of learning which for a long time were steeped in
Aristotelianism and biblical cosmology. In a detailed study Professor Hilde De
Ridder-Symoens traced the slow reception of Copernicus and Descartes.[1] At
the University of Leuven 'Aristotelianism remained the basis of all sciences
till far into the seventeenth century'.[2] In the Dutch Republic 'the Copernican
worldview was not seen as a valuable alternative to the traditional worldview'.[3]
In the 1640s 'the Utrecht professor of theology Gisbertus Voetius denounced
heliocentrism, declaring that it was contrary to the Holy Scripture'.[4] Passions
flared up when René Descartes's *Discours de la Méthode* appeared on the
scene. 'Whereas his ideas', thus Professor De Ridder-Symoens, 'were quickly
received in medical and scientific circles, his metaphysics and epistemology
also immediately provoked fierce reactions particularly among the theologians.[5] No modern Netherlandish philosophers were a match for the great galaxy at the European top, such as Kant and Hegel.

Plakkaat van Verlatinghe, 1581 (Act of Abjuration (sc. of the Spanish King Philip II)). It is accepted that the Act of Abjuration, which has also been called 'the Dutch Declaration of Independence', was well known among the drafters of the American Declaration of Independence.

Against this mediocre background the famous philosopher Baruch Spinoza († 1677) was the exception confirming the rule. He was a lone and lonely figure in the Dutch landscape who became a cosmopolitan esoteric thinker of European fame. He was born in Amsterdam in 1632 of Portuguese ancestry, but belonged to no Dutch tradition of philosophy and founded no school of his own. As a freethinker he was banned by his synagogue, but found refuge in circles of critical Christians. He was reprimanded by Calvinist devines and in 1674 his *Tractatus theologico-politicus* was outlawed. His main work, *Ethica more geometrico demonstrata*, was an idiosyncratic attempt to give ethics a mathematical foundation and was influenced by René Descartes, with whom he corresponded. From all this it is clear that Netherlandish philosophy can claim no higher classification than 'average'.

Theology

For many centuries theology – the Science of God – was the supreme intellectual pursuit, not only among clerics but also among eminent scientists. Isaac Newton, for example, was the author of a voluminous commentary on the Book of Revelation.

The contribution of the Low Countries started with Henry of Ghent († 1293), who taught theology in Paris. He was famous in his time, but nowadays is only known to scholars, who assiduously study, edit and translate his work.[6] In the seventeenth century Bishop Cornelius Jansenius († 1638), professor of theology at Leuven in 1618 and Bishop of Ypres in 1635, wrote a posthumously published book entitled *Augustinus*, the starting point of a controversial worldview known as Jansenism. It advocated a severe, even ascetic approach to Christian morality and was tainted with the doctrine of predestination. It was influential in France, where Blaise Pascal was a follower and where it was associated with Gallicanism, which stood for an independent national Church. In the early eighteenth century Jansenism, combated by the papacy and the Jesuits, was a spent force.

In the nineteenth century the Low Countries again played a role on the theological scene: Neo-Thomism, the revival of the medieval doctrine of Thomas Aquinas, became dominant in Catholic countries, particularly after Pope Leo XIII's encyclical *Aeterni Patris* of 1879. The attraction of St. Thomas's doctrine for modern Catholic philosophy and theology was his attempt to reconcile Aristotle's rational approach with Christian dogma. Making Holy Scripture intellectually acceptable was important in the face of modern science.

The University of Leuven played a significant role in the study of the medieval authorities. In 1882 Désiré Mercier († 1926), the later cardinal, was appointed to the chair of Thomistic philosophy, founded at the request of the aforementioned Pope Leo XIII. In 1881 the University became the seat of the internationally renowned Higher Institute for Philosophy, with Mercier as its first president. Neo-Thomism inspired numerous theologians and philosophers as well as Catholic politicians, but after World War II it had spent its force - Jansenism and neo-Thomism were backward-looking, drawing their inspiration from St. Augustine and St. Thomas Aquinas, so no great innovation was to be expected from that quarter.

The Low Countries produced no illustrious theologians on the European scene comparable to Thomas Aquinas in the Middle Ages, or Luther and Calvin and Carolus Borromeus at the time of the Reformation and the Counter-Reformation. No Netherlandish theologians arose comparable, in our own time, to Dietrich Bonhoeffer, the leading Protestant theologian who was executed by the Gestapo in 1945, the controversial Swiss Catholic professor Hans Küng, or the leader of the critical *Nouvelle Théologie*, the French Jesuit Henri de Lubac, who was forced to give up his teaching in 1950 but rehabilitated by Pope John XXIII.

By way of conclusion it seems justified to place Netherlandish theology in the 'average' category.

Music

The musical record of the Low Countries is unremarkable in spite of a brilliant start. The Netherlandish polyphony of the fifteenth and sixteenth centuries enjoyed international fame. Johannes Ockeghem († 1497) became musical director of King Louis XI of France. Josquin des Prez († 1521) served the Sforzas in Milan and joined the papal choir in Rome. Jacob Obrecht († 1505) was active in Cambrai, Bruges and Antwerp before working, at the end of his life, at the court of the Duke of Ferrara. Adrian Willaert († 1562) joined the chapel of Milan Cathedral and became, in 1527, musical director of San Marco in Venice for the rest of his life. He was the founder of the Venetian School, whose most famous composer, Claudio Monteverdi († 1643) occupied Willaert's post at San Marco in 1614. Jan Pieterszoon Sweelinck († 1621), composer and organist in Amsterdam, was influential in Germany.

The Netherlandish polyphonists were the gifted forerunners of the great Italians and Germans, Palestrina, Monteverdi, Bach and Handel. There was, however, no follow up to this great promise when inspiration ran out. Later centuries merely produced composers like Pierre van Malderen († 1768), known only to erudite scholars. César Franck († 1890) was born in Liège but spent all his life in Paris, and the fact that the ancestral home of the Beethovens stood at Mechelen is only a very indirect contribution to the glory of European music.

So, we will reluctantly put Netherlandish musical composition in the 'average' category.

Medicine and Science

In both these fields the Low Countries present an honourable record. Their achievements in medicine started with Andreas Vesalius in the sixteenth century, followed by Jan Baptist van Helmont in the seventeenth, Jan Palfijn and Herman Boerhaave in the eighteenth, and Joseph Guislain, a pioneer in the humane treatment of the mentally ill, in the nineteenth century. The crowning achievement came when the Nobel Prize for medicine was won by three Belgians, Jules Bordet, Corneel Heymans and Christian de Duve, and by two Dutchmen, Christiaan Eykman and Niko Tinbergen (born in The Hague in 1907, became a British citizen in 1955).

Likewise, the line of scientists started in the sixteenth century, with the botanist Rembert Dodonaeus, the cartographer Gerard Mercator and the mathematician Simon Stevin, the first innovator in his discipline since antiquity. In the seventeenth century Christian Huygens was a mathematician, physicist and astronomer of European fame and a member of the Paris Académie des Sciences.

Here again the twentieth century brought a crowning achievement when a galaxy of Dutch scholars became Nobel Laureates for physics or chemistry, H.A. Lorentz, R. Zeeman, J.D. van der Waals, H. Kamerlingh Onnes, F. Zernike, J.H. van 't Hoff, P.J.W. Derby, P. Crutsen, G. 't Hooft, M. Veltman and A. Geim. In Belgium Ilya Prigogine (born in Moscow in 1917, became a Belgian citizen in 1949) won the Nobel Prize for chemistry, and Jacques Englert for physics.

So, although the Low Countries produced no giants like Galilei, Leibniz, Newton or Pascal or, closer to us, Max Planck or Albert Einstein, their record certainly deserves the epithet 'distinguished'.

Architecture

The Low Countries are rich in cathedrals, town halls, belfries and castles. The oldest go back to the twelfth century, i.e. the Cathedral of Tournai, the Church of St. Servatius in Maastricht and the Count's Castle in Ghent, where the crusader's cross above the gate recalls the trip to the Holy Land of the Count of Flanders, Philip of Alsace. The following centuries witnessed the building in the Gothic style of imposing cathedrals in Antwerp, Brussels, Ghent, Haarlem and Mechelen, as well as the splendid town halls of Bruges, Brussels, Ghent, Leuven, Middelburg, Oudenaarde and Utrecht. Some of them were conceived and built by seven generations of one family, the Keldermans, who were architects, stonemasons and sculptors from the late fourteenth to the mid-sixteenth century. In 1516 Rombout II Keldermans became Emperor Charles V's

Willem van Oranje,
Petit Sablon square, Brussels.
Photo by Jonas Lampens.

Saint Carolus Borromeus church on Hendrik Conscience square, Antwerp.
Photo by Jonas Lampens.

Chief Architect. In 1561-65 the Renaissance style appeared when Cornelis Floris de Vriendt built the magnificent town hall of Antwerp. In the following century the Baroque triumphed in Antwerp with the House of Peter Paul Rubens and the Church of St. Carolus Borromeus, built by the Jesuits Frans d'Aguilon and Pieter Huyssens. Nearer to us some creative architects gained European fame, such as Herman Berlage († 1934) in the north and Victor Horta († 1947) and Henry van de Velde († 1957), two members of the Art Nouveau movement, in the south. Netherlandish architects did not invent the great European styles – Romanesque, Gothic, Renaissance and Baroque of French or Italian origin – but they worked wonders with the common Western heritage, which yields them the 'distinguished' grade.

We have now reached two fields of human endeavour where the Low Countries occupy a seat in the front row, the visual arts and the pursuit of good government. In the course of six centuries Flanders and the Netherlands were the home of superb artists, whose work occupies pride of place in museums, palaces and churches throughout the world. It all began in the fifteenth century with the Old Flemish Masters, Hubert and Jan van Eyck, Rogier van der Weyden, Hugo van der Goes, Hans Memling and Dirk Bouts.[7] After the apocalyptic visions of Jeroen Bosch and the landscapes – sometimes lovely and sometimes ominous – of Pieter Breughel, the great masters of the seventeenth century – Rubens, Rembrandt, van Dyck and Vermeer – astonished the world. The nineteenth and twentieth centuries carried the torch further. Some painters enjoyed local celebrity, such as the Schools of Amsterdam and Latem, but others achieved cosmopolitan status, such as Vincent van Gogh († 1890) and René Magritte († 1967) or, most recently, Luc Tuymans.

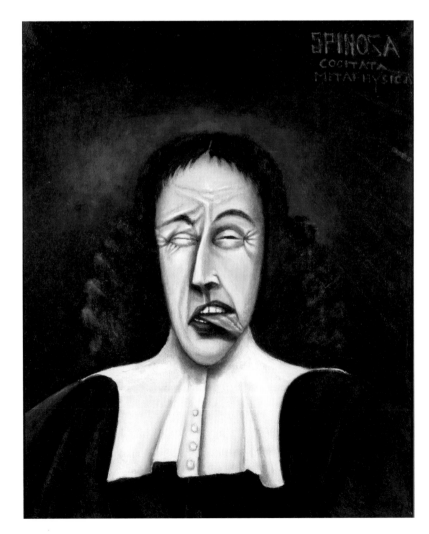

Rachel Baes,
*Les tics de Spinoza
(l'Éthique) ou cogitata
metaphysica*,
Oil on canvas, 1967,
Private collection.

That European art history is unthinkable without them needs no further elaboration. Two points, however, will strike every observer. Firstly the variety of styles, from late Gothic to Renaissance, Baroque and Impressionism, and secondly these artists' sudden entry on the scene: van Eyck's Mystic Lamb was a total revelation – like Athena emerging from Jupiter's head. One wonders how the human mind could create something so marvellous out of nothing.[8] This impressive array of artists, comparable to the great Italians from Giotto to Tiepolo, certainly deserves to be classed as outstanding, for even if European culture lasts for another thousand years, Dutch and Flemish paintings will always be admired.

The art of government: federalism

Justice and prosperity are the sweet fruits of good government, whereas anarchy and corruption are the bitter fruits of the bad. The blessing of *buon governo* and the disasters of its opposite are graphically depicted in the famous allegory by Ambrose Lorenzetti in a fresco of 1338-1340 in the Sala della Pace of the Palazzo Pubblico in Siena. Good government is a cultural achievement to which I now turn my attention, hoping to show the contribution made by the Low Countries to the rise of federalism and republicanism, two pillars of modern constitutional law.

In Europe the Seventeen Provinces of Emperor Charles V were the first federal state. Other countries knew unitary kingdoms (unity often imposed by force, as when in 1707 the Spanish King Philip V punished the rebellious provinces of Aragon and Valencia) or free city states. Switzerland was a loose federation of autonomous cantons, which only became a federal nation state in 1848. In the sixteenth century the Low Countries formed a body politic composed of principalities, each having its own identity, government, parliament, laws, privileges and judiciary, but united by a personal union, as they shared a common ruler. Their union was ensured by the Pragmatic Sanction of 1549, which streamlined their laws of succession. In 1531 Charles V reorganized the central bodies of the Netherlands creating the Council of State, which together with the existing Privy Council and Council of Finance (the three Collateral Councils) formed the national government. Already in 1504 a supreme court of appeal, the Great Council of Mechelen, had been founded. And there was a pan-Netherlandish parliament, the States General, which first met in Bruges in 1464. The Habsburg Netherlands were a distinct state on the European map, but not a kingdom. Charles V was King of Spain and of Germany, as well as Roman Emperor, but in the Low Countries he was Duke of Brabant and Luxemburg and Count of Artois, Flanders, Holland and so on. He was, however, a monarch, so that his Netherlands can best be called a federal monarchy. It was the European prototype of a federal state, combining respect for regional diversity with the advantage of a central government. Like many other lands, the Low Countries produced parliaments and charters of liberties early on, but there is no need to expatiate on this here.[9]

The Revolt of the Netherlands against King Philip II of Spain led to the break-up of his father's inheritance. The ten Catholic southern provinces remained under Spanish rule, while the seven Protestant provinces in the north escaped

Philip's reconquest and were left free and ready for 'the Rise of the Dutch Republic'.[10] The Republic of the United Netherlands was, as the name indicates, a federal state in the footsteps of Charles V. Each of the seven provinces had its own identity, government, parliament and judicature, but there were overarching, central institutions. We have already mentioned the States General, an assembly of the deputies of the provincial states, which was constantly in session. There was also the Council of State, for home affairs, the General Chamber of Accounts and the Monetary Chamber, which controlled the finances of the Union, and finally five Admiralties. Defence was in the hands of the Stadholder, a descendant of William of Orange, the 'Father of the Fatherland'. The Dutch Republic, formally recognized as a sovereign state by the treaty of Munster in 1648, became a great success, whose federal constitution inspired the young United States of America, where it was well known and carefully studied.[11] America in its turn was the model for the Republic of Weimar and ultimately for the German Federal Republic, a successful democracy and federal state in the heart of Europe.

Thus the federalism of the historic Low Countries was an outstanding contribution to European civilization. The irony of it all is, however, that the land of its birth gave up, in the early nineteenth century, its ancient constitution and became a unitary and centralized nation state under King William I.

The art of government: republicanism

In a republic the citizens govern themselves for themselves. In a monarchy the people are lorded over by kings from their palaces and knights from their castles. In a republic, not the 'Sovereign' but the nation is sovereign. The republic was well known in antiquity, most famously through Plato's eponymous work. Throughout the Middle Ages and for a long time afterwards monarchy was the norm (except for a few rural communities in Switzerland), but among the Italian city states republicanism was taken seriously and put into practice. However, after the capture of Florence by Emperor Charles V in 1530, Italian democracy was a thing of the past. Monarchy triumphed in the country, with a kingdom in the south, a papal autocracy in the middle and dukedoms in the north.

Not long afterwards republicanism was given a new lease of life north of the Alps, in the Dutch Republic. In an Act of Abjuration of 1581 the States General of the United Netherlands declared that Philip II was a tyrant and had forfeited the throne. After some futile attempts to find another monarch to succeed him, the States General decided in 1587 to carry on without a king and adopted the republican form of government. It was a revolutionary step, if not entirely without precedent. Republican ideas had inspired Flemish towns in their revolt against their counts, and from 1577 to 1582 Ghent was a Calvinist Republic.

The Dutch made a success of their newfound republic, a tolerant and law-based state, where government was in the hands of elected representatives of the country. For two centuries it was the only country with a republican constitution (with the exception of the ephemeral republic of Oliver Cromwell), an anomaly on the map of Europe.[12]

But after the American Revolution (which was inspired by the Dutch Republic) and the French Revolution (which was not) the republican ideal became

Restoration of the Ghent Altarpiece by Jan van Eyck
in the Museum of Fine Arts, Ghent.

unstoppable and at present four large European countries – Germany, France,
Italy and Poland – are republics, and so are many smaller ones. But what about
the kingdoms – Britain, Spain, Belgium, the Netherlands, Denmark, Norway
and Sweden? Here it is necessary to distinguish between appearances and reality. Those countries do indeed have kings and queens – one even crowned
and anointed by the Church – but they have no impact on national politics.
Their role is ceremonial, opening new kindergartens or offering condolences
to the victims of a railway crash. Power is wholly in the hands of politicians and
elected parliaments. The government even fixes the salaries of the members
of the royal family, and when, as protocol dictates, Queen Elizabeth II reads the
political programme of 'her' government for the forthcoming year, in a solemn
address to the two houses of Parliament, it is not 'her' government nor is the
programme she outlines her text, but one drafted by the Prime Minister.

So shall we call these 'kingdoms' pseudo- or crypto-republics camouflaged by the trappings of royalty, as they are the embodiment of the ancient republican ideology of popular self-government? Are kings and queens useless then? Certainly not, for hereditary monarchy is a visible sign of the identity and unity of the nation. It is anchored in the past, part of the national heritage and stands for continuity and confidence. It also saves the country the turmoil of periodic presidential elections along party-political lines.

Considering this triumph of the republican idea, it can rightly be called an outstanding contribution of the Low Countries to European civilization.

But it is ironic again that, in the early nineteenth century, the pioneering Dutch turned their backs on the republic and converted (or should I say reverted, as they had briefly been a kingdom a few years earlier?) to monarchy, when William, a descendant of William of Orange and a line of stadholders, became king (and a king with autocratic leanings after the fashion of the Enlightened Monarchs). On 3 November 1813 he landed, with British support, at Scheveningen, returning from exile in England, at a time when the French Empire was crumbling. Initially William was styled 'Sovereign Monarch' and on 16 March 1815 he assumed the title of King. In September of that year he made a ceremonial entry into Brussels as King of the United Kingdom of the Netherlands (north and south together again).

In a recent study Matthijs Lok, Assistant Professor of Modern European History, had a critical look at how the Dutch nation so unexpectedly became a kingdom.[13] He showed how William built on the experience of the short-lived Kingdom of Holland under Louis Napoleon (1806-10), a brother of Emperor Napoleon I. Louis Napoleon's kingdom had been a united, centralized and bureaucratic state along, not unexpectedly, Napoleonic lines. King William I even took over a large section of the officialdom of that first Dutch kingdom and, in so doing, took a leaf out of the book of his arch-enemy, Emperor Napoleon. ∎

Dirck van Delen (?), *Interior of the Great Hall at the Binnenhof in The Hague During the Great Assembly of the States-General in 1651*, Detail, 1651, Rijksmuseum, Amsterdam.

'Small Things Grow Great by Concord'

1   H. DE RIDDER-SYMOENS, 'Intellectual Freedom Under Strain in the Low Countries During the Long Sixteenth Century', in: R.A. MÜLLER (ed.), *Wissenschaftsfreiheit in Vergangenheit und Gegenwart*, Basel 2008, pp. 229-48.

2   H. DE RIDDER-SYMOENS, op. cit. p. 237.

3   Op. cit., p. 244.

4   Op. cit., p. 245.

5   Op. cit., pp. 245-46.

6   So recently R.J. TESKE (ed. and trans.) *Henry of Ghent's Summa of Ordinary Questions: Articles Thirty-one and Thirty-two on God's Eternity and Divine Attributes in General* (Medieval Philosophical Texts in Translation, 49), Milwaukee, Marquette University Press, 2012.

7   The term Flemish Primitives that is often applied to these highly cultured artists of genius is both absurd and insulting.

8   Recent research, however, has thrown new light on the role of the painter Melchior Broederlam, who worked in Ypres from 1381 to 1409, as a precursor of the Van Eycks. See C. STROO, 'Broederlam's World of Surface Appearance: Traditional and Innovative Aspects', in: M. DEMEY, M. MARTENS and C. STROO (eds.), *Vlaamse Primitieven tussen visie en materie, Brussels*, Koninklijke Vlaamse Academie voor Wetenschappen en Kunsten, 2012, pp. 67-91.

9   In April 1996 a conference at St. George's House, Windsor Castle, assessed the historic contribution of Britain and the Low Countries to the development of democracy in Europe. The papers were published in John PINDER (ed.), *Foundations of Democracy in the European Union. From the Genesis of Parliamentary Democracy to the European Parliament*, London, 1999.

10 Thus the title of J.L. MOTLEY's famous 3 vols. published in London in 1856. The same author also published a *History of the United Netherlands from the Death of William the Silent to the Twelve Years' Truce*, 4 vols., The Hague, 1860-67.

11 R.C. VAN CAENEGEM, *Historical Considerations on Judicial Review and Federalism in the United States of America, with Special Reference to England and the Dutch Republic*, Brussels, 2003 (Koninklijke Vlaamse Academie van België voor Wetenschappen en Kunsten, Academiae Analecta, New Series, 13). See also C. BONWICK, 'The United States Constitution and its Roots in British Political Thought and Tradition', in: J. PINDER (ed.), op.cit., pp. 41-58.

12 See the encyclopaedic study by Jonathan ISRAEL, *The Dutch Republic. Its Rise, Greatness, and Fall (1477-1806)*, Oxford, 1995.

13 M. LOK, 'The Establishment of the Orange Monarchy in 1813-15. A National Myth', in: *The Low Countries. Arts and Society in Flanders and the Netherlands*, 21, 2013, pp. 208-18.

His Portraits Got the Blues

The Photography of Koos Breukel

A good portrait operates in the field of contradiction, its rhetoric confirms and questions. It creates facts and rises upon them, registers and enchants. It does so in an intangible, simultaneous mix. Nevertheless for Koos Breukel a good portrait is no ambiguous secret. Neither is he a mythologist in the sense meant by Roland Barthes, when he called great photographers great mythologists because they give broader meaning to a face, as in Avedon's portrait of a slave, or Sander's lawyer. It is Breukel's matter-of-factness which makes him a great photographer. He does not beautify, seeking instead, to judge by his photos, a sort of intensified, core reality, the beauty of veracity. He does all this clearly and with great precision.

Among Breukel's three portraits displayed at Bozar in Brussels in early 2015 was that of his mother. Amidst the other photos in *FACES NOW. European Portrait Photography Since 1990*, despite its no-nonsense approach, there was a sublime, undefined quality to this image. At the same time the portrait emanates so many glorious nuances between black and white that it forces viewers in the very act of looking to fit it together like a puzzle. The same portrait was presented more informally at the Museum of Photography in The Hague, where it hung amidst a large circle of family members and friends, placed lower and in a smaller format. In The Hague viewers discovered that Breukel's love for photography came from his mother. She was not a professional, as her son later came to be, deriving his reputation from his unparalleled portraits, but the down-to-earth Dutch woman, as we can see from the photo, conveyed her preference for honest simplicity to the camera and to Breukel himself. She gave him his first camera (35mm single-lens reflex) when he was sixteen and stubborn. He honours her in turn with stubborn veracity. As a boy Breukel did not take to school and his mother probably foresaw the opportunity for him to find some direction in life through photography. When he was twenty he enrolled to study Photography and Photonics at MTS in The Hague (now the KABK, or Royal Academy of Art) and was accepted on the basis not of a diploma but of his portfolio. He showed primarily landscapes, his frankness towards people only developing later on. From a technical perspective it was a solid education. Here he became friends with Eric Hamelink, with whom he set up a studio in Amsterdam-West after graduation.

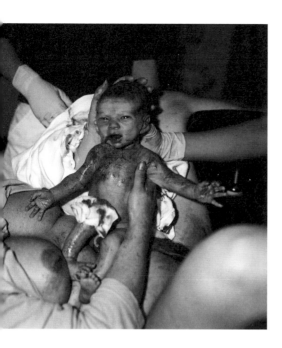

Casper Breukel, Alkmaar 2000
© Koos Breukel

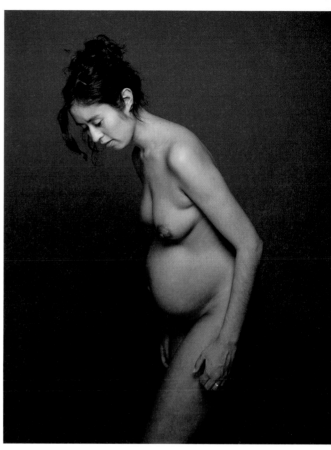

No one lives life unscathed

In 2013 Breukel published *ME, WE*, a substantial volume displaying his own selection of the photos he had taken over thirty years. This is a breathtaking introduction to his work. Recently, in 2015, this won him the Kees Scherer Prize for Best Photo Book 2013/14 in Naarden. The book was launched alongside the retrospective exhibition at the Museum of Photography in The Hague and is arranged in much the same order: Breukel has done no less than map out the life cycle of man. The portrait remains the leading theme, but there are countless photos in which the emphasis is on the entire body, floating in infinitely sparkling seawater, stretched out on the sofa, in the bath, heavily pregnant and suffering the first contractions of labour. The photographer selects an intimate, open point of view, as if reserved only for his children, loved ones and close friends. In essence he approaches people with his direct gaze, more interested in the sharp moments of existence than in external beauty. Babies in the split second they enter the world, bloodied and still attached to the umbilical cord, with wrinkled hands and red feet. That is where life begins and no one lives life unscathed. Even those fortunate enough to grow very old, at the end of the book, appear marked. A couple stand upright, as if supported by the sturdy fabric of their coats. The tone of the blues pervades his work. Not that it is melancholy or despondent; on the contrary, life is openly celebrated here. It can be derailed, however, at a moment's notice, as sickness and death are inevitable

Judith Bloemendaal,
Amsterdam 1999
© Koos Breukel

Sandra and Elf Derks, Bergen 2000
© Koos Breukel

Koos and Riet Breukel, Kijkduin 1993
© Koos Breukel

parts of life. In contrast with Ed van der Elsken, another nonconformist with an inclination towards humanity, Breukel avoids the playful and the reactive. Although like Van der Elsken he grasps the moment of surprise, at the same time he allows the subject to retain a reflective quality, the gaze may briefly slip away or turn inwards. We do not see anyone laughing. There are many portraits in *ME, WE* in which the eyes look straight into the camera, focusing on the viewer, but when the subject looks to the side or slightly upwards, this slows things down by an almost imperceptible breath.

That sense of modesty evidently grew over the years. However, a couple of events in Breukel's life compelled him towards premature seriousness. His life of travel and photographing international and local stars for magazines changed course after a serious car accident in 1992, six years after his graduation. It took place in the Schiphol Airport motorway tunnel. The photographer himself was not driving, but it was his car which caused the accident. From that point on he showed a special interest in people who had endured horrible experiences or were burdened with a handicap. He worked more thematically, for instance in 1997 photographing survivors of the aeroplane disaster at Faro Airport, in which dozens of Dutch citizens lost their lives, and later parents of children who had died in the Volendam café fire next to other parents of Volendam who had lost a child. He also begins to document the progression of illness in two of his friends. Michael Matthews, theatre director and friend of Breukel, asked him to do so, which took courage, on both sides. This resulted in the book *Hyde*, 1996, a coproduction. Matthews wrote the lines of poetry. Seldom has physical deterioration led to such a clarion call as in this photo series. 'Just a thin black line wandering around a big house,' writes the AIDS patient of the skeleton his body has become. It is enclosed in a strange, silvery, scaly skin. 'The illness of time and want / has made me magnificent.' The second half of *Hyde* repeats the first half in the opposite order, but this time in negative, printed on silver paper. Anyone who sees that as an easy way of evoking transcendence is forced to swallow their words on considering the cover: what lies in the hand bears a disconcerting likeness to diseased skin.

A couple of years later his colleague from the very beginning, Eric Hamelink, turned out to be suffering from a brain tumour. The cheerful photos of a good-looking Eric and his girlfriend in the countryside, included in *ME, WE*, are drowned out by a face that loses its beauty, becoming improbably bloated with the medication. I still feel the same sense of disbelief as when I first saw the series. Surely such extreme ugliness cannot really exist? They began to take photos of one another during their studies in 1986 and more than ten years on Koos Breukel continued.

A photo explains nothing

In 1992 Willem van Zoetendaal, then head of the photography department at the Gerrit Rietveld Academie, invited Breukel to come and teach there. He did so until 2003, spanning a period when the department was a hotbed of talent, with names such as Rineke Dijkstra, Hellen van Meene, Charlotte Dumas and Leo Divendal. Van Zoetendaal exhibits excellent judgement, having, not only as a teacher, but also as publisher and gallerist, encouraged many new photographers. Among other things, in 2006 he exhibited Breukel's series *Cosmetic View* and published the book by the same name. This series involves colour portraits of adults and children with eye problems, generally due to illness or accident. Some have their own eyes but little vision, others have artificial eyes. One feels somewhat uneasy staring at the photos for long and we can clearly distinguish the eye which focuses correctly. Moreover the photos are so sharply lit that every scar, blemish, dry patch, birthmark or hanging eyelid is clearly revealed. Mainly, however, you feel like a voyeur for looking to see whether other people can see. Despite the dazzling ambiguity of the girl pictured on the cover, various portraits in *Cosmetic View* lack the tension of Breukel's more successful portraits. These did not make it into *ME, WE*.

A good portrait remains a puzzle for which it is impossible to pin down hard criteria. 'A photo explains nothing,' says Breukel in an interview. 'It maintains the mystery.' His talent enables him to make quick, intuitive decisions. Whether a portrait retains its strength in the long term becomes apparent when it remains hanging on the wall of the studio. 'His studio is a confined space,' writes Van Zoetendaal in *Cosmetic View*, 'containing a wooden, large format camera on a tripod, and a plain background sheet. Although daylight streams in through the roof, it is mainly artificial light that is being used.' Recently he has also worked with a digital camera. People who come to have their photo taken, generally Dutch celebrities, politicians, actors and artists, are often surprised that the severe photos are created in such a homely atmosphere. Studio, home and family life run together.

An interesting observation by Vincent van Gogh on the painted portrait appears in his letter from Arles to his sister in the Netherlands: 'Is such a figure not in all cases something different from a photograph? You see, in my view impressionism is above the rest in that it is not banal and one seeks a deeper resemblance than that of a photograph.' That deeper resemblance is an outstanding example of a motif which the viewer seeks in the work of a contemporary photographer such as Breukel. His fascination, after all, is with humanity as it is and has become, by stumbling and getting up again (only to go down in the end).

A place of honour for the skin

His strength may well be that he succeeds in clothing individuals in something universal or in a certain aura, however vague those notions may be, but meanwhile the individual remains the focal point. As a viewer can you read the depth, the imprint of a person's innate character, in a portrait? Can you read the portrait better if you know someone? This is an unanswerable question. Of those pictured whom I know because they are artists, I notice that they are presented with a twist, their appearance bent into monumental seriousness. This is particularly noticeable where two or three family members appear together. Roy and Céline Villevoye, father and daughter, are presented right next to one another. Nothing in the photo indicates that Roy is the artist with whom Breukel made the long, dangerous journey to Asmat in Papua to stay with a community, resulting in the collective photobook *Tí*. The photo has an innate logic of its own. Sandra and Elf Derks are mother and daughter; you do not see that Sandra is a painter, but you do see the solid balance between *en face* and *en profil* and the fact that both are natural beauties, which makes the photo unusual. You also see the silence which pervades the portrait, the stillness and poetry of momentary nothingness. Photos clearly derive their strength above all from the rhetorical power of what is visually postulated and that is the pure language of imagery.

Roy and Céline Villevoye, Amsterdam 2009
© Koos Breukel

In Van Gogh's time a photo was mainly something for a calling card, a visual identity coupled with a name, and of course recognition still forms an important first step towards reading a photo. A panoramic overview of the photography collection was shown under the title *Modern Times* at the Rijksmuseum in Amsterdam in winter 2014/2015. A high wall was covered in black and white faces by Stefan Vanfleteren, portraits crammed so close that the penetrating profusion was enough to make the viewer's head spin. Close by hung a map with captions. Towards the end of the exhibition the name of Princess Beatrix, the popular former queen, was completely worn out from visitors lingering with their fingers over it while picking out her portrait.

Does this first step apply to Breukel's work too? Many Dutch celebrities have appeared before his lens. Men from politics, women from the world of theatre and art. The dark background and isolated position alone ensure an abstraction which demands a longer look. Actress Sylvia Kristel, for example, appears in such an honest, unglamorous snapshot that you forget for a moment who she is. A hint of sparkle in the gaze raises the photo above the ordinary. Photo historian and friend Hedy van Erp writes in the book that photos were also taken of King Willem-Alexander, presenting him as warmer and more sensitive than the designated official state portrait. Small prints, under embargo, hang in the studio along with photos of the photographer's three children.

The title *ME, WE* is borrowed from Muhammad Ali, the famous boxer. It is the complete text, the back cover states, of an improvised poem which came to him when addressing Harvard students. The title succinctly sums up the relationship with others and is appropriate for a selection of photos culminating in portraits of Breukel's nearest and dearest. The statement, coming as it does from this icon of effective physical power, forms a subtext, with an occasional emphasis on masculinity. In a few places the predilection for sturdy indomitability is so strong that people like Van Zoetendaal and even the critic Lamoree appear to be brothers of the daring agricultural or construction industry labourers who also have a place in the book. We have the male gaze to thank for the equally sublime depiction of a female nude such as Caitlin Hulscher a year before she gave birth to Breukel's eldest son Casper. That male gaze, however, must be curbed in viewing the babies, as the blue marbled skin can only come from a tender onlooker. The skin is in any case a prominent aspect of this work; unique in diversity and meticulously printed on baryta paper, the skin is placed in a position of honour unthinkable in the continual movement of daily life.

National Portrait Gallery

While the majority of the photos in the studio are taken indoors, a mixture of commissioned photos and initiatives by the photographer, the prize-winning book also contains various outdoor photos. The artists' village of Bergen is a favourite location, as is Vinkeveen, a lake with summerhouses near Amsterdam. These images are in no way exuberant, but they are more relaxed and breathe a greater sense of pleasure, with an important role for Breukel's children. In Bergen Breukel photographed his very elderly but girlish colleague Ata Kandó (1913), who once created *Droom in het Woud* (Dream in the Forest) with her children. Kandó had a studio in Paris before she came to the Netherlands as the wife of Ed van der Elsken (a relationship which did not last). Of the many portrait photos he took, that of Rineke Dijkstra is a particularly classic example. He is reported to have asked her to stand still on entering. Wearing her winter coat, her hair half covering her face after her cycle ride over, her observant gaze emerges from the shadow just sufficiently to be present. What an eminent counterpart for the photo she once took of herself during a rehabilitation project, in a swimsuit, with a swimming cap, a paragon of the vulnerability which became her style.

Koos Breukel's fondness for portraitists is clear not only from the fact that he included them in his photographed circle of close friends, but also in his attempt to launch a *Dutch National Portrait Gallery*. He used the Kees Scherer Prize funds to set up an exhibition as an initiative towards an institute which has yet to find a permanent location.

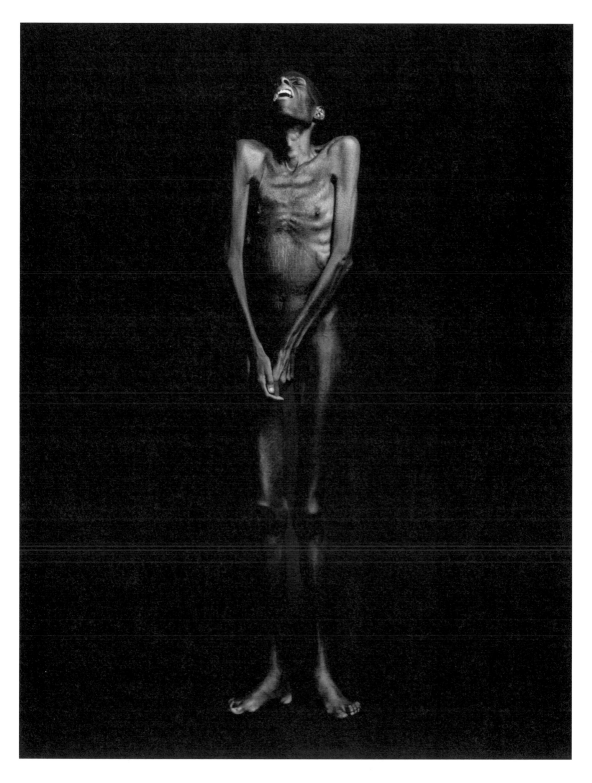

Michael Matthews, Amsterdam 1995
© Koos Breukel

This exhibition, *H2O Humans*, took place in June 2015 in the Commandeurshuis of the Marineterrein in Amsterdam, displaying photos, drawings and videos of close colleagues. The plan for the Portrait Gallery is based on idealism; it 'seeks to contribute to the appreciation of humanity through portrait art. Portraits tell us how we see one another, how we like to see ourselves.' Hopefully soon people less closely tied to the Netherlands will also find a place on the wall.

Lucian Freud, London 2008
© Koos Breukel

No space for mediocrity

When leafing through *ME, WE*, we almost forget the role of passing time, so compressed and concentrated are the moments of life depicted. It is as if memory, inherent in photography, is cancelled out. Breukel goes beyond any-one else in capturing life's decisive moments. He shows his dead father, laid out in the coffin, his mother too, dead and ready to be taken away. This is done in the same modest, succinct manner as his depiction of the living, and, despite his matter-of-fact approach, with great love. For although affection may not be a conspicuous feature of these photos, you only need to look at the photo of Carlien Huijsmans and their daughter Lisa Breukel in Vinkeveen and you know that in this respect Koos Breukel is definitely a mythologist: he takes love as his theme.

There is just one photo in *ME, WE* showing Koos Breukel himself, standing beside his mother as they visit the house where he was born. The parallels between the two are remarkable. Both stand still because the remote shutter release in Breukel's hand needs time to do its work, but activity remains visible in their positioning. Time is visibly suspended. What makes this photo in my eyes the most beautiful in the book are the looks in their eyes. They do not look into the camera, but their attention is drawn to something that lies before them. Their gaze is identical, full of seriousness, concentration, devotion, ex-pectation. It is a gaze that leaves no space for mediocrity. ∎

Translated by Anna Asbury

Magic and the Creation of Illusion

The Design Work of Marcel Wanders

[FREDERIKE HUYGEN]

The work of Dutch celebrity designer Marcel Wanders (born 1963) raises many questions. Is he a superb stylist or is his styling superficial? Is he an artistic designer or a commercial entrepreneur? His exuberance sets us thinking about taste, kitsch and quality. What does celebrity really mean in design? The designer as omnipotent God, a super-brand in which personality and product are seamlessly united? Or is Wanders about entertainment and experience, a melting pot of high and low culture?

In the 1980s Marcel Wanders was a designer seeking his own path through the predominant postmodernism of the day. At the academy in Arnhem he stood out for his talent, commercial and presentational sensitivity, and eagerness to learn. 'In principle I want everything, and I want it all to be very good.'[1] His ambitions were boundless. His breakthrough came in 1996 with the Knotted Chair, a design which reached the press worldwide via Milan. An icon was born and Wanders's career flourished. With customers all over the world and enormous production figures, he became a second Philippe Starck.

Wanders designed all kinds of things: lamps, furniture, vases, pots and pans, cutlery, bathroom fittings, jewellery, office articles, makeup, glasses, clocks, wallpaper, bags, perfume, tiles, towels, electric appliances and tattoos. He clearly enjoys celebrity status and success, but it is less clear how this success should be explained, as making a name and having talent are interchangeable in the world of design, marketing and media.

An all-rounder may be suspected of lack of selectiveness. Does he always perform at a high level? How does he ensure balance between commercial and cultural reputation? Is he after big money and fame? Since Raymond Loewy such designers have stood for style. They cover everything in their own sauce, devaluing their work because they are performing a superficial trick. In the world of high culture, moreover, people look askance at commercially successful artists, questioning their integrity. Do they sacrifice cultural quality and artistic autonomy for commercial value? [2]

Charles Chair, 2015

Knotted Chair, 1996

Love, passion and dreams

Wanders has designed a great deal but he does not work for everyone. His customers are renowned Italian design companies such as Cappellini, Flos, Magis and Kartell, which advance the culture of design and experimentation. He also works with Alessi, Rosenthal, Tichelaar, Baccarat, Christofle and Swarovski, companies from the top segment of the market, which use the name Wanders as a brand within a brand and as a marketing tool, developing designer lines alongside their own ranges. Often these Wanders lines are less interesting because the work is less innovative. For instance, Wanders designs tableware and gifts, simple basics with his signature, for British department store Marks and Spencer.

Most of Wanders's designs, however, enter the market under his own labels, Moooi and Personal Editions. Moooi, founded in 2001, also produces work by other designers. Personal Editions came along six years later for small series and special, unique items. The Moooi furniture varies. Besides ordinary sofas, armchairs and cabinets, this collection offers crazy little tables and lamps, ceramics and home accessories. So Wanders covers the entire spectrum from expensive to cheap and from unique items to mass production. The luxury segment dominates, along with interior products. He is a designer of lifestyle and aspirations. Just as magazines are made for their feel-good factor, Wanders's products appeal to the need for glamour, to possess something special. His motto is 'here to create an environment of love, live with passion and make our most exciting dreams come true'.

Nevertheless he also designs technically and formally innovative products which break with tradition, creating vase moulds by stuffing eggs into a condom (Egg Vase, 1997), for example, and 3D-printing snot (Snotty Vase, 2001). The fibre treatment techniques of his famous Knotted Chair reappear in objects of crocheted cotton fixed with epoxy resin. He has also tried out blow-moulding techniques, for instance using balloons of woven carbon fibre as parts of chairs, making chair legs resembling PET bottles and blowing air into a sandwich layer to form a bag.

Snotty Vase, 2001

Wanders clearly takes pleasure in juggling shapes and decorations: table legs become candelabras or candles, church bells become lamps, and sponges vases. Flower motifs, leaf motifs, Delft blue and curls recur throughout his work, printed, machined, painted or in relief. Walls, floors, ceilings, doors and cabinets, everything is covered and manipulated with an obsessiveness indicating that horror vacui is close on his heels. Wanders's interiors are crowded yet eclectic, perfectly embodying postmodernism, citing everything past and present, mixing and intermingling.

Postmodern?

Nevertheless the label postmodern does not please Wanders. The term reveals the ache of a cynical look at the world. He wants to get past that, and perhaps no aesthetic category exists for his over-the-top interiors. Wanders' swork leaves behind the difference between beautiful and ugly along with any notion of balance or proportion. The word kitsch would be more fitting: imitation, acting expensive, fake and dishonest.[3]

At Wanders's Stedelijk Museum exhibition in Amsterdam in 2014 he put together a room of wonders, a dark environment full of gigantic props, strange furniture and pieces of scenery, with overgrown lampshades, church bells, a cradle and computer photomontage indicating science fiction and gaming. A king-size image of two female faces was made for a luxury apartment building in Istanbul, Turkey. Is it surprising that Wanders has more and more customers in the Middle East? Is his work a perfect fit for the taste of places such as Manama (Bahrein), Qatar and Miami?

Drama, lavish entertaining, revelling in exaggeration, creating fairy tales: Wanders really goes to town when it comes to hotels and shop interiors, and he does so shamelessly and boundlessly, so his work embodies ostentatious consumption and flamboyant play. Sociologist Thorsten Veblen analysed all this in 1899 in his classic book *The Theory of the Leisure Class*. In the better Dutch circles this is taboo, tasteless and ordinary. The wondrous world of Wanders is one of bling, champagne, glamour and money. His work is over-the-top, gilded and decorated, intended to amaze. It is the world of the nouveau riches, the wannabes and wannahaves.

Wanders himself speaks of magic and the creation of illusion. There is a surrealism to it all, a fantasy to fit the digital age. This is escapism, which suits the crisis and other unpleasant world problems. It is enjoyment. Above all, such interiors breathe a strikingly artificial quality, but Wanders challenges us to consider whether ugliness cannot be interesting in itself.

Recalcitrant?

Time and again Wanders takes a stand against modernism, although strict, austere design and the associated moralising ideology are things of the distant past. In the Stedelijk Museum catalogue, the most recent and serious publication on his work, the authors contrast temptation, sensuality, luxury and excess with modernism.[4] But doesn't that lead to difficulty placing Wanders?

Wanders rejects modernism because he considers it rational and cold, claiming that it has burdened us with products man cannot connect with. He stands up for dreams, emotions, meaning, narrative, value, humanity, sustainability, love, beauty and poetry. I believe that Wanders takes all this seriously, but his 'war on design' sounds like ageing recalcitrance and hollow rhetoric.

Value, meaning and luxury goods

Wanders appeals to feeling and emotion, but who or what determines the connection between people and objects? He holds an intriguing conviction that this connection (outside of theatre and fairy tales) is determined by collective memories and familiar archetypical objects, reminiscences of the past living on inside us. In reality it is difficult to predict what an object will mean to a person. The affective value is different from usefulness (utilitarian value). It falls under what researchers call symbolic value.[5] An object can be strongly connected with the memories of another, a deceased family member for instance, but the item can also have personal significance for an individual or their sense of identity, standing for an achievement or sense of self-esteem. Status and prestige also fall under symbolic significance, but are oriented more towards the outside world. Symbolic value is certainly relevant to design objects, which Judy Attfield once beautifully characterised in her study *Wild Things* (2000) as 'things with attitude'. Arrogant things, conceited things, things with pretensions, although Wanders would call them things with personality.

On his website Wanders states that he aims to create value, to touch and connect people. He writes that his audiences wish to get more out of life and that he understands 'their need for surprise, for security, for contribution and growth, for individuality and familiarity'. They want illusion and hope. Here the designer sounds like a guru or life fulfilment coach (Wanders himself regularly attends seminars of this kind). At the same time it sounds unmistakeably like marketing lingo. In order to understand Wanders and his work we must examine the literature on marketing and brands in relation to luxury goods, as the answers are all in there.

The market is hot, as it is continually growing. Trend watchers, economists and other experts cherish high expectations of China, India, Asia, the Middle East, Latin America and Russia in particular.[6] Luxury goods are high quality and expensive, but they are not essential products. They are characterised by rarity, exclusivity, prestige and authenticity, scoring high on the value scale. For the luxury brand the concept of value is crucial, as in order for people to be willing to hand over large sums of money for a product they have to get something in return. Here again researchers into symbolic value distinguish between outwardly oriented significance, associated with social identity, and inwardly oriented, personal significance. On the one hand status and prestige, conformity and the need to impress others, on the other hand the relationship

Mondrian South Beach Hotel Miami, 2008

with personal identity. Researchers studying the luxury market, however, have added two new value categories: experience related to hedonism and experience of interaction with the brand. In doing so they connect a whole range of issues: aesthetics, sensory experience, craftsmanship, uniqueness, authenticity, spoiling oneself and nostalgia.

Research thus confirms the idealistic statement of principle on Wanders's site: the experience must 'have personal relevance for the customer, be novel, offer an element of surprise, engender learning and engage the customer'.[7] Another noteworthy point of the study is that buyers are keen on authenticity, uniqueness and scarcity. Many people require a guarantee in the form of a certificate, signature or limited edition. And finally, interaction-contact between brand and client - has become enormously important in recent years. This can be done online, but generally it happens through events and parties where socially competitive consumers come into contact with people who are trendy or famous, with media figures and creative types. Value creation takes place via networks in which the worlds of art and commerce (including technology and innovation) are increasingly mixed, as in museums, for example.

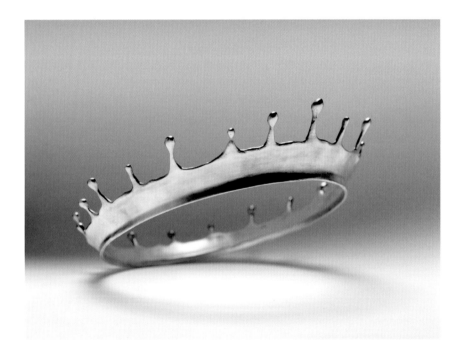

Corona de Agua (Water Droplet Tiara), 2001.
Crown for then princess, now queen Máxima,
made of polished silver.

Wanders is positioned at the thick of it as a designer, cultural figurehead, brand representative and businessman, but he appears not to be entirely aware of his identity as a brand. That brand stands at the centre of the overlapping fields of influence of culture, commerce, media and entertainment, forming a classic example of their complete fusion. We all live in the era of branding, museums included. There is still enormous space for Wanders's luxury brand to grow in many countries, and as a designer he will undoubtedly go a long way yet. As a creative entrepreneur Wanders also seeks to encourage new talent. Wanders wants it all, and he wants it all to be good. As a representative of the creative industry he is a roaring success. That has won him admiration in the Netherlands. He succeeds in operating commercially and without subsidies. Nevertheless, keeping all those balls in the air must be an art in itself. ∎

www.marcelwanders.com

Translated by Anna Asbury

NOTES

1   NOUDI SPÖNHOFF, 'Marcel Wanders, een veelbelovende jonge ontwerper' ('Marcel Wanders, a promising young designer'), in *Items* 7, 1988, p. 21.

2   PIERRE BOURDIEU, *Les Règles de l'art: genèse et structure du champ littéraire (The Rules of Art: Genesis and Structure of the Literary Field)*, éditions du Seuil, Paris, 1992.

3   See an article by NIEK HILKMANN:
     http://www.designhistory.nl/2011/het-begrip-kitsch-in-goed-wonen/

4   *Marcel Wanders: Pinned Up,* in the Stedelijk Museum Amsterdam, 1 February to 15 June 2014.

5   http://www.designhistory.nl/2012/theories-on-people-and-things-2/#fnref-2457-25

6   For this article I used the publication 'Co-creating Value for Luxury Brands' by CAROLINE TYNAN; SALLIE MCKECHNIE and CELINE CHHUON in the *Journal of Business Research*, no. 63, 2010, pp. 1156-1163. The article contains further references to literature on this subject.

7   Op. cit., p. 1158, note 8.

The Low Countries: Growing Apart

Belgium and the Netherlands and Their Attitudes to the European Union

[MARIE-ANNICK MUSCH & HENDRIK VOS]

The creation of the Benelux made Belgium, the Netherlands and Luxembourg the very cradle of European integration. In subsequent European cooperation initiatives, during the 1950s and 1960s, Belgium and the Netherlands were always involved - and usually they were in the front row. Although that did not mean that their interests always coincided or that they agreed on everything, Belgium and the Netherlands, often with Luxembourg, tried for a long time to act together and with one voice on European issues. Since the early 1990s, however, tensions have been increasingly visible in specific dossiers and recently, in particular, it has barely been possible for them to take joint action. Public opinion and especially the attitude of the political elites in Belgium and the Netherlands have begun to differ starkly. When it comes to major European issues, the two countries have grown apart. In this article we look at the history of Belgian-Dutch relations in Europe, examining the pivotal moments. Finally, we try to assess the course the two countries will follow in Europe in the near future.

The Benelux as laboratory

Back in 1944, towards the end of the Second World War, the Benelux was founded in London by the three governments in exile. The intention was to create a customs union and eventually to realise an economic union as well.

In the 1950s, with the foundation of the European Coal and Steel Community (ECSC), and somewhat later the European Economic Community (EEC), a much grander and more ambitious project was launched, involving many more countries including France and West Germany.

The Benelux plans were an important source of inspiration for European integration. This was the development of a customs union and a common market at a higher level now. It is noticeable that Belgian and Dutch politicians played a major role at the start of this integration. The plan to build an economic union at the European level came from the Dutch Minister Wim Beyen, for example, and it was the Belgian Minister Paul-Henri Spaak who led the negotiations that eventually resulted in the Treaty of Rome.

Europa Galante
© Geert Setola

To a certain extent then, the Benelux was quickly overshadowed by these bigger European plans, but it did remain a forum where common positions could be adopted and collective interests defended. Obviously, as export economies, Belgium and the Netherlands were interested in the rapid expansion of an internal market, with strong European institutions to watch over the rules of the game and to prevent the big member states skewing things to their own advantage. They expressed their opinions on important matters in Benelux memoranda.

There were many parallels in the Dutch and Belgian visions of European integration, certainly in the early integration period and in the agenda-setting phase. Nonetheless, there were also some differences in emphasis. For example, the Dutch have always understood the British positions and interests better, while the Belgians have sympathised more with the French viewpoint. As of the 1970s, then, Belgium and the Netherlands cooperated less often in Europe.

The Benelux continued to be a forum for discussing specific matters, such as the water treaties, the high-speed railway line, the deepening of the Wester-scheldt, and suchlike. As Europe changed so did Belgian and Dutch perspectives.

Ceuta (Spanish enclave in Morocco)
Mediterranean. The Continuity of Man
© Nick Hannes

As Europe changed so did Belgian and Dutch perspectives

After the launch of European integration, Belgian-Dutch cooperation gradually became rather less intense. That changed at the end of the Cold War. It soon became clear that there was a large wave of enlargement on its way and that institutional changes were in the pipeline. That meant that Belgium and the Netherlands shared some parallel interests again. The Netherlands certainly wanted to defend the position of the smaller countries, and Belgium was right behind it. The two countries also insisted that expansion of the Union should definitely not occur at the expense of deepening. If necessary it should be possible for a small group to take the lead and to develop a kind of differentiated integration.

In a Europe with more than twenty member states it would also be necessary to present a common front more often. It would be harder for countries to defend their interests individually, so Belgian-Dutch consultations were reactivated. That might perhaps compensate for the relative loss of power that the expansion of the Union would entail. So there was a regular arrangement to organise joint breakfasts before European Summits, at which Belgium and the Netherlands, usually with Luxembourg, tried to harmonize their positions as far as possible.

At the same time, though, the differences were growing. In the course of the 1990s it became clear that the European Union was having a very concrete impact on people's lives. The fault line between the champions of more or less

Europe gradually shifted to a discussion of 'what kind of Europe'. As long as the discussion was about institutional questions and the defence of the interests of the small member states, it was still possible to reach a Belgian-Dutch agreement, but as soon as specific policy questions were discussed the disagreements became very obvious.

Since the 1990s, for example, a wave of liberalisation has swept across Europe. It gained strength in 2000 when the Lisbon strategy was formulated. Its purpose was to make Europe the most dynamic and competitive knowledge economy in the world. Postal services, railways, telecommunications and many other services were exposed, often in phases, to competition, and member states lost their monopoly on organising them. The Netherlands were amongst the pioneers in this debate and it was a Dutch commissioner, Frits Bolkestein, who launched various proposals in the period 1999-2004. In Belgium these initiatives generally met with a lot of mistrust, especially on the political left. In Wallonia, in particular, people had great reservations about this policy.

Another important source of contention in Dutch European policy in the recent past had to do with the budget. In negotiations on the long-term European budget (and certainly during the discussions on the 2007-2013 and 2014-2020 budgets) the Netherlands always championed a smaller budget, less waste and a reduction in agricultural expenditure. This was very different from the

Athens

Mediterranean. The Continuity of Man

© Nick Hannes

Gibraltar
Mediterranean. The Continuity of Man
© Nick Hannes

Belgian point of view. The Belgian government has always emphasised the importance of having a large budget. An ambitious European agenda can only be achieved if Europe has (many) more means. From this philosophy Belgian politicians advocated the introduction of European taxes, as well, while in the Netherlands there was very little enthusiasm for them.

The introduction of the common currency had also exposed some tensions back in the 1990s. The Treaty of Maastricht stipulated that countries must meet strict conditions before they could join the currency union. From the point of view of the Netherlands, membership of the currency union should preferably be limited to the economically strongest countries. Belgium, however, feared a scenario in which the euro would only be introduced in countries like Germany and the Netherlands. Indeed, because of its large government debt, Belgium might miss the boat. When the decision was taken to be flexible about entry into the monetary union, the Belgian government was delighted, while in the Netherlands the decision was received with much gnashing of teeth.

In foreign policy matters, too, Belgium and the Netherlands have frequently found themselves in opposite camps. As far as the Belgian government was concerned, the war in Iraq was a reason to put the expansion of European defence on the agenda, while in the same period the Netherlands was completely behind the British in dismissing any suggestion of stronger European defence, certainly if it would function separately from NATO. Belgium's attempts to set up European military headquarters, in collaboration with Luxembourg, France and Germany, received a great deal of criticism in other member states, including the Netherlands.

So, since the 1990s, fundamental and ideological differences have appeared between the Belgian and Dutch positions on important European questions increasingly frequently.

A crucial tipping point: the Netherlands says no to the European constitution

In discussions on treaty changes Belgium and the Netherlands still managed, in general, to take common positions. But that changed in 2000, when the Treaty of Nice was negotiated. Under the leadership of their then Prime Minister, Wim Kok, the Netherlands pleaded for greater voting power for the Netherlands in decision-making. Guy Verhofstadt, who had just become the Belgian Prime Minister, eventually had to agree to this, but mutual trust between the two countries suffered very serious damage as a result.

Shortly after the Treaty of Nice, negotiations began for what would eventually lead to the European Constitution. For a while the Belgians and Dutch were able to come up with some joint proposals, but it was clear that some points were only really important for one of the parties. In the Netherlands, fear of a power grab by the big member states was very real; Belgium, however, had no problem making agreements with France or Germany.

On 1 June 2005 61% of the Dutch rejected the European Constitution, with a turnout of 63%. Resistance to the Constitution came from very diverse sections of the population. The far left parties called for a no-vote because they thought that European Union policies were too liberal and therefore asocial, and that the Constitution offered no prospect of improvement. Right-wing groups threw completely different arguments into the fray. They were afraid of a further loss of sovereignty for member states. Many of them may also have seen the referendum as a delayed plebiscite on the expansion into Central and Eastern Europe. Immediately after the referendum the Dutch government let it be known that the European Constitution was 'dead' and that an alternative could only be discussed if it differed in form, content and scope from the Constitution. In particular it should not go as far. That clashed completely with the position of Belgium, where the mantra was still 'what's good for Europe is good for Belgium'. In 2006 Prime Minister Verhofstadt went a step further, by explicitly pleading, in a manifesto, for the foundation of a United States of Europe.

During subsequent rounds of negotiations the European Constitution was recycled in the Treaty of Lisbon. Relations between Belgium and the Netherlands were sorely tested in that period. Meanwhile, in the Netherlands, Geert Wilders had become very big politically and had founded the Freedom Party. Resistance to the European Union had also become an important issue. The classic Dutch parties began to adopt some of Wilders's viewpoints and to question European developments more explicitly. The Socialist Party (SP), further to the left than the social-democratic PVDA, increasingly took positions on the European theme too. The rise of eurocritical, eurosceptical and out-and-out anti-European parties has put the initially positive basic attitude of the Netherlands towards European integration under a great deal of pressure. Public and political support for active pro-European policies has shrunk drastically, and at times even turned completely into an attitude that stands for 'less Europe'. In Belgium the tendency in the population to be much more sceptical about integration has grown but, with the exception of the far-right nationalist party Vlaams Belang, the political parties have continued to wholeheartedly defend integration. Now and then there has been some protest - from the Flemish social-democrats of the SP.A, for example - about the overly liberal course of the Union, but integration as such has never been questioned.

So what's the situation today?

According to the Eurobarometer at the end of 2014, 42% of Belgians were positive about integration. In the Netherlands that figure was 37%. Only 22% of Belgians had an explicitly negative attitude, as opposed to 26% of the Dutch. The Dutch population, then, is more critical of Europe than the Belgian population, though the difference is not particularly spectacular. The days when Belgium had massive numbers of Europe-fans are over. In 2014 there were ten member states in which a larger portion of the population had a positive attitude towards integration than in Belgium.

At the political level, there are still noticeable differences between Belgium and the Netherlands. The general discourse about Europe is more critical and more negative in Dutch politics than in Belgian politics. Belgian political parties continue, with the exception of the far-right Vlaams Belang, to take a basic position that is very positive towards integration. Parties like the ecologists (Groen) or the social-democratic SP.A sometimes fiercely criticize certain policy choices, but do not question integration as such and will never in principle advocate 'less Europe'.

In the run-up to the elections of 2014 the main focus was on the attitude of the Flemish nationalist N-VA. It would have to speak out explicitly on European issues for the first time. Some observers predicted that the N-VA would take a strongly eurocritical direction, but that did not happen. There were a variety of calls for a change of course in Europe, but the N-VA never pulled out all the stops, as Geert Wilders did in the Netherlands. The N-VA politicians who were elected to the European Parliament eventually joined the fraction to which the British Conservatives belong, but they emphasised that they wanted to continue to play a positive and constructive role. The next period will reveal the extent to which they actually do that and what standpoints they take in specific dossiers.

In the Netherlands there is still a certain scepticism amongst the classic parties and a plea for 'less Europe' is much less unusual. Meanwhile, two PVDA politicians occupy important European positions: Jeroen Dijsselbloem is the Chairman of the Eurogroup and Frans Timmermans is the First Vice-President of the European Commission. It is noticeable that they both come under fire in Belgium, and not least from their ideologically related socialist sister parties, because of their limited ambitions. Timmermans is accused of wanting to reduce the impact of the Union by subjecting the European market to fewer rules. Dijsselbloem, on the other hand, is criticised because he pleaded for

Melilla (Spanish enclave
in Morocco)
© José Palazón

Translated by Lindsay Edwards

more budgetary discipline during the euro crisis and does not want to develop more solidarity mechanisms at the European level.

Protection of interests

Belgium and the Netherlands have a long history of cooperation in Europe. After the Second World War they stood side by side at the cradle of integration. They had every interest in the creation of a large market and wanted the continent to be organised so that the big countries would not be the only ones to have a say.

As European integration became more important and more substantive decisions had to be taken ('what sort of Europe?'), more and more differences emerged. In the Netherlands political parties on the outer edges of the political spectrum began to define themselves as euro-critical or euro-sceptical, and for a while now the classic parties have to some extent followed suit. Although even amongst the Belgian population criticism is growing, the Belgian political parties continue in general to defend a pro-European course. To what extent the N-VA will continue to do this is yet to be seen. The N-VA will definitely not adopt Geert Wilder's position, but it is possible that it will take a more critical stance, comparable to that of the classic Dutch parties, like the VVD.

In any case, Belgian-Dutch cooperation in Europe is no longer so obvious these days. There have been many incidents in recent years and differences of opinion in all sorts of dossiers. At the same time, Belgium and the Netherlands have not completely grown apart either. The simple fact that Belgium and the Netherlands are neighbours, that they share an important part of their history and as a result know each other well, makes it 'natural' to have regular consultations and, where possible, to look for agreement. The glue that binds Belgium and the Netherlands is, after all, pretty good insight into each other's background, priorities and sensitivities. Fundamental and ideological differences of opinion cannot be swept under the carpet, but they should not prevent the formation of thematic alliances. Indeed, in today's large European Union this is the main way in which interests are defended. ■

The Magic of Charcoal

Rinus Van de Velde, Rising Star in the Flemish Art World

'A James Dean skilled with charcoal' is how one critic characterised Rinus Van de Velde at the start of his career. It was an apt comparison, because this young artist displays an almost provocative virtuosity. A lot of hype soon developed around his work, which consists mainly of monumental charcoal drawings. Wherever he exhibited, collectors, curators, critics and enthusiasts fell under the spell of his images, the insistent presence of his figures and the obvious skill with which it is all put down on paper. But what lies at the heart of this fantasy world? Why does the artist himself appear as a character in almost all his works? And where does one situate these drawings in the adventurous art scene that has managed to reach out from Flanders to an international audience in recent decades? We shall try to answer these questions in this article.

Rinus Van de Velde (Leuven, 1983) was no child prodigy. Although in the course of time he conceived a huge admiration for Picasso, who was able to draw a bullfight so masterfully when only six years old, Van de Velde himself only became interested in art as a teenager. It was sparked off by a visit to an exhibition on Fauvism in Paris. The energy that radiated from the works by Matisse and his fellows made a deep impression on this young visitor, although as he freely admitted he did not understand much about it. He wondered where this vitality originated, and how these silent canvases could have such a powerful effect on him. He sought answers in books, firstly the catalogue of the exhibition and then in more general works on art history, including E.H. Gombrich's *The Story of Art*. On the basis of the artists' lives and background, he gradually started to understand something of their work. Without realising it, he had found the key to a world that would take a lasting hold on him.

A quick and light medium

As a result of his experiences in Paris and his subsequent increasing interest in art, Van de Velde decided to study art. He opted for sculpture at St Lucas in Antwerp, attracted mainly by the physical work involved. But the complex and protracted work process soon started to pall on him. In the course of his work

Rinus Van de Velde, *An investigation into the hyperpersonal ...*, 2015,
Charcoal on canvas, artist frame, 210 x 250 cm,
Courtesy Tim Van Laere Gallery, Antwerp

he discovered that drawing suited him much better, because it enabled him to achieve a result sooner.

'Drawing is a quick and light medium that suits my temperament better,' he says. 'I was soon doing one work a day. Drawing gives me more of a sense of freedom than painting. When you paint you have to face up to a powerful tradition, from Van Eyck to Gerhard Richter. Whatever you do, you soon find yourself working in the style of one or other great predecessor. This applies much less when it comes to drawing. Drawing has by tradition served an auxiliary purpose. Most drawings are sketches or preliminary studies from which a painting or other work will later emerge. I find that a shame, because drawings are worthwhile as works of art in their own right too. My drawings are intended to be fully-fledged, independent works of art. Which is how I arrived at these large formats, although initially my drawings were much smaller.'

Van de Velde made his debut with drawings in coloured pencil. Their small format enabled him to work in series and to hang the sheets in each series alongside one another on the wall so that a story could take shape. In the early period he learnt a lot from looking at other artists' work. 'Copying what you think is good is the best way of finding your own direction,' he says. It was only after a few years that he evolved towards black and white, larger formats and charcoal as his main medium. His most recent drawings often reach three metres long and two high – in 2014 he even drew a panoramic view of the city that was ten metres long. He prefers to work on canvas, using charcoal on a coating of plaster, which gives him every opportunity to introduce contrasts and nuances into his scenes. The result is that his charcoal drawings often have the quality of a painting, though they also evoke the atmosphere of old film stills, or of an old black and white strip cartoon. Many of Van de Velde's works show dark scenes illuminated by bright light.

The myth of artisthood

Van de Velde initially worked on the basis of found images. His archives contain thousands of photos cut out of old magazines such as *National Geographic* or simply taken from the internet. He is not interested in photos that he can easily identify: each image has to have something odd about it to be suitable for use. Van de Velde is keen to emphasise that his work is imaginary. This enables him to travel to a different place or time and step into the shoes of other artists, scientists, sportsmen and adventurers. For instance, you encounter both the painter Elsworth Kelly and the poet Vladimir Mayakovsky in his drawings, as well as the volcanologist Haroun Tazieff and the chess-player Bobby Fischer. Although he describes his work as 'a fictional autobiography', it is only partly about himself. It is more the case that the artist is a character in his own stories. He wonders what it would be like to paint like Elsworth Kelly, and what he would have been doing in Mayakovsky's day. The fantasy world he draws gives him the opportunity to explore new possibilities of reality.

One of the more important themes in Van de Velde's drawings is the myth of artisthood. In the early days he was fascinated by the painter Jean-Michel Basquiat, who died prematurely and whom he learnt about through the film on his eventful life. Someone else who also had a major influence on him was Rodney Graham, who, like Van de Velde, is fond of putting himself in another character's shoes and then inventing a story around it. In the monumental charcoal drawings Van de Velde presented at the Venice Biennale in 2015, he portrayed himself amidst a set of fake Andy Warhol Brillo boxes. What does it mean to be an artist, and what makes an artist's work original and special? These questions form a *leitmotif* in his oeuvre.

A shrewd career

Rinus Van de Velde's career is a perfect example of those of today's young artists. After studying at St Lucas he took various jobs. For instance, for a time he toured as a technical assistant with Meg Stuart's dance company. This introduced him into a creative environment and left him sufficient free time to draw. He also worked as a driver for the Antwerp artist Guillaume Bijl, who pointed the way to the HISK, the Higher Institute of Fine Art, in Ghent, where talented young artists are given two years to work under the guidance of established artists, museum people, art academics and curators. This institution played an important part in Van de Velde's development. 'At the HISK I learnt to understand and explain my work better,' he says. 'As a young artist you work mainly intuitively. At the HISK you learn to see structures in your work, to establish a framework for it and to express it clearly in words. Which is extremely important in the art world. At the same time you are given time to eliminate your weak points. What is more, at the HISK you come into contact with people who may be able to give you the opportunity to exhibit; but in my view it's the wrong approach if you only take the course to build up a network.'

Van de Velde started exhibiting in 2004. Four years later he was given his first show in a museum: at the S.M.A.K. in Ghent, Belgium's leading museum of contemporary art, he showed a series of drawings about a fictional artist under the title *William Crowder – 40 years of sculpture*. After that things went very quickly. Van de Velde's work found its way to arts centres and galleries in Spain, the Netherlands, Brazil and the United States. In 2009 his work was shown at Art Basel Miami. In 2015 he took part in the Flemish Community exhibition in the Palazzo Nani Mocenigo at the Venice Biennale. His first major solo exhibition is in 2016, at the S.M.A.K. In the meantime he has found a base at Tim Van Laere's gallery in Antwerp, where he has shown several series that have attracted a lot of attention. Even the music world has discovered his work: the well-known Flemish singer Raymond Van het Groenewoud chose one of Van de Velde's drawings for the cover of his album *De laatste rit*.

Rinus Van de Velde, *Driving on the highway, I can't help but wondering where all the other roads go*, 2015,
Charcoal on canvas, artist frame, 154 x 233 cm
Courtesy Tim Van Laere Gallery, Antwerp

Rinus Van de Velde, *It's all about rescheduling my desire*, 2015,

Charcoal on canvas, artist frame, 210 x 325 cm,

Courtesy Tim Van Laere Gallery, Antwerp

An uninhabited island

In 2014 a well-illustrated book on Rinus Van de Velde's work was published by Hannibal. It includes two series that provide a good impression of the artist's unusual subjects and methods.

The first series, *The Story of Frederic, Conrad, Jim and Rinus*, is about the experiences of Van de Velde and his friends in a commune in the woods. So as to work as realistically as possible, and above all to remain in command of the scene he was going to draw, he built the whole of the setting himself, together with his friends. In addition, to get as close as possible to the atmosphere of a film image, the scenes were lit by a professional lighting technician. The photos were only taken when the whole setting was ready and the characters in their positions. They then provided the basis for Van de Velde's charcoal drawings. This means the work of art is the end product of a process that involves much more than pure drawing. As he himself says, Van de Velde made it 'absurdly difficult' for himself, but the quality of his drawings is probably due in part to these intensive preparations.

The cast of *The Story of Frederic, Conrad, Jim and Rinus* comprises four cliché characters: the artist, his art dealer, a writer and a philosopher. A story takes shape around these characters, as in a soap or a sitcom. The events are in themselves trivial: you see the friends playing chess, holding a discussion, loafing about and having a bit of a tussle. Yet Van de Velde is able to give a poetic quality to each scene. To achieve this he uses such film techniques as close-ups and tight framing. And above all he is a master in the evocation of moods, the depiction of action and capturing striking details. The viewers have to feel the realism, but they must also see that each work of art is a construction.

The second series, *The Islander*, is located on an inhospitable island in the sea. Van de Velde built the setting for this series himself too, and in fact exhibited it together with the drawings in a Berlin gallery. The exhibition is about a young man – the artist himself – who is washed ashore on a desert island. As always, Van de Velde starts fantasising about what might happen in this sort of situation. Whereas the atmosphere in *The Story of Frederic, Conrad, Jim and Rinus* was primarily sultry, in *The Islander* it is all about misfortune and adventure. The elements are unleashed, the castaway suffers great hardships. Until a lifeboat moors at the island, containing three characters who are not entirely unknown to us...

Rinus Van de Velde, *They call themselves Bossie and Marty – I have never asked their real names or where they come from, supposing they preferred to remain anonymous*, 2015,
Charcoal on canvas, artist frame, 210 x 230 cm,
Courtesy Tim Van Laere Gallery, Antwerp

An obsession with drawing

Drawing is an obsessive occupation for Van de Velde. He engages in it every day and it calms him. And, like Cindy Sherman, he is his own constantly available model. In a series of self-portraits, for example, he presents himself as a tennis-player and as a miner, or while cleaning his shoes or drawing in his studio.

But however obsessively engaged with images Van de Velde may be, at the same time he is aware that images cannot be trusted. Which is why he adds extensive subtitles to many of his drawings. He thinks them up together with a friend. This is quite unusual in visual art. 'I don't like simply sending images out into the world and leaving their interpretation to the viewer,' he says. 'For each drawing I want to give an indication of what I intended and of the story behind it. Even if most people do not read the subtitles, they still make me feel good. Though I must add that the stories are not the most important thing to me. The setting is at least as essential as the plot. And each story is in the first place a reason for drawing. For me, drawing is the beginning and the end.'

By opting to draw in charcoal, Van de Velde occupies a distinct position in the art scene of the Low Countries. Just as Luc Tuymans and Michael Borremans have given a new impulse to painting, and Berlinde De Bruyckere injects her sculptures with an unprecedented expressive power, Rinus Van de Velde rejuvenates drawing and shows its new potential. In the case of all these artists, an original formal idiom is combined with sound traditional skills. This is probably the explanation for their undeniable success, not only in the Low Countries, but also far beyond. ▪

Translated by Gregory Ball

Rinus Van de Velde, *Some part of me knew something was out of joint...*, 2015, Charcoal on canvas, framed, 310 x 540 cm
Courtesy Tim Van Laere Gallery, Antwerp

The Reform-Resistant Belgian Welfare State

[KRIS DESCHOUWER]

One of the iconic election posters of post-war Belgium is from 1995. It shows the President of the Flemish socialist party, Louis Tobback, looking straight at the voters with only the simple message: 'Your social security'. The 1995 elections had been called early by outgoing Prime Minister Dehaene, because he wanted the backing of the voters to continue with his centre-left coalition and the planned reform of the welfare state. This focus on the welfare state and on its possible reform was certainly not unique for the 1990s. In the 1970s and 1980s already the sudden increase of unemployment had made adjustments necessary. The Verhofstadt government that came into power in 1999, after Dehaene, launched the notion of an 'active welfare state', and more recently the question of the future of the pension scheme and the price of health insurance were (once more) on the agenda. Indeed the welfare state has been on the agenda almost constantly for the past four decades.

This almost permanent focus on and debate about the functioning and the financing of the welfare state is of course not a typical Belgian phenomenon. All welfare states have been, since their full deployment after the Second World War, confronted with pressures that have triggered heated debates and subsequently led to adaptation and change. Yet welfare states are not all alike, and therefore the kind of pressures that they encounter and the way in which they deal with them can vary quite extensively.

A continental model

In *The Three Worlds of Welfare Capitalism* (1990) Gøsta Esping-Andersen suggests a distinction between three types of welfare regimes or three types of welfare state. He draws the boundaries between them by looking at the way in which benefits are financed, the degree to which they are accessible and generous, and the extent to which they affect the social structure of society. The liberal regime (as in the US, the UK, Australia or New Zealand) is characterized by fairly limited benefits aimed at avoiding poverty and is financed by taxes. The social democratic regime, on the other hand, though it is also tax-financed, is much more generous and offers a very solid protection against

Uw sociale zekerheid.

LOUIS TOBBACK. SENAAT

the loss of income from employment. This is the regime found in the Scandinavian countries. Belgium belongs (with the Netherlands and Germany, among others) to a third type, labelled the conservative or continental type of welfare state. Here the benefits are financed by payroll contributions and they are linked to a person's former income or to a family relationship with someone who has contributed. Special arrangements for specific groups (like civil servants) are also typical for this model. The division into three welfare regimes is of course quite crude, but it does point at relevant differences in the basic logic of a welfare state.

Whether one of these types is developed in a particular country depends to a large degree on the political coalition that has initiated it. The continental regime is typical for countries where the welfare state was put into place by a coalition of social democrats and Christian parties (or of Christian parties alone).

The Belgian welfare state was put into place towards the end of the Second World War. Its origin was an agreement between the employers' and workers' organizations that had started negotiations during the German occupation. By bringing these two groups together, a typical 'continental' grand coalition was formed, and the agreement was rapidly implemented by the post-war governments. By bringing representatives of workers and employers together, the two major parties of the period – the Christian democrats and the socialists

– were also immediately involved. In the Belgian context this also meant the creation of a coalition of the largest political group in Flanders (Christian democrats) and the largest political group in Wallonia (socialists).

This coalition established a system of social security that is based on compulsory payroll contributions by both salaried workers and their employers. In a later phase – in the 1950s – a similar system for the self-employed was gradually developed. Under this system unemployment benefits and pensions are (or at least were in the early days) closely linked to the level of income earned. So social security in Belgium works very much like insurance. As with other continental systems, it has its obvious weak points. The most important is the fact that it relies on income generated by the active workforce and not on general income tax. In the first place this directly affects the cost of labour. Hiring personnel is more expensive because the total cost includes the contributions to be paid into the social security system. In the second place a system that relies on payroll contributions is very dependent on the extent to which the working age population is employed. High unemployment or early retirement tend to erode the very basis of the system and to have a negative impact on the ratio between those who work and contribute to the system and those who receive benefits.

Path dependency

Welfare regimes belong to a category of policy structures that are difficult to change. They are a complex set of rules and mechanisms and financing methods that – once put in place – become very sticky. The longer a system exists, the more difficult it becomes to rebuild even parts of it from scratch. Further developments, additions and changes become *path dependent*, which means that the decisions and (financial) commitments made in the past heavily influence the kind of policy that can be developed and limit the policy choices open for future coalitions.

On top of this path dependency, welfare state policies face other obstacles to change. The most obvious is the fact that welfare benefits are of course popular, which means that when citizens vote they are not likely to support parties that announce radical changes or cuts. Political parties know that they are taking electoral risks if they announce that kind of policy. This does not mean that changes to welfare policies are impossible, but that they are likely to be slow and that they require from the parties a convincing story about adjustments in the short run being needed to safeguard the system in the longer run. This is easier in times of crisis.

As regards the Belgian welfare system, we have to take into account two extra elements that slow reform down. In the first place Belgian political decision-making in social and economic matters has a strong *corporatist* flavour. This means that organized interests not only mobilize to defend their members' interests, but that a number of larger ('representative') organizations are directly involved in preparing, making and implementing the policy. For the welfare state this is reflected from the outset in the fact that these 'social partners' themselves negotiated the founding agreement, and in the fact that some of the benefits are paid out by the organizations themselves (trade unions and health insurance 'mutuals') rather than directly by the state. A National Labour Council with equal numbers of workers' and employers' representatives provides the government with advice on social policies. And interprofessional agreements between the peak organizations are made legally binding by the government. The management of the social security system is in the hands of these same social partners. This gives the social and economic policy a broad and solid legitimacy, but it also builds in hurdles for decision-making. If consensus is needed between the social partners, the absence of consensus means that no policy can be developed unless – as will indeed happen more and more often – the government takes over and imposes changes on the social partners (which will still be very much involved in the implementation).

Since the coalition that founded the welfare state was also in fact a coalition between the north and the south of the country, the increasing tensions between the two regions have important consequences for it. During the postwar period Walloon industry was in decline, while Flanders was increasing in economic strength and thereby fiscal capacity. As a result, debates on social and economic policies and on social security policy in particular always have a strong regional flavour. Welfare state policies have a different impact in each of the regions, which creates different policy demands in Flanders and Wallonia. But, more importantly, the welfare state is a system of redistribution from those who contribute to those who receive, and if one aggregates indi-

Achille Van Acker, Socialist Prime Minister (1945-1946; 1954-1958),
'Father' of the Belgian Welfare State.

vidual contributions and benefits per region the conclusion can only be that the richer region is subsidizing the poorer one. One of the recurrent themes in the debates about the structure of the Belgian state is the question of whether social security should remain a federal matter or whether, on the contrary, it should be organized on a regional basis. However, the Belgian federation is based on power sharing between the two language groups at the federal level, so governing requires an agreement or at least a compromise between the views and demands of them both. The Belgian state is a typical *consociational democracy* with the two language groups each being a strong veto player. On issues related to social security, this obligation to find a middle ground acts as another effective brake on attempts at radical reform, unless – which is unlikely – it does not affect the substates of the federation unequally.

While all welfare regimes face path dependency, the Belgian system – because of the corporatist and consociational nature of its political decision-making – displays a few extra mechanisms that contribute to the avoidance or slowing down of change. The social partnership requires a good social climate, which means that in periods of economic crisis – exactly when pressures on the welfare state increase – agreements are more problematic. Yet here one can find an interesting pattern in the history of the Belgian welfare state. Changes to the system have indeed been introduced, but often precisely during periods in which the social climate was *not* good and social partners were not able to reach an agreement amongst themselves. The social partners were then overruled by the government, which is itself of course a body in which Flemings and Francophones need to agree on major policy choices.

The government takes over

The first difficult period was the 1970s and the 1980s. The impact of the oil crisis in the 1970s had confronted Belgium with rising unemployment rates and therefore increasing pressure on the social security system. The central state had to increase the (still relatively small) proportion of money from general tax income that is added to the payroll contributions, while the budget of the central state showed huge deficits. In this difficult economic climate the relations between the employers and the trade unions were very poor. Yet changes and adjustments to the welfare system were needed, not only because of the economic crisis, but because various societal and economic developments meant that society was no longer what it had been immediately after the war. The improvements in medical care and therefore also higher life expectation, the increasing participation of women in the workforce, the gradual change from an industrial to a service economy, and the changing structure of households and partnerships all demanded at least some fine-tuning of the welfare system.

Since the social partners could not agree with each other in these difficult times, the reforms of the social and economic policy and the social security system were to a large extent imposed by the government, without the formal agreement of the social partners. The centre-right governments led by Prime Minister Wilfried Martens between 1981 and 1987 actually went even further and asked parliament for special powers, allowing the cabinet to rapidly push though policies and ask for parliamentary approval at a later stage. Yet while

Charles Michel, Liberal Prime Minister (2014-),
attacked with Belgian fries by an activist, crying 'Away with austerity'.

there was no formal agreement from the social partners, the government had kept open the lines of communication within the Christian pillar, with informal and secret gatherings of key figures, including the leader of the Christian trade union Jef Houthuys. The Martens governments were able to devaluate the Belgian franc, link the evolution of the cost of labour in Belgium to that of the most important competing countries, raise social security contributions (by abolishing upper limits for higher salaries, among other measures), reduce the unemployment benefits for some categories, and reform the financial management of social security by bringing all the income and expenses of the different sectors into one single budget.

The 1980s can now be seen as a turning point. Leaving the social partners who were at the origin of the welfare state out of these reforms certainly did not mark the end of the social partnership in Belgium. Constant contact, negotiations and formal agreements per sector or for all sectors remain important ingredients of social and economic policy-making in Belgium. But when an agreement cannot be reached the government takes over and, if necessary, ignores the social partners. That happened in the 1980s and has been repeated several times since.

When the Christian democrats and the social democrats were back in government together, from 1987 to 1999, the cabinet tried at crucial times to get the formal backing of the trade unions and employers. The so-called Global Plan of the Dehaene I government – working hard to reach the Maastricht norms for joining the euro – once more introduced some changes to the way the welfare state functioned, although they were rejected by the socialist trade union. Among the changes were a longer waiting time for school-leavers before they could receive unemployment benefits, the non-adjustment of wages to inflation caused by the rising prices of tobacco and fuel, and the computing of pensions on the basis of average income during a whole career rather than on the income at the end of it. Meanwhile the government also strengthened the so-called second and third pillars of pensions. The second is a pension scheme based on capitalization and financed by the employers and the third is an individual insurance or capitalization for which tax incentives are given. It is interesting to note that the government moved forward not only without the agreement of all of the social partners, but it also – like the centre-right governments of the 1980s – asked parliament for special powers.

When, in 1999, the Christian democrats were removed from power for the first time since 1958 and a 'purple' government of liberals, socialists and greens took over, with the liberal Guy Verhofstadt as Prime Minister, the programme that brought the liberals and socialists together was labelled the 'active welfare state'. One of its key goals was 'activation', which means that more people should be activated and convinced to enter and to stay in the labour force. It was made more difficult to take early retirement and a bonus was introduced for those who did not; likewise, the unemployed were checked and monitored more closely to make sure that they could enter or re-enter the labour force. The economic situation was better in the early 2000s, which should have made a broad agreement between government and the social partners easier. Yet Prime Minister Verhofstadt, who had previously often criticized the informal power of the social partners, opted for open debates and public round tables involving the social partners among other participants. When the second Verhofstadt government put its 'Generation Pact' (with the pension reforms) on the table, it failed – again – to convince the employers and trade unions to agree with it.

The current government, formed in 2014 – with the socialists removed from power for the first time since 1987 – has put forward a programme of austerity for which it has quite obviously not received the backing of the trade unions. Once again the cabinet has simply moved forward, introducing an increase in the retirement age from 65 to 67, for instance, and further reducing the availability of unemployment benefits for young people who have not yet worked.

The Belgian welfare regime belongs to the continental or conservative category because it was set up by an alliance of Christian democrats and social democrats. These were the two major political forces in the country, together obtaining almost 75% of the vote in 1950. Both parties were at the centre of a network of organizations to which the most important representatives of the employers and the workers also belonged. In 2014, however, the Christian democrats and socialists together held only 37% of the votes, and relations between the parties and the representatives of the workers and the employers have become much looser than they were before. One might therefore also expect a move away from the basic structure and policies of the welfare state.

The many smaller and sometimes larger changes and adjustments to the welfare state have not, however, fundamentally altered it. There certainly have been numerous smaller alterations, corrections and fine-tuning. Some benefits are more difficult to obtain, but more minimal protection measures have been introduced too. Social security is still based on payroll contributions and therefore remains vulnerable to low employment rates. But Belgium has not become a liberal-type welfare state and neither has it become a social democratic-type welfare state. It remains a continental model that requires broad agreements – with or without the ex-ante approval of the social partners – to introduce adjustments. One hears once in a while that the trade unions and health insurance 'mutuals' should not be so deeply involved in managing the social security system, but they are still solidly there. Likewise, since the 1980s there have been debates about the automatic adjustment of wages and welfare benefits to keep up with inflation (the so-called *indexing* of wages) but, apart from some minor changes, that system is still in place too. Those who defend the basic features of the system do however believe that it is gradually being dismantled, while those who are not happy with some of those basic features believe that the in-built resistance to change will be detrimental in the long run. The first opinion is voiced more loudly in the south (Wallonia), while the second is heard more often in the north (Flanders). The welfare state is and remains a compromise built on corporatist and consociational mechanisms. It is a compromise with which nobody is really happy. This must be Belgium. ■

Train Strike in Belgium, 6-7 January 2016

The Rebuilding of the Dutch Welfare State

[RUUD KOOLE]

The Dutch welfare state is going through a series of radical reforms. The most prominent is currently the transfer of the delivery of a number of social provisions from central to local level. This 'localisation' of the welfare state marks the last step for the moment in a longer process of reconstruction and retrenchment of Dutch social security arrangements, which began in around 1980. This brought an end to the welfare state as a societal model that was built after the Second World War. The quest for a different welfare state is still in full swing.

The building and expansion of the welfare state (1945-1980)

The development of social security arrangements is not a post-Second World War phenomenon; the origins of the welfare state have a long history (De Swaan, 1988; De Beer, 2015). However, it was the misery caused by the crisis in the 1930s, followed by the Second World War, which prompted post-war politicians to start building a system of social security arrangements that was unprecedented for its time. The Netherlands changed from lagger to leader in the social domain.

The changing political situation played an important role here. The Netherlands has always been a country of political minorities; no single party has ever held a parliamentary majority. From the end of the nineteenth century, four political 'families' dominated the political playing field: liberals, socialists, Catholics and Protestants. From the start of the twentieth century, these four political families each built up their own network of civil-society organisations, described as 'pillars' (*zuilen*). This process of 'pillarisation' meant that the electoral landscape was also more or less frozen in stasis for a long period. Immediately after the Second World War, an attempt was made from the left of the political spectrum to break through this pillarised system, but without success. One change that did take place, however, was the start of the long-lasting participation in government by the social democrats (PvdA). The party joined the national administration for the first time in 1939, and after the Second World

Willem Drees, Socialist Prime Minister (1948-1958),
'Father' of the Dutch Welfare State.

War joined forces with the Catholic People's Party (KVP) to form the heart of
a series of 'Roman-Red' coalitions, which from 1948 onwards were led by the
social democrat Willem Drees. The party also battled in the elections to win
the votes of the large group of Catholic labourers. The result was a situation
of 'upward rivalry' (Van den Berg, 1992: 39) which went a long way to fostering
the building of the welfare state, as Catholics and social democrats sought to
outbid each other with their proposals to expand the system of social provisions. One of the first and best-known measures was the introduction of a state
old-age pension, first as a contingency measure (1947) and later formalised in
legislation (General Old Age Pensions Act (AOW) – 1956). When the Roman-Red
collaboration came to an end in 1958, the welfare state was expanded further,
leading in the 1970s to an extensive system of insurance-based arrangements
and provisions, all aimed at income protection. This system broadly consisted
of three categories:

1. Employee insurance
Insurance for employees to provide benefits to cover events such as illness
(Health Insurance Act / *Ziektewet* – 1930), unemployment (Unemployment
Act / *Werkloosheidswet* – 1949) and incapacity for work (Invalidity Insurance
Act / *Wet Arbeidsongeschiktheidswet* – 1967). These provisions were funded
from contributions paid by employees.

2. Social insurance
A universal arrangement to help citizens to meet basic needs when they
were unable to do so themselves (Social Assistance Act / *Algemene Bij-
standwet* – 1965). Funded by central government.

3. National insurance

Insurance for everyone, funded from the public purse, which was filled by contributions paid by employees (with the exception of child benefit, which is paid from tax revenues). Examples are the state old-age pension (1956) and child benefit (1962).

The system was based on a set of ideas that was developed in the middle of the twentieth century. The misery of the 1930s and the Second World War greatly increased the need for social arrangements. There was a broad consensus that market failures created a need for government intervention. Keynes dominated the economic thinking of the time. Income protection was important as a means of sustaining domestic consumption. In Dutch government circles, too, the ideas propounded by the British economist Beveridge, who had published his *Social Insurance and Allied Services* in 1942, proved influential. The country had to be rebuilt, and in a way that was socially responsible. The broad coalitions led by Drees achieved this in a period of relatively limited government resources. The social arrangements in this first period of building the welfare state reflected this, being limited to mitigating pressing need and shortages.

This changed during the period of expansion starting in the mid-1960s, with the focus increasingly shifting from simply mitigating pressing need to meeting other goals as well (Schuyt, 2013). The burgeoning economy in the 1960s made the Netherlands a very prosperous country, which also found itself sitting on large reserves of natural gas, the proceeds from which largely went to the government. The number of social arrangements expanded further, but the scope of existing arrangements was also greatly broadened. For example, as early as 1967 the Invalidity Insurance Act abandoned the distinction between incapacity for work caused at work or elsewhere for employees in the private

Ruud Lubbers, 1986.
'Let Lubbers finish his job'.
Christian-Democrat Prime Minister
(1982-1994)

sector. In 1976, the Act was expanded further to include the self-employed, civil servants and those who had been disabled since birth. The generous social benefits suited an atmosphere in which the government also provided generous tax breaks for things such as home purchase and awarded substantial grants to civil-society organisations of all kinds. This prompted the sociologist Van Doorn to refer to the 'unlimited expansion of our free provisions' (Van Doorn, 1978: 159).

The crisis and the rebuilding of the welfare state (1980-2015)

The Netherlands was faced with an economic downturn in the 1970s. Two oil crises hit this very open economy hard. Unemployment rose sharply and the public finances came under pressure: gas revenues and increased borrowing were not enough to prevent the government's budget deficit rising to 10.7% in 1982. This also cast doubt on the affordability of the Dutch welfare state. Social security spending had grown steeply, from 4% of GDP in 1950 to 17% in 1983 (De Beer, 2015). Although the new Constitution in 1983 gave a prominent place to basic social rights, there was talk of 'crisis', 'unaffordability' or 'stagnation' of the welfare state. The changes that had taken place in the political landscape since the middle of the 1960s meant it was impossible to find a consensus on how to put the public finances in order. Self-reinforcing technological, economic and social developments in the 1960s had changed Dutch society within a short space of time from a pillarised, fairly conservative society to a depillarised, open society (Koole and Daalder, 2002). Processes of individualisation and secularisation also had an impact on the political landscape. The growing number of floating voters led to the 'de-freezing' of the party system. The confessional parties saw their support shrinking and new political parties were launched, aided by the highly proportional electoral system that has existed in the Netherlands since 1917. The consensus-based style of doing politics also temporarily disappeared. In this atmosphere of polarisation, it was not easy to find common ground in a joint approach to tackling the economic crisis.

In the early 1980s, the centre-right administration led by Prime Minister Ruud Lubbers, which proclaimed itself a 'no-nonsense' government, stepped in. Civil service salaries and social security benefits were cut and, under heavy pressure from the government, trade unions and employers' organisations forged an agreement in Wassenaar in 1982, in which pay moderation was linked to employment-sustaining measures such as a reduction in working hours. The common aim was to create more jobs. This agreement marked the beginning of a return to consensus politics, including between employers and trade unions (the 'social partners'). Traditionally, the social partners had had an important voice in the Netherlands in the formulation of terms of employment. This 'neo-corporatism' had come under pressure during the period of polarisation in the 1970s; antagonism led to inertia, which was only overcome in the early 1980s. Later, the Wassenaar Agreement was often seen as the basis for the economic recovery in the 1990s, especially by the social partners themselves. Their method of consensus-based negotiation also gained international renown, under the name 'polder model'.

The reality is perhaps slightly more complicated. The confrontational style was indeed replaced in the early 1980s by negotiation (Visser and Hemerijck, 1997), but the power relations shifted to the disadvantage of the trade unions. First, the large budget deficits forced the government to intervene, and spending on employment conditions and social provisions could not escape the axe. As a result, the position of the trade union movement changed from offensive (aimed at the expansion of provisions) to defensive (focused on preserving what had been achieved). This ultimately made it harder for the unions to connect with the younger generation, who saw this defensive strategy as a defence of the interests of an older generation. Second, the changing political relations undermined the position of the trade unions. Secularisation had weakened the position of the Christian political parties, who lost voters mainly to the growing liberal party (VVD). This in turn weakened support for Christian trade unions from the Christian democrats, not only because of their reduced size, but also because the confessional parties (which in 1980 merged to create the Christian Democratic Appeal (CDA)) found themselves competing electorally with the liberals. It seemed as if the 'upward rivalry' with the social democrats in the 1950s had made way for a 'downward rivalry' with the liberals, with parties competing to curtail social provisions. The 'social wing' of the CDA came off worst. Third, the international political discourse was increasingly coming under the influence of what came to be known as 'neoliberalism', which had as its central tenet 'less government, more market'. Keynes was replaced by Hayek. This ideology provided a fillip for proponents of a slimmed-down government apparatus in the Netherlands. They also argued that globalisation made this a necessity.

The combination of the need to reduce the budget deficit, the changed political landscape and the new ideological discourse impacted on the welfare state arrangements. As elsewhere, the central feature of the revamping of the welfare state in the Netherlands was the perceived need to make the system less generous (Pierson, 2001). But just as important were the changes taking place in society itself. The post-war welfare state was in tune with the society of the time, which was built around the traditional household model with a male breadwinner. The social security arrangements were designed to provide income protection in times of illness, unemployment or incapacity for work. But society began to change in the 1960s. Family life changed; women began working en masse, albeit mostly part-time. Lifestyles and labour market patterns also changed radically. The upshot was that the traditional arrangements of the welfare state were increasingly out of kilter with the changed society. Questions were raised as to whether the existing arrangements were not focused too heavily on risks that no longer existed to the same degree, whereas new risks received too little attention (Engelen and Hemerijck, 2007). Government policy, influenced by growing Europeanisation, increasingly moved away from the idea of 'protection' towards a focus on 'empowerment' and participation. In his Speech from the Throne in 2013, the King of the Netherlands observed on behalf of the liberal/social-democrat (VVD/ PvdA) coalition that 'the traditional welfare state is slowly but surely evolving into a participation society'. The Speech placed great emphasis on the need for people to take their own responsibility (Troonrede, 2013). However, this policy direction provided only a partial answer to the new division that had arisen in society: that between the 'insiders' of the traditional welfare state (with permanent full-time jobs) and

the 'outsiders' in the growing group of flexible workers, the self-employed and people without work.

This statement by the King accordingly sparked off a great deal of discussion. It was argued from several quarters that this was an attempt to disguise a cold (neo) liberal policy of austerity as some kind of lofty ideal. This cannot be seen in isolation from the political landscape in the Netherlands at the time, which changed yet again after the turn of the millennium. The great electoral instability opened the way for the rise of successful nationalist/populist parties: first the LPF party headed by Pim Fortuyn, and later the PPV party led by Geert Wilders. This latter party, in particular, links a xenophobic and anti-Islamic stance with the notion of defending the traditional welfare state. On the left of the political spectrum, the Socialist Party (SP) – also a staunch defender of the traditional welfare state – has become a feared competitor of the social-democratic PvdA. These peripheral parties exert electoral pressure on the mainstream parties which, each from their own standpoint, are nonetheless convinced that the welfare state has to be modernised. Society has changed, they argue; the costs are too high and the international environment means there is no choice but to modify the social system and deregulate the labour market. At the same time, existing arrangements are resilient and any attempt at change is highly path-dependent (Hemerijck, 2007, 2012; WRR, 2006). The result of this interplay of forces is a major but gradual, and austere, rebuilding of the welfare state.

The localisation of the welfare state

Despite all the attempts to curtail social security, public spending on the care sector (both cure and care) has continued to rise, from 9% of GDP in 1972 to 16% today (De Beer, 2015). Population ageing and the development of expensive medicines and treatments are contributory factors here. 'Market forces' were seen as part of the solution, with care insurers being given a stronger negotiating position vis-à-vis care and drug providers with a view to achieving cost reductions, under the mantra 'better care at lower cost'.

That same goal drove the decision by the present VVD/PvdA coalition under Prime Minister Marc Rutte to give local authorities a bigger role in the social domain. From 2016, local authorities will be responsible for the delivery of youth welfare services, care for the long-term sick and for guiding hard-to-place people into work. It is no coincidence that the legislation framing this latter objective is called the Participation Act. These three decentralisation operations (3D) build on earlier decentralisations in the preceding decade. The shift has been so massive that it is sometimes referred to as the 'localisation of the welfare state' (Bannink et al., 2013). The hope is that placing responsibility for these policy domains at local level will improve quality by integrating what were previously separate strands of the care and support system and placing them in the hands of decision-makers who are familiar with the local situation. At the same time, this operation is driven by a strong desire to save money. For example, after 2015, local authorities will have to deliver elementary domestic help with 40% less money than in the past. The integrated approach is intended to deliver synergy, but above all individual citizens will be expected to do more for themselves.

Concerns have been expressed not just about the speed with which these changes are being implemented, but also about the ability to achieve the austerity targets without affecting quality. That is now the primary focus of the political debate. For example, is it legitimate to largely shut down access to special benefit arrangements for young disabled persons or to sheltered employment? As well as 'participation', should 'protection' not also continue to be a central goal of social policy?

However, the decentralisations also impinge on the structure of the Dutch state as a whole. In the decentralised 'unitary state' that the Netherlands has been since 1848, responsibilities are now being devolved on a large scale to local authorities. Should those same local authorities then not have additional powers to raise taxes (Rfv, 2013)? Is democratic legitimacy for these tasks adequately regulated at local level (Nehmelmans, 2014)? And how much policy freedom do local authorities really have in practice? Might formal policy freedom be nullified by 'implicit centralisation' (Van Berkel and De Graaf, 2011; Van den Berg, 2013)? As an example, in 2015 the new Participation Act has already become slightly less decentralised due to the harmonisation of a number of rules in order to assuage the concerns of employers (SC, 2015). The debate about the principle of equality is also important here (Rob, 2006). How acceptable is it that local policies differ from each other on an issue as important as the application of basic social rights? In practice, therefore, harmonisation could mean that formal decentralisation turns into de facto (re)centralisation.

The debate about the rebuilding of the Dutch welfare state is in full spate, driven largely by these decentralisation operations in the social domain, and shows no signs of abating. The configuration of the new welfare state is still the subject of heated political argument. But the Dutch term *verzorgingsstaat* ('nurturing state'), the unfortunate Dutch translation of the English term 'welfare state', is less and less appropriate for describing recent developments. Alternatives have been proposed, including 'social investment state', 'activating guarantee state', 'participation society', but there is currently no consensus on a new term. Yet there is no doubt that the Dutch welfare state is evolving in a more austere direction, comparable to that of other European welfare states, even though each of them is following its own, historically determined institutional path. ■

REFERENCES

Bannink, D., H. Bosselaar and W. Trommel (ed.) (2013), *Crafting Local Welfare Landscapes*. The Hague, Eleven.

De Beer, P. (2015), 'De grote golf van Jan Pen', in: *Socialisme & Democratie*, Vol 72, nr 5 (November), pp. 5-21.

De Swaan, A. (1988), *In Care of the State. Health Care, Education and Welfare in Europe and the USA in the Modern Era*. Oxford, Oxford University Press.

Hemerijck, A. (2007), 'Contingente convergentie. De doorontwikkeling van de Europese verzorgingstaat', in: Ewald Engelen, Anton Hemerijck and Willem Trommel (eds.), *Van sociale bescherming naar sociale investering. Zoektocht naar een andere verzorgingsstaat*. The Hague, Lemma, pp. 83-125.

Hemerijck, A. (2012), *Changing Welfare States*. Oxford, Oxford University Press.

Koole, R. and Daalder H. (2002), 'The Consociational Democracy Model and the Netherlands', in: *Acta Politica*, Vol 37, Spring/Summer 2002, pp. 23-43.

Nehmelman, R. (2014), 'De Stelling', in: *Tijdschrift voor Constitutioneel Recht*, October, pp. 324-332.

Pierson, P. (ed.) (2001), *The New Politics of the Welfare State*. Oxford, Oxford University Press.

Rfv (2013), 'Lokaal belastinggebied', letter from the Financial Relations Council to the government, 26 March 2015 (http://www.rob-rfv.nl/documenten/uitbreiding_lokaal_belastinggebied.pdf).

Rob (2006), *Verschil moet er zijn. Bestuur tussen discriminatie en differentiatie*. The Hague, Council for Public Administration.

Schuyt, K. (2013), *Noden en wensen. De verzorgingsstaat gezien als historisch fenomeen*. Rotterdam, Faculty of Social Sciences. Inaugural lecture.

SC (2015), 'Participatiewet wordt iets minder decentraal', The Hague, Sdu, no. 14 (15 September 2015).

Troonrede 2013 (Speech from the Throne). Located at: https://www.rijksoverheid.nl/documenten/toespraken/2013/09/17/troonrede-2013

Van Berkel, R. and W. de Graaf (2011), 'The Decentralisation of Social Assistance in The Netherlands', in: *International Journal of Sociology and Social Policy*, vol. 26, nos. 1-2: 20-31.

Van den Berg, Joop Th.J. (1992), '"Een geschiedenis van grote vraagstukken, grote noden en grote mannen en vrouwen". Politiek historische context van de sociale zekerheid', in: J.Th.J. van den Berg et al. (eds.), *De SVr 40 jaar: einde van een tijdperk, een nieuw begin?*, Zoetermeer, pp. 29-45.

Van den Berg, Jurre (2013), 'De spagaat van de gedecentraliseerde eenheidsstaat', in: *Beleid en Maatschappij*, Vol. 40, no. 2: pp. 205-220.

Van Doorn, J. A.A. (1978), 'De verzorgingsmaatschappij in de praktijk', in: J.A.A. van Doorn and C.J.M Schuyt (eds.), *De stagnerende verzorgingsstaa*t, Meppel/Amsterdam, pp. 17-46. Also in: J.A.A. van Doorn (2009), *Nederlandse democratie. Historische en sociologische waarnemingen*. Amsterdam, Mets & Schilt, pp. 139-161.

Visser, J. and A. Hemerijck (1997), *A Dutch Miracle: Job Growth, Welfare Reform and Corporatism in the Netherlands*. Amsterdam, Amsterdam University Press.

WRR (2006), *De verzorgingsstaat herwogen. Over verzorgen, verzekeren, verheffen en verbinden*. Netherlands Scientific Council for Government Policy. Amsterdam, Amsterdam University Press, 2006.

Translated by Julian Ross

Revealing Concealment

On the Visual Artwork of Krijn de Koning

[DOROTHEE CAPPELLE]

Anyone who has ever built or renovated a house will tell you that the first step in your not-quite-finished home feels like a step into another world, one in which the perspective seems slightly changed, where the light falls a little differently, where you feel larger or smaller than normal. A house whitewashed from floor to ceiling with no internal doors, furniture, curtains or colours does not feel like a new house, but like a hushed, geometric construction in the midst of the chaos of the world racing by, mildly surreal, as if you had suddenly dropped down a rabbit hole in an architectural model. What if that bright white world were to receive an injection of colour? Not just any colour, but loud ones: blood red, bright blue, grass green or lemon yellow? What effect would that have on the construction? And on you?

That is precisely what Dutch environmental artist Krijn de Koning (born in 1963 in Amsterdam) does. He introduces geometric constructions, ranging from monumental to minuscule, into an existing environment, decks them out in lively colours and invites the viewer to set to work. The viewer has no backstory or obvious starting point. De Koning simply formulates a proposal; entering the labyrinthine constructions, examining the work of art and its surroundings from different angles and considering the effects, shaping the work of art in the viewer's mind. The effect is different for everyone. Krijn de Koning's art is only complete when it is experienced. Above all it emanates freedom, while at the same time having a special physical and psychological impact. That sounds terribly abstract, theoretical even, but de Koning's work could hardly be less so.

Environmental artist in heart and soul

In 1983 Krijn de Koning embarked on a course in audiovisual design at the renowned Gerrit Rietveld Academie in Amsterdam. Five years later he moved to Ateliers '63 (in Haarlem at the time), later moving on to the Institute des Hautes Études en Arts Plastiques in Paris, where he was taught by Daniel Buren among others.[1] Buren clearly made his mark on the young de Koning: the use of expanses of colour and preference for intervening in the environment – minimalist or not – are obvious examples.

Krijn de Koning, *Land*,
work for the Edinburgh Art
Festival, Edinburgh Collage
of Art (UK), 2013
© Krijn de Koning

De Koning's work can be seen in well-known Dutch museums such as the Stedelijk in Amsterdam, the Centraal Museum in Utrecht, the Vleeshal in Middelburg and the Boijmans van Beuningen in Rotterdam. Given the nature of his work, these are often, but not always, temporary exhibitions, although the artist also does permanent installations, for instance in public spaces such as the redeveloped Nuon Energy site behind the RAI Exhibition and Convention Centre in Amsterdam, about which de Koning made the following remark to the newspaper *Het Financieel Dagblad*: 'It's as if it simply doesn't exist. (...) All attention at this location is focused on what happens around the Nuon site. It needs something doing with it. It should draw attention. It's a cliché that those closed grey blocks have to be ugly. It's a question of how you present them and how you look at them.'[2] It is this last point which forms the essence of his work and applies as much to an ugly environment such as the Nuon site as to an attractive one like the gothic Vleeshal or Nieuwe Kerk in Amsterdam.

In 2007 de Koning was awarded the Sikkens Prize, an international prize for individuals and organisations working originally and creatively with colour, created by the foundation behind the paint manufacturer Sikkens. In doing so he followed in the footsteps of Gerrit Rietveld (first winner of the prize in 1959), Theo Van Doesburgh, Le Corbusier and Donald Judd, artists with whom he has been compared more than once. In past years the prize has also gone to recipients such as the Rijksdienst voor de IJsselmeerpolders (a government organisation responsible for the polders reclaimed from the Ijsselmeer lake) in 1979 and the well-known shopping chain Hema in 2004. This prevents it from being seen as a 'real' art prize, but that ambiguity and open character makes the prize particularly fitting for de Koning.

Since 2010 de Koning's work has increasingly been on show outside his home country, including installations at the Chapelle Jeanne d'Arc in Thouars and the Abbaye de Corbigny in France. The Dutch artist clearly sees religious sites as a good setting for his work, or is it the other way around?

In 2008 de Koning's work was exhibited in Paris and Budapest. The following year visitors to the Belgian Beaufort Triennial had the opportunity to admire his art on the Belgian coast and another year later he made it to New York. In 2014 de Koning set to work again at the Belgian open-air folklore museum Bokrijk, as well as exhibiting in France, Austria and at the British Folkestone Triennial. There is plenty of diversity in the path Krijn de Koning has taken.

Publications on de Koning frequently refer to De Stijl, Mondrian or Rietveld, influences unmistakeably present in his work, although it must be said that de Koning does not colour within the lines nearly so strictly as his illustrious forebears. The work of Krijn de Koning is more playful, freer, perhaps even more ambiguous, despite its tightly geometric character. Emotion and atmosphere play as important a role in his oeuvre as colour, plane and physical space.

On his website[3] de Koning presents himself as the maker of installations, drawings, sculptures and architectural works. In my view this description, extensive as it may sound, is too restrictive. It fails to do justice to the role he gives the viewer, the importance of experience for his art, from feel and atmosphere to the technical and rational. De Koning is a multidisciplinary artist, but he is every bit as much a director who steps in, steers and lets go again. He is also a composer, as Michel Gauthier rightly notes in his contribution 'Passage in het werk' ('Passersby at work') in the catalogue *Krijn de Koning – Binnen Buiten / Inside Outside*.[4] De Koning does not just give his works titles, he also numbers them as a composer would. His website now displays a list of 168 works (on 30

Krijn de Koning, *Land*, work for the Edinburgh Art Festival,
Edinburgh Collage of Art (UK), 2013 © Krijn de Koning

November 2015). Numbered 'opera', be they abstractions of his smaller works such as the replicas he presented at his regular gallery, Slewe in Amsterdam,[5] or his manipulated photos. De Koning also composes new works of art with volumes and colours as if they were notes and rhythms. The term 'environmental artist', however, seems the most appropriate, summing up the diverse aspects of his work, the different roles of artist, work of art and viewer, as well as the immense importance of the environment for his art, far better than any other artistic term.

Krijn de Koning, Work for the Rietveld Wing,
Centraal Museum Utrecht, 1999 © Ernst Moritz

Straightforward complexity

A crucial work within Krijn de Koning's oeuvre is the site-specific *Image for the Centraal Museum Utrecht* which he created for Sjarel Ex, a member of the Sikkens Prize jury and the museum director at the time. It was presented in 1999 and consists of a construction or composition involving interwoven spaces made of wood and acrylic paint. The work nestles over two floors of a wing of the museum, inviting the visitor to enjoy the different experiences of the artistic space of the artwork and the museum surrounding it. The image appears rather chaotic – unlike most of de Koning's other installations – but fits beautifully with the sense of history in the location. After all, this building once housed not a quiet museum but one of the oldest psychiatric institutions in the Netherlands, the Willem Arntsz House. De Koning makes virtuoso use of history and surroundings, bringing the experience intuitively to the visitor. In *Amsterdam Weekly*, Ex remarks, 'De Koning added extra walls to make a criss-

Krijn de Koning, Work for the Rietveld Wing, Centraal Museum Utrecht, 1999 © Ernst Moritz

cross of spaces. With this complexity of architecture and colour he created something that suggests complete craziness.'[6] That suggestiveness is crucial. De Koning hints, rather than insisting, whispering softly to viewers or nudging them in the right direction.

Taking a completely different but equally effective approach, he entered into a dialogue with the environment at Edinburgh Art Festival in 2013. In *Land* he presented a sort of podium with different levels, enabling the visitor to view the works in the Sculpture Court at Edinburgh College of Art completely differently. The sculptures, the location and their history are seamlessly integrated into the piece. Here the bright splashes of colour he is so famous for are conspicuously absent, apparently incorporating his own artistic history. In older pieces he used wood shades or white, leaving the raw materials visible from time to time. Here he repeats this in stylised form. Is that a statement? A way of wrong-footing those familiar with his work? Surely not. It simply suits the space of the academy. De Koning often makes his choice of colour, shape and proportion intuitively.[7]

The work in Edinburgh particularly emanates peace and contemplation, while at the same time inviting the visitor to investigate. The same is true of de Koning's installation for the Nieuwe Kerk in Amsterdam, a gigantic rhomboid platform mounted five metres up, diagonally above the altar. Visitors were able to climb onto the new platform to see the church, stained-glass windows and pulpit from a completely different perspective. In the middle of the floor was a construction in which visitors could wander and lose themselves, leading towards a crypt and the ground floor.

For Krijn de Koning, however, art does not always need to be cerebral or monumental. From time to time some humour or even kitsch is allowable. The beach huts and the work around the Victorian grotto which he produced in 2014 for the Turner Contemporary's Summer of Colour Festival and the third Folkestone Triennial are examples of this. Small works also make up part of his oeuvre. In 2012 he exhibited a series of small to medium-sized sculptures, *Models*, at Amsterdam's Slewe Gallery. On the one hand the models, drawings and photos are a reflection of his own research, his artistic experiments, because of course a downside of his temporary, monumental and site-specific installations is that, once dismantled, only the sketches, images and miniature versions remain to remind us of what has been.

At the same time they invite the visitor to set to work, albeit in a completely different manner from his building-sized installations. One model consisted of five parts which each appear quite unusual on their own, but which can be combined in endless different ways to make new miniature architecture. Visitors were able to work on them too, feeling and handling the different parts, learning to look differently, to think in shapes and to experiment, just as they did as children playing with a box of building bricks. One work particularly expressed this playful, childlike character in de Koning's work. The artist bought a 1970s

Krijn de Koning, Work for the Nieuwe Kerk, Amsterdam, 2010 © Ernst Moritz

Krijn de Koning, *Dwelling*,
work for the Turner Contemporary Margate and the Folkestone Triennial (UK),
2014 © Thierry Bal

dolls' house on the online sales site Marktplaats, one with the bright colours he uses in his own work. De Koning transformed the dolls' house into a sculpture barely distinguishable from his large-scale, monumental designs in existing buildings, except in its proportions, illustrating how a playful fantasy world and reality become entangled. De Koning's art is simultaneously complex and yet straightforward.

At the end of 2015 Krijn de Koning presented a new series of smaller works in his regular gallery. These pieces are more abstract and colourful than the previous series; life-size, three-dimensional puzzles which the viewer can look over, under and through. De Koning has plenty more to say and we are all too happy to be coaxed along into his captivating, colourful universe. ∎

1   www.nieuwekerk.nl/nl/#/nl/de_kerkmeester/2010/biografie.htm?m=99

2   Edo Dijksterhuis, 'De wereld anders ingekleurd. Beeldhouwer Krijn de Koning krijgt prestigieuze Sikkensprijs 2007 uitgereikt' ('The world coloured in differently. Sculptor Krijn de Koning receives the prestigious Sikkens Prize 2007', *Het Financiële Dagblad*, 1 December 2007.

3   www.krijndekoning.nl

4   Michel Gauthier, 'Passage in het werk', *Krijn de Koning – Binnen Buiten / Inside Outside*, Rotterdam, 2000, pp. 85-125.

5   For example, the exhibition *Models*, Slewe Gallery, Amsterdam, 2012.

6   Marinus De Ruiter, 'Complex Interiors', *Amsterdam Weekly*, 6-12 December 2007, p. 7.

7   See also the video interview at http://www.slewe.nl/videos?id=365.

Translated by Anna Asbury

Krijn de Koning, *Shafts and corridors*,
Courtesy Slewe Gallery Amsterdam, 2016 © Peter Cox

Let There Be Light

Discovering Eindhoven

Back in the 1880s, when Van Gogh was plodding through the Brabant potato fields, Eindhoven was just a small Catholic town. Now it is the fifth largest city in the Netherlands, with an acclaimed modern art museum and a world-class design academy.

I thought I knew the city. Many years ago, I got off the train to take a look around. It struck me as a rather soulless place compared to other Dutch towns. Hardly surprising when you learn that the centre was heavily bombed by the Allies during the Second World War. All I can remember is dull post-war architecture and a large blue Philips sign hovering in the sky.

I caught the next train. Not thinking that I would ever go back. But then I did. And I discovered that Eindhoven has changed.

The blue Philips sign, now a protected monument, is still up there. But the huge multinational electronics company that once dominated the city has left town and turned out the lights.

You can thank globalisation for that. After shaping Eindhoven for almost a century, Philips moved its production base to Asia in the late 1990s. Then it transferred the company headquarters to Amsterdam, leaving just the research and development department behind in Eindhoven. And then it stopped making most of the things it used to make.

It was a terrible blow when Philips left, a local art dealer told me. For more than a century, the company had dominated Eindhoven, like General Motors in Detroit. Philips was involved in everything from providing workers' housing to sponsoring classical concerts.

The first thing I saw when I stepped out of the station was a statue of Anton Philips, one of two brothers who founded the company, looking solid and serious in his heavy overcoat.

'You should take a look at the railway station,' the art dealer told me. 'It's modelled on a 1950s Philips radio.' I was doubtful at first, then I noticed that the station clock looked like a tuning dial and the concrete tower to the left could almost be an aerial.

Fifty thousand light bulbs for the Tsar

That's just the beginning. On a walk through the centre, I passed the Philips Museum and the Frits Philips concert hall. Then I came across the Philips Dorp, a model urban district built in the early twentieth century for factory workers who had migrated here from poor rural areas like Drente and Friesland. Two brick columns on either side of the road marked the boundary of the workers' settlement. PHILIPS, it said on one column. DORP, read the other.

The company had its own healthcare system, long before other Dutch companies, along with a final-salary pension scheme. It operated a company bus service, a bakery, a technical school and Etos, a discount cooperative store for employees.

Even the local football team PSV Eindhoven was founded by Philips in 1913 for its workers (the initials stand for Philips Sport Vereniging). Some of the finest Dutch players like Ruud Gullit and Ruud van Nistelrooy once wore the distinctive PSV strip with the company name prominently displayed on the front.

The company started out in 1891 in a former textile mill. It is now the Philips Museum. Opened in 2013, it tells the story of Gerard Philips, who studied electrical engineering in Glasgow before setting up a small company to produce carbon filament light bulbs.

In 1898, Gerard Philips won a major contract to supply the Tsar of Russia with 50,000 light bulbs for the Hermitage. Gerard sent a message from Russia with the good news. His employees in Eindhoven must have assumed it was a mistake, because Gerard had to send a second telegram that left no one in any doubt. 'Vijftigduizend, cinq mille, fünfzig tausend,' it said.

By 1900, Philips was employing 400 people in Eindhoven, many of them young girls with nimble fingers who could thread the fragile filaments. Forty years later, Philips had 25,000 employees on its payroll, in a town that numbered 113,000. At the company's peak in the 1970s, it was employing 400,000 people across the world.

It is no exaggeration to say that Philips changed the way people lived in the twentieth century. With the invention of the light bulb, factory labourers could work longer hours, the company pointed out. Its street lighting would reduce the number of road accidents, Philips wrote to the Dutch queen after her car was involved in a road accident.

By the mid-twentieth century, Philips dominated the market in consumer products, moving seamlessly from light bulbs to radios to television sets. By the 1960s, Philips was riding high on the consumer revolution, manufacturing products like the Philishave electric razor, vacuum cleaners, cassette players and compact discs. It even created its own record label to ensure that teenagers had pop songs to play on their new Philips equipment.

The company liked to engage in promotional stunts, like illuminating the Eiffel Tower in 1937. It went on to create a pavilion at Brussels Expo 58 to demonstrate the world's first multimedia experience, called Poème Electronique. More recently, Philips lit up New York's Empire State Building using the world's most efficient light bulbs.

The company's sleek image was reflected in the industrial buildings it constructed. Dominating the city centre is the Lichttoren, the Light Tower, a striking 1909 modernist building topped off with a seven-sided tower where Philips once tested light bulbs. The sleek white building next door, known as De Witte Dame, or The White Lady, was built by Philips to manufacture radio tubes.

The company went on to develop a huge industrial site called Strijp S where it put up a series of Bauhaus-style concrete and glass factories. It also funded the construction of a sleek observatory on the edge of the city park, and unveiled a striking flying-saucer shaped building known as the Evoluon.

Completed in 1966 for the company's 75th anniversary, the Evoluon marked a high point in Philips history. It was a stunning, futuristic building designed by the Eindhoven architect Leo De Bever and the company's chief product designer Louis Kalff. Conceived as a technology museum (and a showroom for Philips products), it once attracted half a million visitors every year.

But visitor numbers began to fall sharply in the 1980s, and the Evoluon finally closed down in 1989. Not long after, the company began to cut production in Eindhoven. It stopped making televisions, DVD players and almost all the other products that had made it famous, closed its factories and fired thousands of employees (it now employs about 120,000 people).

'You need to dismount when your horse is dead,' announced the head of Philips, Frans Van Houten, during a press conference in 2014. 'What was relevant twenty years ago is no longer relevant today.' The focus in future would be on lighting and healthcare devices, he said, standing in front of a screen with enlarged photographs of the two stern Philips brothers who had founded the company.

Twenty years ago, the distinctive Philips logo – a shield with stars and waves in a circle – appeared on CD players, televisions and record players in almost every home. 'When I was growing up,' a Dutch friend told me, 'Everyone had a Philips television in their front room, so you could walk along the street with a Philips remote control changing the channels as you went along.'

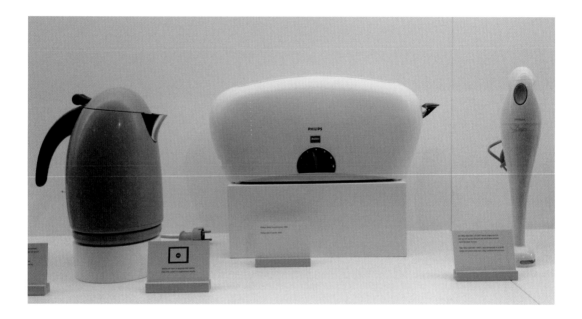

Design

No more. My hotel room in Eindhoven had a Samsung television, a Bosch coffee maker and a Princess hair dryer. Nothing was made by Philips. It was like visiting Wolfsburg and seeing everyone driving a Toyota. Worse still, the company was planning to drop its sponsorship of PSV Eindhoven's shirts. Soon you would only see the logo when you changed a light bulb or glided into a hospital scanner.

The company didn't just ditch its products. It dumped the town it had built from almost nothing (and whose new logo resembles the waves on the Philips shield). By the late 1990s, Eindhoven was starting to look like a city without a future. With rising unemployment and the highest crime rate in the country, many young people left to look for work elsewhere. But then something interesting happened. In the course of a few years, this depressed company town turned itself into a smart design city.

You can see the results in the vast Strijp S factory district where Philips built several huge factories to assemble radios in the 1930s. It used to be known as the Forbidden City because of the high security fences that surrounded the site. But, by the end of the twentieth century, the Verboden Stad had become a graffiti-sprayed urban wilderness.

In 2004, the Trudo housing association took over the site. Working with the city council and the Dutch national heritage organisation, it drew up a master plan to redevelop Strijp-S (now written with a hyphen). The Dutch architect and urbanist Jo Coenen, a graduate of Eindhoven University of Technology, was put in charge of the project.

Trudo has transformed Strijp-S into an inspiring post-industrial quarter where old Philips factories are now occupied by loft apartments, design studios, pop-up shops, kids' workshops and a 3D print factory. Little now remains of the company that once occupied this site, apart from an exhibition of old radios and a Philips clock with the letters P-H-I-L-I-P-S instead of numbers.

One of the many new projects is Urban Shopper, a vast industrial hall in the Anton building where twenty creative startups occupy small cabins with round roofs made from transparent corrugated plastic. The businesses include a hairdresser, a shoe shop, and a vintage store. Some look as if they are struggling to survive, but others look as if they have hit on a product that people want to buy.

On wasteland behind the factories, the New York architects LOT-EK have stacked 250 rusted shipping containers to create a mini urban district called The City. The aim is to encourage artists, galleries and small shops to settle in this industrial warren of alleys and walkways.

Early in 2015, another startup called Broeinest opened in a raw industrial building known as the Glasgebouw. Created by the young architect firm Atelier to the Bone, it provides a flexible space for an emerging generation of nomadic designers and architects. As well as offering a space to meet, Broeinest provides drawing tables, a laser cutter and a café.

The most recent development is a vast indoor food hall called the Vershal van Veem which opened in late 2015. Located in another impressive industrial building, this vast space is occupied by stalls selling homemade soup, local meat and Dutch cheeses as well as craft beer produced by the in-house brewery Brouwerij Van Veem.

Much of the creative energy behind this transformation has come from young designers who studied at Eindhoven Design Academy, DAE. Founded in 1947 as a school of industrial design, the DAE developed a revolutionary approach in the 1980s that turned it into one of the world's top design schools. It went on to produce some of the country's best-known designers, including the collective Droog Design, Hella Jongerius and Studio Job.

In the past, graduates would head to Amsterdam or Berlin to pursue their careers. But some now stay on in Eindhoven, settling into one of the old Philips buildings. One of the first to realise the city's potential was Piet Hein Eek, who moved his studio into an abandoned industrial building formerly occupied by the Philips ceramic factory. Here he has opened a shop where he displays his quirky bohemian furniture made out of multicoloured fabrics and salvaged wood.

A more recent graduate, Rocco Verdult, has developed a radical vision of design. He doesn't believe in creating products, but prefers to shape social interactions. Verdult tours Eindhoven with a mobile disco to spark off spontaneous dance events, stages unexpected happenings in dreary waiting rooms and walks around depressed neighbourhoods encouraging locals to contribute to a story.

Several abandoned Philips factories in the city centre have also been renovated, including the Light Tower. The ground floor is now occupied by a vast café, Usine, with a raw industrial interior, while the rooms in the light tower have been converted into stunning hotel lofts. Next door, the Witte Dame has become home to the Design Academy, public library and MU art space.

Facing the Light Tower, the Italian architect Massimiliano Fuksas has added a striking glass and steel dome known as the Blob. Opened in 2010, the five-floor building is currently occupied by the Dutch concept store Sissy-Boy. It includes a stunning café on the upper level furnished with wooden tables and chairs by Piet Hein Eek.

On the same square, two organic structures lead down to a new underground bike garage with space for 1,700 bicycles. It forms part of a sophisticated new cycling infrastructure which has transformed a city once dominated by cars. The most imaginative element of the city's bike plan is a spectacular circular cycle bridge called the Hovenring suspended above a busy motorway intersection.

The World's smartest city

The city's skyline is also changing. Once dominated by a statue of Christ with outstretched arms, it now features the slender Vesteda Tower built in 2006 by the Eindhoven architect Jo Coenen in the style of the Flatiron Building in Manhattan.

The city authorities have recently commissioned art installations to liven up some dull squares, including an amusing work by Claes Oldenburg and Coosje van Bruggen, on the far side of the station, which features a huge bowling ball scattering ten yellow pins across a park.

Eindhoven also has one of the most inspiring contemporary art museums in Europe. Founded in 1936 by the cigar manufacturer Henri van Abbe, it was designed to show that Eindhoven was more than just an industrial town making radios.

Originally located in a sober brick building, the museum now has a striking modern extension with large glass windows overlooking a pond. In this beautiful setting, it displays a huge collection of works by El Lissitzky, land art by Hamish Fulton and Richard Long, and eighteen striped paintings by Daniel Buren.

With its new emphasis on art and design, Eindhoven has become a much more interesting place. Yet it remains a city based on technology, as the OECD recently acknowledged when it ranked Eindhoven as the world's smartest city, based on the number of patents registered per head of population.

As darkness fell on the city of light, I set off by bike from the station in the direction of Nuenen. I wanted to look at the new Van Gogh cycle path created by the artist Daan Roosegaarde in 2014, which features thousands of tiny lights embedded in the path that glow at night. The idea was inspired by Van Gogh's painting *The Starry Night*, which he painted in June 1889, one year before he died.

It was impossible to find in the dark Brabant countryside. Next morning, I headed out to the village of Nuenen, where Van Gogh lived for two years. Here he painted the local church, a country cottage, and the famous group of Dutch peasants known as *The Potato Eaters*.

The village has created a Van Gogh trail as well as opening a Van Gogh museum (although it has no original paintings). Facing the museum is a café called De Aardappeleters where you can buy Dutch fries served with mayonnaise.

I thought about those potato eaters of 1885 sitting in a dark room lit by a single flickering oil lamp. Within a few years, people like them would be working for Gerard Philips in his light bulb factory on the Emmasingel, helping to turn Eindhoven into the world's smartest city. ■

Silent Witnesses on the Table

Still Lifes Today

The still life is alive and well in art. Most contemporary Dutch and Flemish artists regard the Christian message as outmoded, but some do not mind a bit of moralism, as long as it's ambiguous and only implied. The lusts and burdens of earthly sensuality should keep each other in balance.

The still life is not a fashionable subject, one would think. The displays of fruit, game, flowers and skulls which were painted in the seventeenth century are so famous that they have become clichéd. One would not expect a twenty-first century artist to elaborate on this genre, since the first rule is to be original. Yet the genre is booming.

Last year the largest still life of all times was completed in the new market hall in Rotterdam: the *Horn of Plenty* by multimedia artist Arno Coenen (born 1972). In Coenen's digitally designed panorama, giant fruits, loaves of bread, fish and other traditional ingredients of the still life whirl around a dazzling white sun. Coenen calls his monumental still life an ode to the old masters of sixteenth- and seventeenth-century Dutch painting. In a number of important aspects his explosion of edibles is in fact just the opposite of a still life: everything is moving, free of gravity and without a blemish. In a traditional still life the objects displayed lie literally still, mostly on a table. There is often the suggestion that the expiry date of the wares is close at hand. Sometimes a broken flower indicates the decomposition that will inevitably come. Coenen's *Horn of Plenty* looks more like an ode to supermarket advertising than a warning of the approaching end. Nearly all product advertisements are indebted to the still life tradition, even though, of course, they carry a commercial rather than a religious message: one is no longer admonished to invest in imminent eternity but in consumption in the here and now. Coenen's work takes this advertising imagery, derived from art but now freed from its perishability, back to art. Whether he wants to comment on the phenomenon of advertising or our consumer society as well is doubtful.

Gijs Assmann, *Vanitas (for Karin)*, 2009, ceramics, iron, wood, found objects, paper bird, 58 x 46 x 38 cm, Collection Margeet De Koster and Fred Velders, Den Haag.

An ambiguous genre

Since time immemorial the still life has been an ambiguous genre, in which attraction and repulsion often vie for precedence. While the reminder of death can be to some an incentive to lead a more virtuous life, to others it can be a license to enjoy the life of the moment with abandon. Whether each classical still life was painted with quite such an edifying intent is however debatable and some art historians doubt it. The still life is also known as a rewarding field of research for studious and experiment-minded painters who were undoubtedly more interested in the anatomy of a carcass or the way light was reflected on a glass than in propagating virtue. Nonetheless, for centuries the genre has been linked to Christian morality.

Contemporary still life has disconnected itself from both Christian morality and painting. These days it is a theme that pops up everywhere: in photography (Elspeth Diederix, Krista van der Niet, Scheltens & Abbenes), in sculpture and installation (Merijn Bolink, Tim Breukers, Koen Theys), in drawing and collage (Erik Mattijssen, Ruth van Beek), in video and new media art (Sara Bjarland, Les Oiseaux de Merde) and even in performance art and theatre (Uta Eisenreich, see further).

Painter and sculptor Gijs Assmann (born 1966) made his first vanitas sculpture while still at the Amsterdam Rijksakademie, as a present. *Vanitas (for Stephan)* (1992) became the first of a large and still-growing series of portraits in vanitas form. A selection of eighty-nine works can be seen on Assmann's website.

'I was educated with the idea that you must behave as if you had thought up everything yourself,' he says. 'But I want to show that my work is part of a larger tradition. The message of transience in still lifes attracts me too. That balance between *memento mori* and *carpe diem*.'

Assmann originally created ceramic vanitases, but gradually started using all kinds of materials. He also, more and more often, added his own ingredients, like coconuts, sausages and doorstops, to the usual vanitas components.

The general moral admonishment of the traditional vanitas becomes a coded morality with him, tailor-made to suit the person he is portraying, who can then be subjected to identification and interpretation by each individual viewer. 'They are declarations of love with a critical undertone. Like the messages written to accompany presents given at Sinterklaas (the feast of Saint Nicholas) in the Netherlands which, though they include some gentle ridicule or criticism of the recipient, are accepted as long as they are tongue-in-cheek. Not that I want to judge anyone. But I do long for an art that, like in the Middle Ages, doesn't just serve as a commodity but also brings about a confrontation in one's daily life with difficult subjects like mortality.

For the past three years, Wouter van Riessen (born 1967) has been engrossed in Van Gogh's sunflower paintings. Meanwhile, based on the numerous sketches he has made of these famous paintings, he has painted twenty immaculate comic strip-like still lifes with flowers. Van Riessen's colourful, evenly painted bouquets, devoid of shadow, would be just right for a spacecraft. His flowers have an object-like, surrealistic quality.

'I like it that Van Gogh painted three versions of his *Vase with Five Sunflowers* that are all very similar, in a relatively short period of time,' says Van Riessen. 'He doesn't make a definite statement about how these flowers look, but gives different options, each with small alterations which change the flowers' ap-

pearance. I have amplified what he has done. I experience his flowers as facial expressions without faces, or as postures. There is a tired sunflower among them that is in the autumn of its life. Two other ones have a certain gaiety. Together the sunflowers form a chorus, in which the separate voices can still be distinguished. I see a parallel with my self-portraits. At different times you can have quite different feelings.'

All of Van Riessen's work – which also consists of drawings, photographs and prints – deals with the human inclination to bring things to life through the imagination. Van Riessen finds the still life interesting in as far as it lends itself to this. 'When an image remains a *nature morte*, I don't find it interesting. When there is room for your own projection, you become mystically connected to things. You can draw the world closer to you.'

For exactly this reason the fame of the sunflowers is important to Van Riessen. Since the viewer can easily recognize the reference, it is immediately clear that he is looking at a retake, an interpretation of an existing composition. This carries with it the implicit invitation to interpret Van Riessen's paintings just as freely. Van Riessen guards the suggestive power of his paintings - he wants to evoke but not to specify. 'When, for example, I see something bat-like in one of the sunflowers, I'm not going to develop the bat, but will just try to capture that bat-like quality.'

Dirk Zoete (born 1969) actually portrays himself by giving shape to the world inside his head. His drawings, tableaux with masks and costumes, scale-models and installations, as grim as they are absurd, are reminiscent of Ensor's work. The vanitas theme pops up regularly, in his self-portraits for example, in which Zoete's face has already turned partly into a skull.

Among the works with the collective title *Flemish Voodoo* (2008) are numerous skulls, often in the company of bread. There is for example an ink and charcoal drawing on which a floating skull, pierced by nails, seems to be eating a slice of bread. More slices of bread are flying around – enough of them, should the hollow-eyed one be hungry. But what good are they to someone who

Koen Theys,
The Vanitas Record.

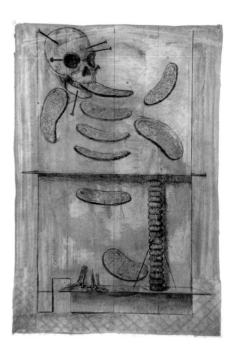

Wouter van Riessen, *Fifteen Sunflowers in a Vase*, 2013,
Acrylic paint on linen, 74 x 58 cm,
Collection Akzo Nobel Art Foundation.

Dirk Zoete, *Skull and Bread*, 2008,
Printing ink and charcoal on paper, 140 x 100 cm.
© Dirk Zoete

is, after all, just a skull? Just as the many piercing nails can't hurt Van Zoete's skulls, his loaves of bread can't feed them. His works evoke associations with religious torture, offerings and the ritual of the Eucharist, but with Van Zoete all means of conquering or warding off death seem in vain.

A messy festive explosion

Painter Sander van Deurzen (born 1975) chose the still life tradition to catch the spirit of the times. During his academy years Van Deurzen made installations. But having often thought that he had done something new, only to discover later that this was not the case, he opted after his final exam for what he himself calls 'a radical turnaround to painting'. 'I decided then to commit myself more to art history,' he says. 'I wanted to apply the old themes in art to topical matters. I also use landscape and portrait, but the still life suits me best because of the sense of tranquillity and transience.'

His still lifes are inhabited by toy and game figures with wildly extended limbs, blowsy Buddha figurines, dripping heaps of pudding and messy bits and pieces. Often the knickknacks and sweetmeats are gathered beneath looped garlands that hang over them threateningly. You would rather not get caught up in them. Here and there in the foreground it may be quiet, but in the background, as a rule, things are in motion. Cartoonish and disproportionate flies regularly bother the objects – a reference to the subtle lifelike flies which proclaim imminent decay in seventeenth-century still lifes.

The toys entered Van Deurzen's work after he found a box full of imaginary creatures and fairy-tale heroes at a flea market. Many of them are protagonists from the Disney stable, obtainable as a bonus with a Happy Meal. 'I recognized the vanitas theme in them. Every month McDonald's produced a new series of, let's say, ten different figures. So the children had to eat more hamburgers to get them. Then the old ones could be discarded. The turnover rate fascinated me.'

Although he is aware of the adverse effect that the overproduction of cheap consumer goods has on the environment, he is careful not to burden his paintings with moral messages. 'I find the classical vanitas pedantic. I want to shed light on both sides of our era. There's also this festive explosion, the freedom of being able to buy anything.'

The things Van Deurzen portrays are becoming gradually less recognizable. 'More and more often I try to capture the vanitas quality in the brushstrokes. I lay on the paint quite wet, so that the forms seem to melt. They spread out like melting ice-cream.'

The language of things

Of a whole different order is the both anarchistic and analytical work of Uta Eisenreich (born 1971), an artist of German descent who studied in Amsterdam and continues to work there. Eisenreich uses photography, installation art and performance. Her interest in still life dates back to her time at the academy and had its origins in her experience at home with housework and child rearing. 'Because of the birth of my son the question of how thinking is formed, how you explain things to a child occupied me. My final exam project in 2000 dealt with unsuccessful systems for clearing up. On a carpet I made a diagram in the form of a pie in which I put household items into categories like "toys" and "edible things". But then, where would you put an edible toy? If I am not able to organize a kitchen cupboard, I thought, then organizing on a large scale in science can't be possible either. Reality is so polymorphous, it can't be caught in a single system.'

In 2010, in collaboration with the graphic designer Julia Born, Eisenreich made the photo book, *A not B*, a kind of semiotic picture book for all ages based on the Wechsler Intelligence Scale – an intelligence test for children that presents them with ever-changing combinations of items from a suitcase and has them describe the relationships between them. Eisenreich's book contains photos of eggs, matches, ladybugs, pins, fruit, deflated footballs, teapots, Post-it notes, ash trays and a lot of other things. Her plain graphic compositions give these commonplace objects an aura of enormous importance. But what do they demonstrate? What do they symbolize, of what are they derivatives? The book has an obstinate, cheerful, liberating air of investigation. Language, signs, objects - what refers to what, when does something become readable, when is something self-evident? Why do we use things for packaging our purchases? What do we project on our food and our possessions?

Tim Breukers, *I LOVE YOU*, 2014,
Clay, 23 x 11 x 23 cm, Private collection.

Uta Eisenreich, *A not B # 11: Bananadrama*, 2010.

Eisenreich is presently collaborating with the performance artist Eva Meyer-Keller and singer-songwriter Miss Kenichi (Katrin Hahner) in a production based on the theatrical text *Objects Lie on a Table – A Play* (1922) by Gertrude Stein (1874-1946). Eisenreich and Meyer-Keller, with visual artist Rebecca Sakoun, had previously based a shorter performance on it called *Things on a Table* (2015). Stein moved in the progressive artistic and literary circles of early twentieth-century Paris and was friends with painters like Cézanne, Picasso and Matisse, who all three revitalized the still life through cubism. Stein's wild, poetic text full of puns is noticeably influenced by their painterly quest and Stein's kaleidoscopic textual collage fits in well with Eisenreich's unsettling humour. Stein replaces objects with language; Eisenreich replaces language with objects. Their visual still-life marriage in *Things on a Table* produced alternating effects of recognition and alienation that were overwhelming. The audience sat in front of a screen on which a table, which was being filmed on the right side of the room, was projected. While Stein's text was being recited, hands on the table were busy constantly creating new arrangements of objects. Sometimes the things were what they seemed, other times they stood for something else. They transformed from thing into symbol and back again, as the public's eye was directed from one interpretation to another with the help of words and theatrical manipulation.

Aukje Koks (1977) likewise plays with collective and personal symbols in her work. To her, painting and writing are very closely related. In 2012 she made an installation for the exhibition *Time, Trade & Travel* as part of a collaboration between the Stedelijk Museum Bureau Amsterdam and the Nubuke Foundation in Accra, Ghana. Partly as a result of Pieter de Marees's travelogue from 1602, Koks became intrigued by the way in which the objects brought from Ghana by seventeenth-century Europeans acquired a totally different function and status, often with strong symbolic connotations, and by how European traders tried to take advantage of this.

At Belgian and Dutch flea markets Koks bought objects of the kind that colonial traders used to take with them to Ghana in those days: a copper pan, a rope, a strainer, a knife, keys. She used this collection as an idiom to portray sayings of the Ghanaian Ashanti, like: 'The ears of a chief are like a strainer, there are more than a thousand ways to them'. She also discovered sayings that related to the relationship between the Ashanti and Europeans: 'If there had been no poverty in Europe, then the white man would not have come and spread his cloths in Africa.'

Table theatre

To summarize then: the still life is still being used as a bearer of coded moral messages, but it is being done in a new way. Unequivocal piety is no longer part of it. The contemporary still life provides a handle for (self) examination, analysis of the human spirit and the spirit of the times and the exploration of our changing relationship with our mortality, our possible soul, our possessions and eternity – but without reaching any compelling conclusions.

Yet even though the artists no longer uphold a standard Christian conviction, they seem to consciously make use of the moralistic image of the genre, even as they prefer to leave us with conjectures and questions rather than conveniently arranged conclusions. By their choice of still life they seem not only to indicate that their work can be understood symbolically and have possible moralistic connotations, but they also ensure that it becomes part of the impressive chain of still lifes in art history. In this way they invite the audience to compare their contemporary displays of objects with all those other arrangements of things that have been immortalized through the centuries.

The still life is especially suitable for this game of looking back and forth, since the genre deals invariably with concrete goods that are depicted on a domestic scale. In the defined area of the table theatre the similarities and differences between various eras and places are clearly visible. For until the end of time, our food and our possessions will not only testify to our existence but also to our desires and fears. New elements are concerns about our garbage with regard to the environment, our consumer society, and the promise of digital perpetuity. Our tendency to measure our status and happiness by material things is undiminished, as is our concern about what we have and what we think we need to make the most of our existence. The still life will most certainly be rediscovered again and again by many artists as an ideal genre to confirm, unveil and examine who we are and who we want to be. ■

Translated by Pleuke Boyce

Digital Humanities and Low Countries Culture

[REINIER SALVERDA]

The beginning of the virtual world may seem like prehistory today, yet it was only 1990 when Tim Berners-Lee invented the World Wide Web. His vision was to build a digital global brain in an interactive information sharing community, which would overcome the obstacles of the real world, in particular physical distance, time zones, geographical barriers, national borders, and differences of language and culture.

By 1995, when I first went online at University College London (UCL), myriads of websites were out there already, offering instant access to any subject under the sun. Every day, millions of people around the world were sharing more information than all the world's encyclopedias and dictionaries together. Growth has been explosive ever since, and today personal computers, laptops and tablets are everywhere; so too are mobile phones, the social media and an ever-growing array of intelligent apps – all part of a constantly innovating digital architecture which connects us to anything anywhere anytime.

Just a mouse click away, this virtual world constitutes an incredibly rich resource. And so far, humankind has shown itself remarkably versatile in handling this new domain. Our fingertips, eyes and brains have adapted; and learning today is increasingly driven by playful exploration and peer interaction via the social media. Facebook's impact - with its 1.3 billion users, from very many, very different cultures, who are nonetheless in direct contact everyday – is massive, generating instant global trends, new forms of understanding and cooperation, sharing games, blogs and videos as well as the fierce debates that mark the fault lines of modern global culture. In the process, WiFi has become a basic necessity of life, and the original notion of an information superhighway has morphed into a vehicle serving many other purposes – infotainment, glamour and hype; spreading values, improving logistics, as well as increasing online sales; piracy, identity theft, plagiarism and other fraud; cyber attacks, encryption, war games, and global surveillance of people's behaviour and private lives. And today, with the arrival of virtual reality, its new visualizations and other sensory experiences, the next step may be upon us.

All this, however, has not come about without some rather costly learning curves – witness how the ambition to have the domain of Dutch government and administration fully digitised from 2017 has run into serious problems.

New defence computer systems are not fit for purpose; newly developed digital systems for social security are causing enormous cost overruns; and about half of all Dutch primary schools do not have a proper internet connection. The lesson being learnt the hard way here is of the basic need to put every effort into designing properly working and cost effective systems for the public domain, which actually deliver the required services and meet the interests of both society and its citizens.

Digital humanities for Low Countries culture

Within the domain of arts and culture, the field of digital humanities (DH for short) was defined recently by Jane Winters, the new Professor of Digital History at the Institute of Historical Research in London, as 'applying digital tools and methods to humanities research and coming up with new and interesting ways of doing things as a result' – a deceptively simple formula for a whole new world of investigative and imaginative possibilities.

Digital humanities began in Italy in the late 1940s, when the Jesuit father Roberto Busa (1913-2011) pioneered the use of the computer for text searches in the massive works of St Thomas Aquinas. Busa´s *Index Thomisticus* ran to fifty-six printed volumes in the 1970s, was then issued on CD-ROM in 1989, followed by a web-based version in 2005. Today, many universities have a centre for digital humanities, where people are delivering new courses, handbooks and research, and sharing their results through scholarly publications and discussion of innovative ideas and best practice on the relevant online platforms, such as *Debates in Digital Humanities*, the *Digital Humanities Quarterly* (DHQ), *Digital Scholarship in the Humanities* (DSH), and the *Journal of Digital Humanities*.

A major new development in the Netherlands is the construction of a digital research infrastructure for the humanities called CLARIAH (i.e. **C**ommon **L**ab **R**esearch **I**nfrastructure for the **A**rts & **H**umanities). This four-year project, launched in June 2015 and directed from the Huygens Institute in The Hague, is carried out by a nationwide consortium which brings the digital capacities of the humanities research institutes, universities and research councils together with those of the National Archives and the Royal Library, as well as the immense audiovisual collections of the museums and *Beeld en Geluid*, in the media park at Hilversum. In Flanders, meanwhile, there is the active research community DHu.f which, based in Antwerp with a link to the Huygens Institute, brings together a wide range of research groups in Flanders and beyond, working on Low Countries literature, visual poetics, medieval and archaeological studies, computational psycholinguistics and translation.

Big data is the key word here. As in Britain, where the UK Web Archive of the British Library holds some 2 billion resources today, so CLARIAH´s focus will be on large scale collections, in particular in the three fields of social and economic history, audiovisual media studies, and text and language studies.

In language studies, the Nederlab project for the study of structure, variation and change in language builds on the expertise gained in several earlier projects which are now coming together: the Language Portal for the linguistic investigation of Dutch, Frisian and Afrikaans; the linguistic databases of the Institute for Dutch Lexicology and the CLARIN project for innovative language resources; as well as the Endangered Languages Archive (TLA) at the Max Planck Institute for Psycholinguistics in Nijmegen, which preserves the vanishing voices and oral cultures of some 120 very endangered languages from around the world. In 2015, this archive was the first digital-born heritage site to gain official recognition in UNESCO´s Register of the Memory of the World.

Meanwhile, in the field of history, many major collections have already been or are being digitised, archival records held in the huge colonial archives of the Dutch East and West Indies Companies (VOC & WIC), the Dutch Prize Papers in the British National Archives in Kew, and centuries of Dutch shipping data on the Baltic trade in the Sound Toll Register in Copenhagen. Over the coming years the immense Amsterdam City Archives, with their 20 million documents from 1656 till the present (of which so far only 7% has been digitised), will become available in digital form. Together with the ongoing digitisation of many other important archives, in Antwerp, in New York, in Cape Town, India, Indonesia and Japan, this will provide a far wider empirical basis for research, and will revolutionize – in scale, in depth and in detail, through visualization as well as by analytic, theoretical and experimental modelling - our understanding of Low Countries history and culture.

Handling data of such diversity and magnitude will require the use of advanced digital tools for cross- and multidisciplinary research. Very useful in this respect is the historical-geographical infrastructure of the HISGIS project of the Fryske Akademy. Working with the University of Amsterdam, the National Institute for Cultural Heritage (RCE) and the National Land Register (Kadaster), HISGIS is building a digital geographic grid covering all of the Netherlands down to the individual plot, digitised to an accuracy of within one metre. Feeding unlimited ranges of historical information of any kind into this infrastructure makes it possible to undertake totally new kinds of research into correlations between, and modelling of, the available data. One result of this has been the painstaking reconstruction of how, through centuries of *impoldering* in the Middle Ages, the Frisian monasteries continuously expanded their land holdings - thus laying the foundation for the wealth and power of Fryslân, with its own stadholder, as an independent province within the Dutch Republic, with its own language, Frisian, today available in Google Translate. When, next, HISGIS links up with the historical databases mentioned above, this will make it possible to investigate both the general patterns and the detailed workings of the important Frisian contribution to the maritime, economic and political history of the Netherlands.

Impact: issues and expectations

Going beyond the projects just mentioned we can see how the digital revolution is already having a massive impact on the humanities.

At a practical level there are implications, priorities and decisions to be taken on what to retain in our archives, libraries and museums - plus how and where to store it, and for how long, but also, what to forget and discard,

Holland House Library,
London,
September 1940

and why. It also matters for what purposes we build our infrastructures, what technologies are adopted, and what practices will develop - of collaboration in harvesting and sharing of data; of protocols on sustainability, security and retrievability of digital data; of rules on plagiarism and privacy. Useful guidelines are set out in the new National Strategy for Digital Heritage, drawn up in 2015.

A crucial issue here, which goes well beyond humanities research and directly affects Dutch international publishers such as Elsevier and Brill, is: What principles to adopt for the world of information? Should it be fair trade or free trade? The free trade view is that information is a matter of enterprise, business and profit, of copyright, property rights, money and patents. The alternative is to start thinking from the viewpoint that knowledge and information is a common good which belongs to all mankind, and that international sharing offers a better way forward. Brill now offers open access solutions at all levels of publication, while Dutch academics are campaigning actively for fair open access for humanities publications. For a wider perspective on this issue – working on the principle that information and discoveries should benefit everyone on the planet, especially in the field of education, languages, cultures and society – there is UNESCO with its Information for All Programme (IFAP) and its Recommendation on Universal Access to Multilingual Cyberspace.

As for the impact of DH, the CLARIAH infrastructure is expected to become a major instrument for accessing and exploring Dutch culture, its heritage, arts and humanities. Just as in the Dutch Golden Age, when the microscope made possible all kinds of new discoveries, so today DH is bringing new ways of doing research, with vast new capacities for modelling, pattern analysis, experimental data manipulation and theory testing. These new techniques and the discoveries they produce will generate new vistas for humanities research, in any field within the arts, humanities and social world that we may be interested in, from abstract art and nomadic literature to Sumerian medicine.

Much more is at stake here than just technical innovation. As Peter Burke sees it, we are witnessing a great leap forward, from the *Encyclopédie* in the eighteenth century to our *Wikipedia* of the twenty-first. Back in the eighteenth century, as we know from Robert Darnton, the biggest bestsellers produced by the pirating international publishing industry were books with forbidden information, often combining philosophy and pornography. Today, what we find on the internet is that sex is the biggest magnet; and developments are driven by curiosity, imagination and desire, by freely sharing information and knowledge, as much as by competition, power politics, fear, greed, and the human hunting instinct.

In this wider perspective, DH can be expected to engender very significant new potentialities in the cultural field, in music, in art, in museums, in entertainment and heritage, in the media, in literature, in publishing and in our everyday lives. And as we are delving more deeply into the virtual world of meaning, sound, image, values and imagination, new ventures will arise to enhance our capabilities with ingenious apps in order to help us realize Prospero's dream, connecting us to a million *Midsummer Night's Dreams*, and going far beyond the wildest imaginings in the science fiction of Edgar Allan Poe and Jorge Luis Borges.

The contribution from digital humanities

The question, then, is not whether the digital revolution will transform the humanities, but rather how. So what should we expect of digital humanities in the near future?

Here, it may be of some use to take a look at the policies and strategies we have in place for this digital future. At the national level, the Netherlands now has its Agenda for Science, while at the European level there is the agenda of Horizon 2020. In both these agendas, however, the humanities have been allocated a rather minor position, with some pious words about creativity and about their possible societal relevance. But the dominant issues in those agendas are health, food, mobility, business, industry and cutting edge innovations in sciences and technology. As a consequence, crucial policies and standards risk being defined without sufficient input from the humanities.

They do have a contribution to make though. Of basic importance is the insight that however big our data, and however massive and powerful our research tools, in the end we will always need the high level skills of close reading - such as the deciphering and decoding of very heterogeneous document material; weighing its relevance, truthfulness and significance; engaging in linguistic and lexicographic analysis; together with critical interpretation and an assessment of what is its point in a historic or other context. To my mind, therefore, what we really need to develop in digital humanities are innovative techniques and methodologies for close reading, building on the skills of philological examination that have been developed in centuries of humanities scholarship, as they are being practised today by a scholar such as Franco Moretti in his essays on *Distant Reading* (2013).

A step further would be to consider the increasing symbiosis and interaction between, on the one hand, digitally enhanced humans and, on the other hand, humanised robots. The size, scope and complexity of the information around us are constantly increasing, so the question arises: How do we manage? Are we really still in control, as users, designers, organisers and builders of our

information systems? Or, are we becoming mere extensions of those systems, subject to their rules and the way in which they are structured? Here, to help us out, robots are becoming increasingly necessary. Everywhere today new technologies are being developed and adapted specifically to deal with human beings, such as the provision of care for humans by robots, which is presently being introduced in Singapore. The corollary is to humanise and socialise these robots so they can adequately engage with us. In his Paris laboratory, Pierre-Yves Oudeyer (2006) is doing just that, by giving his robots language, and the freedom to try and develop, through playful interaction, the necessary basic mechanisms of vocal mimicry, language play, metaphor and poetry. In my view, cross-over phenomena, such as human enhancement through smart apps and with intelligent robots that can handle language and communication, are a very important theme for digital humanities to explore.

A humanist perspective

Michel Foucault may have predicted the end of the humanities, but today DH, the digital revolution and the virtual world are offering a new beginning.

In the process, our humanities research and how this is being done will undoubtedly be transformed. What will not change, however, is the age-old question: What about us humans? In this respect, the significance of digital humanities is that they offer new ways of investigating our many and very diverse human faculties, talents, endeavours, ambitions and desires, our own mental makeup, along with our cultural heritage, languages, storytelling, literature, imagination, and so on.

Today, these issues are as fascinating, and as difficult to understand and to resolve, as they have ever been. But they matter immensely for our understanding of human nature, and for the future of humankind. It is our common humanity which, in the end, is the deepest wellspring of our disciplines. So what I expect we will see is how the humanities will go on reinventing themselves, as they have always done - and as they are doing again today, in the era of digital humanities. ■

FURTHER READING

Berners-Lee, Tim (1999). *Weaving the Web*. London.

Burke, Peter (2012). *A Social History of Knowledge,* vol. II: *From the* Encyclopédie *to Wikipedia*. Cambridge.

Darnton, Robert (2009). *The Case for Books. Past, Present, and Future*. New York.

Moretti, Franco (2013). *Distant Reading*. London.

Oudeyer, Pierre-Yves (2006). *Self-organization in the Evolution of Speech*. Oxford.

Schreibman, Susan et al. (ed.) (2004). *A Companion to Digital Humanities*. Oxford.

Warwick, Claire et al. (eds.) (2012). *Digital Humanities in Practice*. London.

PLATFORMS, COMMUNITIES AND DEBATES

Debates in Digital Humanities – www.dhdebates.gc.cuny.edu/debates

Digital Humanities Quarterly (DHQ) – www.digitalhumanities.org/dhq

Digital Scholarship in the Humanities (DSH) – www.dsh.oxfordjournals.org

Fair Open Access for Humanities Publications – www.openlibhums.org

Frontiers in Digital Humanities – www.journal.frontiersin.org/journal/digital-humanities

Journal of Digital Humanities – www.digitalhumanities.org

DIGITAL HUMANITIES FOR LOW COUNTRIES CULTURE

www.brill.com – Brill Online Books, Journals, Newsletters in the Humanities

www.clariah.nl – CLARIAH – Common Lab Infrastructure for the Arts & Humanities

www.delpher.nl – full text search engine Dutch books, journals and newspapers

www.dighum.uantwerpen.be – DHu.f (Digital Humanities Flanders)

www.dbnl.org. – Digital Library of Dutch Literature

www.edata.nl – *E-Data & Research*, online DH-newsletter of DANS (KNAW)

www.hisgis.nl – Historical-Geographical Information System NL (HISGIS)

www.nederlab.nl – Nederlab

www.taalportaal.org – Linguistics of Dutch, Frisian and Afrikaans

www.openlibhums.org – making Open Access in the Humanities a reality

www.unesco.nl/memory-world-programma-en-comite – Documentary Heritage NL

Felix Nussbaum, *Selbstbildnis mit Judenpas* (Self-Portrait with Jewish Passport), 1943
© Felix-Nussbaum-Haus, Osnabrück

Chronicle

Architecture

The Markthal in Rotterdam by MVRDV © scagliobrakkee

Life After Rotterdam
Dutch Architecture Edges Its Way out of Crisis

2014 was Rotterdam's year. The city spent decades rediscovering itself after the reconstruction, in search of a pleasant city atmosphere. Sixty years on, that process seemed complete. The new station was opened by the Queen of the Netherlands in 2014 - with a majestic lobby designed by Jan Benthem of Benthem Crouwel Architects as its crowning glory. This was followed by the largest office building in the Netherlands, De Rotterdam, by Rem Koolhaas, who also contributed the Stadstimmerhuis in 2015 to house municipal services. The cherry on the cake, however, was unveiled on 1 October 2014: the Markthal by MVRDV, a colourful gateway or vault, where the Queen received the exuberant kisses of market vendors. All these buildings were labelled architectural highlights, and not only in the Netherlands. So what's all this about a crisis in Dutch architecture? Or among Dutch architects? The fact that Rotterdam can now be declared complete as a figurehead of urban planning is in fact an ominous sign. What next?

Dutch architecture is reaping what it has sown over the last twenty-five years, its quality praised to the skies at home and abroad. After the previous crisis in the 1980s an unprecedented period of boom took place, fuelled not least by government measures, including an architectural institute and fund, both also based in Rotterdam, and Architectuur Lokaal, a centre of expertise for local initiatives. The time was ripe for it too. In 1991 the 'Vinex operation' started up, with the aim of building as many as 634,000 houses on the outskirts of the cities, new residential districts with surprisingly diverse architecture to meet a changed need: that of flexible, spacious housing in beautiful suburban surroundings.

The current architectonic crisis is different from that of thirty years ago, as it is caused by a surplus of residential buildings as well as utilities, offices and shops. Architects are affected by concurrent movements, such as the closing of care homes and nursing homes, mergers of municipal authorities and in particular the inexorable demise of the office market. Business parks no longer pay off, and are largely left vacant without prospect of improvement. Rem Koolhaas's celebrated building De Rotterdam was planned fifteen years ago (called the MAB tower at the time). The colossus, uniting offices, a hotel and leisure facilities, is finally finished, but leaves behind the towers where the municipal authorities have been housed until now.

Another paradise for architects is entering a transitional phase. After three decades of build-up, Almere - the new city in the province of Flevoland - is having its doubts about making the leap to becoming a true big city. Population growth has slowed. The only remedy comes in the form of self-build plots in the new district of Poort. Self-builds are like lifebelts for architects, although the architect's task is reduced to that of an intermediary between municipal government, banks and suppliers, involving more advice than design. A new form of consultancy is born. Standardisation has made way for individualisation and buyers decide what they will have. People are no longer interested in terraced houses, preferring a detached *notariswoning*, with its classic features and hipped roof, a 1930s villa or a farmhouse, none of which require an architect.

For sixty years Rotterdam was a Valhalla for developers and urban planners, a laboratory, operating differently from The Hague or Amsterdam. Architects were able to design new cities almost from scratch. At the Venice Architecture Biennale 2014 the Dutch pavilion looked back on this utopia, designed by Jaap Bakema (1914-1981). He was responsible for the first shopping promenade in Europe, the Lijnbaan. Countless architects have had the opportunity to contribute to the reconstruction of the destroyed city. Many of them began their careers here, including Mecanoo, Rem Koolhaas, Jo Coenen, MVRDV, Ben van Berkel and before them Maaskant, J.J.P. Oud (1890-1963), Willem van Tijen (1894-1974), Brinkman & Van der Vlugt and Wim Quist. The city also became the international base for many Dutch architects, who set off in droves to China, Qatar, Germany and Spain. What was their secret? It was their new twist on modernism, no longer as dogmatic as Jaap Bakema with his Lijnbaan, but playful, perhaps even ironic. They were open to new symbols which were particularly welcome in rising economies.

The Schieblock in Rotterdam by DUS Architects
© O. van Duivenbode

One of the unique qualifications of Dutch architecture of the last twenty years has been its public domain roots. Rem Koolhaas can be seen as an ambassador of Dutch architecture, possibly surpassed by Adriaan Geuze of West8, who has transformed urban areas from Copenhagen to Madrid and was responsible for the pleasant square and park in front of Rotterdam Station.

Over the past five years architects' firms have frequently remarked that there will never be a time like this again. Apart from the odd Markthal, 'iconic' buildings are things of the past, now seen as an inappropriate form of self-congratulatory architecture. Instead, converted industrial heritage has become relevant, for instance creating cultural clusters showcasing the raw traces of the past, as in the Energiehuis in Dordrecht and the ENCI power station in Roermond in the province of Limburg.

The country is also teeming with small-scale initiatives. The 3D Print Canal House in Amsterdam-Noord and the Schieblock in Rotterdam particularly spring to mind. The former is a building gradually emerging from a 3D printer, based on a design by DUS Architects. The Schieblock is a feat of repurposing based on a property from the 1970s, previously presumed a lost cause, on the edge of Rotterdam's Hofplein. It has been turned inside out, with a roof garden for drinking beer and exercising. For a while a city farmer operated on the roof and it has acquired a wooden bridge con-

necting it to the old Hofplein station, the Luchtsingel or 'air canal'. The money was cobbled together from crowdfunding. Once again it is not a case of inspiring architecture; aesthetics is the last means of expression. The architecture, by architect firm ZUS, sprang from dissatisfaction with the emptiness of the building while it awaited demolition and rebuilding. That could take another decade, the architects thought, and meanwhile nothing would happen. Unused premises at the edge of the city centre are like open wounds, detracting from the quality of life.

It is reassuring to see that architecture is temporary and that this gives it significance. The demolition of 1980s office colossi in and around city centres has had a serious impact, with disruption from the large quantities of building waste and disturbance to living standards lasting years. Temporary architecture circumvents this danger. Dutch architecture has wrestled its way through the crisis with small-scale projects which impress in a different way from those of twenty years ago. They are as colourful as a bouquet of wild flowers, while avoiding being purely cosmetic or trying too hard to attract admiration. It will take some getting used to, but in the end they might just give new meaning to the concept of architecture.

JAAP HUISMAN
Translated by Anna Asbury

Economics

The Beer Giant with Belgian Roots
AB InBev and SABMiller Merge

The largest brewery in the world, Belgian-Brazilian AB InBev, is merging with the second largest, South-African-British SABMiller, to create a beer giant which will leave all other brewers far behind. A few figures: 30% of all beer sold will come from the new group, with the Dutch company Heineken trailing far behind with a market share of 9%. Almost 60% of all beer profits worldwide will flow to the new beer conglomerate. The company will have 224,000 people working for it, producing at least 220 brands, including such resounding names as Stella Artois, Jupiler, Corona, Budweiser, Beck's and Pilsner Urquell. Who are the most important shareholders? A couple of aristocratic Belgian families.

The history of the world's number one brewery dates back to 1366, when beer was brewed in Den Horen, a tavern in Leuven. For a long time the brewery was run by the Artois family, transferring via marriage to the De Spoelberch and De Mévius families. In Belgium their Stella Artois brewery competed for many years with Piedboeuf, which started up in 1853 when Jean-Théodore Piedboeuf began brewing beer in the cellar of the old castle of Jupille. Marriage alliances made the Van Damme family the main shareholder of Piedboeuf.

For decades Artois and Piedboeuf competed to outdo one another, both taking over small brewers all over Belgium and thus growing into the two most important breweries in the country. In the 1970s Artois and Piedboeuf took over the bankrupt Brasseries de Ghlin at the request of then Minister of Finance Edmond Leburton. The De Spoelberch, De Mévius and Van Damme families then began trading shares amongst themselves in absolute secrecy, while their beers continued to compete. In 1987 Artois and Piedboeuf merged to form Interbrew, with 60% of the Belgian beer market.

International expansion proceeded rapidly. In 1995 the Canadian brewing group Labatt was taken over for 57 billion francs (1.4 billion euros), a gigantic sum at the time, by Belgian standards at any rate. Interbrew became a world player and floated on the stock market in 2000. In 2004 the company took another important step, fusing with the Brazilian group AmBev to create InBev. In 2008 it took over the largest brewery in the US, Anheuser-Busch, for 45 billion euros. AB InBev, the largest brewing company in the world, was born. Now it is set to take over the second largest brewery in the world, SABMiller, for 92 billion euros. The Belgian dynasties De Spoelberch, De Mévius and Van Damme, who now have around 200 descendants, will be the largest shareholders with 24%.

For a long time the De Spoelberch and De Mévius families played a leading role in the beer conglomerate, but for some years now the key figure has been Alexandre van Damme, whose fortune is estimated at 3.2 billion euros. Some suggest that is a serious underestimation, claiming that he is richer than Albert Frère, making him Belgium's wealthiest citizen. His money is by no means only tied up in AB InBev. Two years ago, for example, he invested 585 million euros in the coffee manufacturer Douwe Egberts. Interestingly the Columbian Santo Domingo family pumped 275 million euros into Douwe Egberts at the same time. The Columbians were already an important shareholder in the second largest brewery in the world, SABMiller, with which AB InBev is now merging. Clearly it's a small world.

Douwe Egberts is not Alexandre van Damme's only other investment either. He is passionate

STELLA ARTOIS

She is a thing of beauty

about football and a shareholder in RSC Ander-lecht. He generally invests through the 3G Capital fund, managed by Jorge Paulo Lemann, Marcel Herrmann Telles and Carlos Alberto Sicupira, the Brazilians who owned brewery AmBev and be-came shareholders of AB InBev after the merger with Interbrew. Their investments are focused on the food and drink sector, including the American hamburger chain Burger King and ketchup manu-facturer Heinz. Once in a while rumours circulate that they would like to make a bid for Coca-Cola. Evidently the sky is the limit.

The new beer conglomerate will be managed by the Brazilian Carlos Brito, CEO of AB InBev since 2005, who operates from New York, although the head office of the merged group will remain offi-cially located in Leuven. Brito's business style is well known, involving cutting costs where possible. That's not likely to change, as the primary reason for the merger between the first and second larg-est companies in the beer world is to create added value for the shareholders. Those Belgian dynas-ties will reap the financial benefits.

EWALD PIRONET
Translated by Anna Asbury

Iconoclasm as a War Strategy
Past and Present

A raging mob tore through the Low Countries in the middle of the sixteenth century. They destroyed church interiors, monasteries, chapels and abbeys, smashed statues from their plinths, slashed paint-ings with lances and left books and robes irrepara-bly destroyed. The unprecedented destructive urge of the Protestant Reformation had enormous con-sequences for the religious and cultural heritage of the region. It also marked the symbolic beginning of a long struggle, which would ultimately lead to the redrawing of maps and a split from the Roman Catholic Church. The Iconoclastic Fury (Beelden-storm) is an important episode in the history of the Low Countries, and one which shows striking par-allels with more recent conflicts.

On 31 October 1517, Maarten Luther nailed his famous 95 Theses to the door of the Schlosskirche (All Saints' Church) in Wittenberg, an act that is widely regarded as the catalyst for the wave of ref-ormation which spread rapidly through large parts of Europe. Charles V, whose dominions included the Low Countries, responded harshly and repres-sively, but ultimately unsuccessfully: he was una-ble to prevent the onward march of Protestantism. More and more people fell in with Luther's ideas and those of his successor, John Calvin. The Cal-vinists increasingly preached in public, and their sermons drew large numbers. On 10 August 1566, one such sermon in the village of Steenvoorde (now in Northern France, twenty-five kilometres from Ypres), led by a Protestant refugee who had recently returned from England, got out of hand. At the end of the sermon, twenty members of the listening crowd rampaged through a nearby mon-astery, and the first images were destroyed. In the ensuing weeks and months, groups of iconoclasts vandalised large numbers of church and monas-tery interiors throughout the Low Countries.

The aim of the first Reformers was to get rid of Church practices that they regarded as abuses: the selling of indulgences, the external display of

Jan Luyken, *The Iconoclastic Fury in Flanders and Brabant*, 1677-1679, etching © Rijksmuseum, Amsterdam

power and wealth and the encouraging of believers to worship icons. All that pomp and splendour distracted churchgoers from the true faith, which in the views of the Reformers should be based not on external appearances but on inner perception. They drew their inspiration from the second of the Ten Commandments: 'Thou shalt not make unto thee any graven image, or any likeness of any thing that is in heaven above, or that is in the earth beneath, or that is in the water under the earth'.

The reason so many people were attracted to these Protestant preachers was not just the religious message of simplicity and piety that they preached. The movement undoubtedly had a base. Even more than the espoused doctrine, the masses blamed the Church and the state for the widespread socioeconomic misery throughout the region. It is not a coincidence that the Iconoclastic Fury began in the countryside, where people were living in poverty. The public rage stemmed mainly from their aversion to those in power: the Church of Rome and the strict, absolutist Spanish authority that was established in the Low Countries.

The reaction to the widespread destruction was not long in coming. After a short period of trying to appease the Protestants, the Spanish King Philip II dispatched the Duke of Alva with an army to restore order to the Low Countries and punish the guilty. The Iconoclastic Fury was therefore also the cradle of the Eighty Years' War, which ultimately led to the break-up of the Low Countries into a Dutch Republic in the north - the Republic of the Seven United Netherlands - and the Southern Netherlands. Catholicism rapidly re-established itself in the south. Churches and monasteries that had been stripped bare were once again adorned with imagery, even more richly than in the past.

The history of Christianity is marked by a continual oscillation between revering icons (and thereby the external display of power) and striving for a pure, 'icon-free' Church. The history of iconoclasm is in fact by no means a purely Christian phenomenon: Islam and Judaism have also seen many iconoclasts in their history. The plundering of important cultural symbols and the destruction of monuments, books or works of art has always been an important element of warfare and, as recent conflicts have shown, that is still the case today. The destruction of the images of Buddha in Afghanistan by the Taliban (2001), or the widespread destruction of cultural heritage in Syria by Daesh, show that history constantly repeats itself. As in the past, today's iconoclasts are not protesting against the images themselves, but rather the value that their enemy attaches to them. By destroying works of art and precious objects, they hope to destabilise or bring down societies or religions. The link with the Iconoclastic Fury of 450 years ago is not difficult to see.

ELINE VAN ASSCHE
Translated by Julian Ross

A Daesh warrior destroying a sculpture on the city gate of the former Assyrian capital Nineveh

Language

'Dutch Translation in Practice'
Essential Strategies for Translation and a Wealth of Resources

This practical and comprehensive translation handbook is aimed mainly at learner-translators from Dutch to English with CEFRL level C in Dutch and native or near-native competence in English. As the authors point out in their introduction, globalisation, EU enlargement and the European Commission's New Framework Strategy for Multilingualism (2005), plus student mobility and multilingualism, have led to an increased interest in translation and a need to rethink teaching. Some 27 million people worldwide speak Dutch, either as a mother tongue or as a second or foreign language. Yet when Dutch texts are translated into English, the most widely spoken language in the world, with an estimated 1.8 billion speakers, they become accessible to a much larger public. Hence the importance of training good Dutch–English translators.

Dutch Translation in Practice can be read from beginning to end or can be dipped into as needed. That said, as chapter one sets out the authors' approach and outlines the basic principles of translation, it is certainly advisable to take it as your starting point. There are nine chapters in total, each built around a particular theme reflecting contemporary life and culture in the Low Countries. The themes range from people and places to Dutch language and culture, literature, employment, finance and economics, media and communications, art history and exhibitions, fashion and design and, lastly, the Earth, energy and the environment.

As mentioned, chapter one lists the various steps involved in translation: firstly, an initial read-through of the text with research and reflection on the target audience; secondly, an analysis of the various linguistic features of the text plus word and sentence meaning; and thirdly an assessment of the style of writing, and the importance of style for the target text and its audience. After the initial assessment, step four is to make a first draft of the translation. The fifth and final step is to read through and revise the translation, an absolutely essential step, for which time should be set aside, as the authors point out. Chapter 2 offers a summary of the revision procedure and the conclusion to the book explains in more detail how to go about it, including strategies for dealing with tight deadlines when it might not be possible to revise every word.

Each chapter starts with a page or two of introduction to the chosen theme and then offers two texts on that theme which one of the authors has at some time been asked to translate. Some of these texts come from the Netherlands and others from Flanders, while in chapter 2 there is a text from Surinam, so they illustrate a wide range not only of subjects but also of both styles and vocabulary. Readers are taken through an in-depth analysis of each of the texts. The format is always the same, firstly, decide on your translation strategies and techniques: what are the first things you notice about the text, and what do you know about the target audience for your translation and how it will affect your translation? These aspects are then discussed at length, offering background information and a wealth of resources - most of them online and therefore easy to access - which can be used for the research necessary for the text concerned.

In step 2 of the analysis, text and language, there is a discussion of various words and expressions occurring in the text that may be unfamiliar or difficult to translate, including names, subject-specific terminology, compound nouns and so on, as well as advice on working out the infinitive of verb parts. Complicated sentences are broken down into clauses to aid comprehension and facilitate translation, with strategies for dealing with structures that differ in Dutch and English. Step 3 is a stylistic analysis of the text and an assessment of the style appropriate to the target text, bearing in mind that the style appropriate to the target audience might differ from that of the source text. Finally, after the discussion of each of the texts there is a sample translation of it.

Between the two texts and their treatments there is a practical tips section in each chapter which provides a more in-depth discussion of some of the translation issues, thorough background information and more resources. Sometimes the emphasis is on source text comprehension and sometimes on target text production. Punctuation is also dealt with, stressing the importance of correct punctuation for comprehension.

Chapters close with a third text, for which a sample translation is offered at the end of the book. In the concluding pages there is a list of grammatical terms and a section on useful resources for problems that the authors have not covered - grammars, reference works on translation and online translation resources. Finally, an index that includes the various topics dealt with and the different points of language and grammar makes for easy reference.

To sum up, *Dutch Translation in Practice* is a really excellent, comprehensive and useful textbook that teaches the development of translation strategies to guide decision making during translation and offers a wealth of resources for reference. If readers apply the advice and use the information contained in it, they are certain to achieve what the authors regard as the goal of translation: to produce texts in English that function effectively for the purpose for which they are required. A must-buy for (aspiring) Dutch-English translators. Beware though, a quick look at online vendors reveals that prices vary hugely from very expensive to very reasonable, so be sure to look at a variety of different sites. Some sites also offer an electronic version, which makes searching for information very easy.

LINDSAY EDWARDS

Jane Fenoulhet & Alison E. Martin, *Dutch Translation in Practice*, Routledge, Oxford, 2015.

Dutch and Other Languages in Seventeenth-Century Britain and the Dutch Republic
Two Monographs by Christopher Joby

What we have before us here are two substantial scholarly monographs by one British academic, both focussing on the history of Dutch in contact with other languages, in the Dutch Republic of course, but especially also in early modern Britain. Both adopt the cultural-historical perspective on European multilingualism as developed in Peter Burke´s seminal contributions, and combine this with Peter Trudgill's approach to historical, socio- and contact linguistics. And both remind us how near England has always been, in close contact and competition with the Low Countries. Just two days´

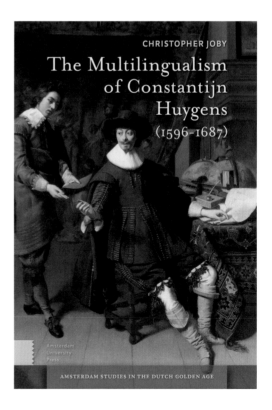

sailing across the North Sea, it was for centuries the Protestant ally of the Dutch in Europe, though often also a fierce rival in politics, in enterprise, trade and commerce.

The first of Christopher Joby's books presents a historical case study of the multilingualism of Sir Constantijn Huygens (1596-1687), whose wonderful portrait by Thomas de Keyser (now in the National Gallery in London) graces its cover. Dutch statesman and man of letters, servant to the House of Orange and Renaissance humanist scholar, Huygens's contribution to Anglo-Dutch relations during the Golden Age was handled in 1962 by Professor Fred Bachrach CBE (with a second volume edited in 2013, by Evelien Bachrach and Ad Leerintveld). Joby, therefore, can concentrate fully on this 'truly remarkable early modern polyglot', who wrote poetry and letters playing in and with the eight languages he mastered - Dutch, French, Latin, Greek, Italian, Spanish, English and German (plus a little Hebrew and Portuguese).

Language and languages take centre stage here, in seven detailed and attractive chapters on Huygens's multidimensional multilingualism - successively, on his acquisition of those languages; on the keen ear he developed for different languages, dialects and their uses; on the use of language(s) in his vast official and private correspondence, in thousands of his poems, in his translations, in his comedies and in language play; on his use of Dutch, alongside Latin, French and also Italian, in writings about music, science and architecture; on the way in which he presented himself through all these languages - sometimes mixing them up, sometimes shifting back and forth between them - as a learned and playful Erasmian humanist; and on the education, including language learning, of his children.

Joby's second book, with a portrait of William and Mary on its cover, goes far beyond the elite multilingualism of high-ranking individuals such as Huygens. Instead, it makes a formidable contribution to the historical sociolinguistics of English-Dutch language contact in early modern Britain, by focussing on the use of Dutch in a range of societal domains.

The period studied by Joby in this social history of language is the long Golden Age, beginning with the establishment in 1550 of the first Protestant Dutch Church, in Austin Friars in the City of London (still functioning today), and ends with the death in 1702 of the Stadholder-King William III, the first (and last) to unite the two countries under one ruler. This was indeed a very significant period, even though there have been other waves of Dutch-Flemish immigration which merit further investigation, both before 1550 (the Flemings who under William the Conqueror came to settle in the land of Madoc in southern Wales) and after 1702 (with the wars of Napoleon, and later the First and Second World Wars).

For documentary evidence on the British language situation during the seventeenth century, Joby's book extends well beyond what we know from the many Dutch loanwords in English. What he presents here - for the first time - is a huge collection of primary sources and archival documentation concerning the localities, communities and domains where, and the purposes for which, Dutch was used, in letters, wills and many other forms of communication. On this basis Joby demonstrates how the Dutch language - or rather, the various 'Dutches' concerned - had a very substantial presence in early modern Britain, across not just England but also in Scotland and Wales, where the language was used in everyday contact and competition with English, French and Latin, in many different social domains - in the church, in education and learning; in immigrant communities and their government; in domestic matters and the world of work, crafts and commerce; in court culture, literature and translation; as well as in diplomacy, military and naval matters.

Joby's two books make a major contribution to research into the social, linguistic and cultural historical dimensions of early modern multilingualism. As his findings demonstrate, there is a clear need for rewriting the standard histories of early

Literature

Émile Verhaeren
The Only National Poet Belgium Has Ever Had

If someone were to be nominated as the greatest Belgian of all time, it would surely have to be Émile Verhaeren (1855-1916). He was a man who wrote in French but who was regarded as a Fleming; and who died in the First World War as a staunch defender of gallant little Belgium. A poet with his boots on, fighting for the cause, indefatigably mounting the barricades for his fatherland; last bastion of civilisation in the face of the Teutonic barbarians; falling to his death under the wheels of a train at Rouen station in France, uttering the perfectly cast last words: 'Je meurs...ma femme...ma patrie' ('I am dying...my wife...my homeland').

In these famous last words, which are almost certainly apocryphal, Verhaeren's love for his wife, for whom he had created the monument *Les Heures claires* in 1896, goes hand in hand with his love for his homeland. They are appropriate words for a 'symbolic' death: a man who sang the praises of the leviathans of the New Age was crushed to death by one of those very machines. There can surely be no doubt, then, that this was the greatest Belgian of all time. Except that Verhaeren's name did not even appear on the 'Flemish' list of 111 nominees a few years ago in the quest for the greatest Belgian. And on the list of French-speaking Belgians, his name languished in a very modest 67th place.

Flemings who write in the French language fall between two stools today: too Flemish to be French-speakers and excluded by those who believe that 'the language is the nation'. It is unlikely that Verhaeren ever knew the Dutch language. Some remnants of the Flemish from his childhood may possibly have remained, the language spoken with other boys in the streets of his childhood village of Sint-Amands on the River Scheldt, and at village fairs; but there will not have been much of it, and the Jesuit priests at the Sint-Barbaracollege school in Ghent will have done a thorough job of eradicating what little there was. At the same time, Verhaeren's French was regarded in Paris as ex-

---

modern Dutch, and also of the English language, where the contribution from Dutch - amongst other languages with a significant influence on English - has been seriously underrated.

Both books come with an exemplary scholarly apparatus of references, notes, bibliography, and index. Both also contain uncommon illustrations regarding their subjects - maps, letters, paintings, poems, manuscripts, the Dutch house on Canvey Island, the Dutch Church in London and Huygens´s Dutch translations of John Donne. And both were published within a few months of each other, in prestigious book series, by two of the most reputable academic publishers in the Netherlands.

Not many researchers can pull off such an impressive double act. But Christopher Joby, who is Assistant Professor in the Department of Dutch at Hankuk University of Foreign Studies in Seoul, South Korea, just went and did it.

We owe him a great debt of gratitude for these two new and fascinating standard works.

REINIER SALVERDA

Christopher Joby, *The Multilingualism of Constantijn Huygens (1596-1687)*, Amsterdam Studies in the Dutch Golden Age, Amsterdam University Press, 2014, 350 pp.

Christopher Joby, *The Dutch Language in Britain (1550-1702). A Social History of the Use of Dutch in Early Modern Britain*, Brill's Studies in Language, Cognition and Culture, vol. 10, Brill, Leiden, 2015, 451 pp.

otic and savage, but it would be wrong to think that Verhaeren learned French late or with difficulty. At home, the Verhaeren family spoke French, and the priests trained him well. Verhaeren's idiosyncratic idiom is more likely to have been a deliberate stylistic device: 'une incorrection volontaire' ('a deliberate inexactitude'), as his biographer Jacques Marx claims.

We now know the truth. The young state of Belgium, which celebrated its 50th anniversary in 1880, sought its legitimacy against its large French neighbour by giving itself a glorious 'Flemish' past. *Les Flamandes* ('The Flemish women'), Verhaeren's debut published in 1883, fitted in perfectly with this strategy. If we are to believe Jacques Marx, Verhaeren also deliberately chose this Flemish identity, constructing it rather than emanating from it. For Verhaeren, Flanders was a literary market segment that he could feed with the landscapes of his youth: the broad, meandering River Scheldt, the heavy, pregnant skies, the 'solid beauty' of the women of Flanders, were all given a place against the backdrop of the mystique and sensuality which it was now obligatory to ascribe to Flanders - the two extremes of the fleshly and the pious. Flanders was a splendid alibi for Verhaeren. He was a Fleming, but one who preferred to be outside Flanders.

In his biographical essay from 1910, Stefan Zweig consecrated Verhaeren's position within the still young and prosperous Belgian nation. Verhaeren was nothing more or less than the very incarnation of the nation; proud of his Flemish roots and at the same time in the vanguard of industrial progress. The Belgian race was powerful, vital and sensual, active and industrious. Verhaeren, with all his contrasts, epitomised that: he was a child of the city and an inhabitant of the earth; Catholicism and socialism fought for supremacy within him. He was the prophet of the 'Belgian soul', the bell-ringer who had earlier called on the people to defend their territory and who now exhorted them to realise their own power with conscious pride.

But perhaps Verhaeren's literary strategy was not quite so deliberate. He may simply have had a flair for good timing. There are writers who are ahead of their time or who lag behind it. And there are writers who express their time, because they coincide with it or happen to be on the crest of the wave when it rolls over the beach. Verhaeren falls into this latter category. It may be that this makes him literally 'dated', in the sense of inextricably linked to a particular moment in time. What is in any event beyond dispute is his extraordinary capacity for empathy, for sharing in the suffering and the emerging forces of his time.

He became the first bard to sing the praises of the brutal grandeur of the factories and the spreading tentacles of the towns which were swallowing everything in their path. He was at once fascinated and horrified, but also saw that human progress could only come from the towns and cities. This was where masses of people, misery, movement, experience, labour, industry, science, revolt and

Theo Van Rysselberghe, *The Lecture*, 1903, Oil on canvas © Museum voor Schone Kunsten, Ghent.
Émile Verhaeren is wearing a bright red coat. Some of the other participants: Maurice Maeterlinck (seated first from right),
Félix Fénéon (leaning on the mantelpiece) and André Gide (head in hand, across from Verhaeren).

ideas came together. The clashes between them would give birth to the future, to a new world and a new earth. 'Le monde est trépidant de trains et de navires' ('The world is pulsating with trains and ships'). It is no surprise that the futurist Marinetti saw a forerunner in the Verhaeren who wrote *Les Villes tentaculaires* (1895).

Verhaeren's maturity as a poet in the 1890s brought the wide circulations and the fame. His work was read in Paris and in London, and the meeting with Stefan Zweig in 1902 opened the eyes of the German world to his oeuvre. Zweig did more than anyone to spread Verhaeren's fame in Europe. His biography of the poet was published in 1910 and was immediately translated into French.

Verhaeren was now frequently away from Belgium. He had lived in Paris since 1899, giving rise to the revealing comment: 'Je m'exile pour que la nostalgie de mon pays m'inspire mieux' ('I have exiled myself so that nostalgia for my country will inspire me the more'). He toured Germany and Russia, where he was even recognised in the street, delivering lectures on 'la culture de l'enthousiasme' which virtually became his trademark.

When war broke out in 1914, Verhaeren was ready for his final role. No *Innere Emigration* for this artist who wanted to express *his* time, who wanted to *be* his time. And this was a time which reeked of nationalism and militaristic hysteria. This European realised the bankruptcy of his humanitarian ideals and became an ardent patriot who discovered that he hated Germany. This convinced internationalist, who had once been the cultural conscience of Europe, had become a blinkered nationalist. When the Belgian King Albert I summoned the poet to De Panne, behind the front line, Verhaeren inspected the Belgian troops in the company of the royal couple. The rebellious poet, who had long been poet laureate, now became a propagandist who would serve his country and his sovereign as a loyal vassal.

Yet the artist that Émile Verhaeren was, can't easily be claimed; not as a symbolist, an anarchist; nor a monarchist or socialist, nor as a troubadour for Flanders. His genius lay in his ability to connect, whilst remaining rooted firmly in the local, with the great ideas and ideals of the time, and in some cases to initiate those ideas himself.

He was perhaps the only - and certainly the last - national poet that Belgium has ever had. But in order to become that, he could not survive the First World War. Belgium saw its finest hour between 1914 and 1918, its first and last transcendental moment in its more than 180 year history. Abroad, Belgium evoked admiration (Gallant Little Belgium) and sympathy (*La Belgique martyre* - The martyrdom of Belgium). The monarchy - the glue which bound together the structure of Belgium - also enjoyed its strongest period at this time, with its Knight-King watching over the nation, and with the poet laureate standing at his side on the beach at De Panne. But by 1918, that momentum was gone for good.

Verhaeren died at the right time, then. And he knew that the River Scheldt would remain faithful to him. In 1927 his body was returned to the place of his birth, the riverside village of Sint-Amands. He now lies there together with his wife beneath a black granite sarcophagus, for all the world standing ready to sail up the river at any moment like a container ship. It is worth a visit.

LUC DEVOLDERE
Translated by Julian Ross

English translations of some of Emile Verhaeren's oeuvre may be found in *Poems of Emile Verhaeren: Selected & Rendered into English by Alma Strettell, with a Portrait of the Author by John S. Sargent* (1915), Cornell University Library, Ithaca (NY), 2009, 106 pp.

In Honour of a Forerunner
The First Gay Novel in Modern World Literature

In 1904, twenty-three-year old Jacob de Haan wrote a novel called *Pijpelijntjes*. It was written in the naturalistic style of the French writer Émile Zola. De Haan depicted the day-to-day life of two men who lived in the Amsterdam neighbourhood the *Pijp*. The only difference with many novels from that era is that the two men had a sexual relationship. It is known as the first book ever in Dutch and world literature – that is not pornography - in which an author wrote so clearly about two men who were involved in a same-sex relationship. The other main reason the book is important is that de Haan portrayed the two characters as if it were the most common thing in the world to write about. Thirdly, he published it under his own name and not with an alias or anonymously. The title gave away that the book was not a common story; for all readers it must have been obvious that, with the storyline set in the Amsterdam neighbourhood the Pijp, it also had another connotation, as *pijpen* is the Dutch verb for *to perform fellatio*.

De Haan dedicated his book to another writer and medical doctor, Arnold Aletrino (1858-1916). For the in-crowd it was clear that the bisexual protagonist Sam, with his sadistic disposition, looked very much like Aletrino. The antagonist Joop very much resembled de Haan. It is an understatement to say that Aletrino was not happy about the publication. He bought as many books as he could lay his hands on and destroyed them. Aletrino never acknowledged that the main character was modelled after him. He called the main character perverse and he called de Haan 'the most depraved and unreliable individual I have ever met'. The first publication of *Pijpelijntjes* is known as one of the rarest books in modern Dutch literature.

A few months after the initial publication, de Haan published a second edition, but this time he left out the name of Aletrino and any allusions to his friend and changed the names of the two main characters to Koos and Hans. Several critics wrote

Maurits de Groot, *Portrait of Jacob Israël de Haan*, November 1918, burin © Universiteitsbibliotheek Amsterdam

reviews, but all were disgusted by the openly homosexual relationship between the two characters. P.L. Tak, the chief editor of newspaper *Het Volk*, for which de Haan worked, fired him, and the writer was likewise sacked from the primary school where he taught. Life became very difficult for him. In a *Public letter to P.L. Tak*, de Haan sought justice and reconciliation.

In the introduction to his second novel, de Haan also tries to solve the misunderstandings about his first controversial novel. '*Pijpelijntjes* was not confiscated by the police or by a public prosecutor, nor was the edition stopped due to other reasons. I am still content, as a literary artist, to have written *Pijpelijntjes*, although my life as a member of society has become much more difficult. As soon as circumstances allow me, I will publish the second part of *Pijpelijntjes*, which I have finished writing'. Unfortunately, it has never been published and the manuscript has never been found.

De Haan also sought support from well-established Dutch writers such as Frederik van Eeden and Lodewijk van Deyssel; they would not support de Haan publicly, only privately. He did find support, however, from Belgian novelist Georges Eekhoud, who wrote the prologue for his second novel. Eekhoud claims that 'the novel will establish de Haan's name forever as a literary artist'. He saw it as a very important document in which the psychologist de Haan writes about deviant inclinations, i.e. *uranism* (homosexuality). Eekhoud says of *Pijpelijntjes*: 'De Haan wrote tactfully and with moving authenticity about the lives of two 'nerve-unhealthy' young men, who belong to a group of the extremely dejected, and who are deprived of love. At last scientists, and especially those involved in literature, are showing a bit more fairness towards these people'.

Eekhoud continues: 'Law and public opinion have to take into account that this deviant inclination is not *perversité*, but *perversion*' (The distinction in the French connoting the difference between moral character - the former, and sexual aberration - the latter). That is to say, that people need a certain predisposition in order to develop this, which, in many cases, is an illness. This is a scientific fact and must end the involuntary prejudice due to which people are despised and judged. The only thing for which one can blame these people is that Their beliefs have given them homosexual feelings and inclinations. Everyone who loves justice and mankind will hear with deep satisfaction that the deviant, in his quest for Love, is therefore not a criminal, but indeed often times will be unhappy. He is neither a violator of mankind, nor does he deserve to be disdained as someone who was born with a physical handicap. It is someone who is gifted by Mother Nature in an unfortunate manner'. The scientific fact Eekhoud speaks of undoubtedly refers to the findings of Magnus Hirschfeld (1868-1935) who founded his Humanitarian Committee in

The *lewaje* or funeral of Jacob Israël de Haan in Jerusalem, July 1924.

1897 with a view to doing research in order to defend the rights of homosexuals.

However, de Haan continued writing and published a few short stories in literary magazines, and was able to publish a second novel in 1908: *Pathologies*, a novel in the European literary decadent tradition of the Englishman Oscar Wilde's *The Picture of Dorian Gray*, as well as that of the Dane, Herman Bang, and the aforementioned George Eekhoud. Some works of another famous and successful Dutch writer and novelist, Louis Couperus, may also be counted in this tradition. This time de Haan went even further and the two main characters partook in a homosexual sadomasochistic relationship. Hardly anyone reviewed it; it was, critics thought, simply too disgusting.

De Haan carried on writing poems and started studying law. In 1912, he went to Russia and visited several prisons to investigate the situation of political inmates. He also published his findings in a book, *In Russian Prisons*. He founded a committee to protest the situation in them too. De Haan began working as a professor of law at the University of Amsterdam and became a specialist in the field of legal significance. Amnesty International mentions de Haan as one of its forerunners.

Raised as an orthodox Jew, de Haan became interested in socialism as an adolescent and later in Zionism, adding *Israel* to his last name. Emigrating to Palestine in 1919, he then became an anti-Zionist and started writing as a correspondent for the Dutch national newspaper *Algemeen Handelsblad*. In 1924 de Haan was murdered in Palestine for his anti-Zionistic ideals, just shortly before his intended return to the Netherlands.

De Haan's two novels, short stories and poems were not in great demand during his life, and after his death the man and his work were largely forgotten. Yet a very small group of people saw the importance of de Haan's work and founded the De Haan Society in 1952 in order to give him the credit they felt he deserved and to make his work better known. The society published a few short articles in limited editions, but were unable to introduce de Haan to a large public. The society died a slow death, but in 1967 J. Meijer published a biography of de Haan. However, Meijer was mostly interested in his politics and stance on Judaism, not his literature. In 2015 Jan Fontijn published a complete biography.[1]

The novel was finally republished for a larger public in 1974, when the publication right expired, fifty years after de Haan's death and seventy years after its first publication. In 1975, L. Ross and R. Delvigne released a new edition that includes a short introduction to this controversial novel, explaining why it was of such importance. Subsequently, Ross and Delvigne would publish most of de Haan's literary work, even the short stories that de Haan had published in lesser-known magazines and newspapers. The result was that, after so many years, de Haan was finally recognized and rediscovered by important Dutch critics as a writer who wrote beautiful novels and poems about men loving men. In 1987 the city of Amsterdam erected the *homomonument*, a symbol for gay emancipation in the Netherlands and abroad. It would be the first monument of its kind in the world. A pink marble triangle with a text atop reads: *Naar vriendschap zulk een mateloos verlangen* (Such an endless desire for friendship). The words are Jacob Israël de Haan's.

In 1996, a new De Haan Society was founded. Again it is a society dedicated to introducing the general public to the importance of de Haan's literary legacy. In recent decades streets have been named for de Haan as well. On 26th February 2013, another monument to commemorate de Haan was inaugurated in Zaandam, the town where he had lived with his parents, across from the synagogue where his father had been a cantor.

De Haan's *Pijpelijntjes* was translated into Czech in 2006 and into Serbian in 2011. Only a few poems have been translated into English. For the very first time a complete chapter has now been translated into English and can be read by an international public.[2]

BONNY WASSING & MARC NASSAU-WOODWORTH

1 Jan Fontijn, *Onrust. Het leven van Jacob Israël de Haan* (Unrest. The Life of Jacob Israël de Haan), De Bezige Bij, Amsterdam, 2015.

2 You can read the chapter 'A Beloved Student' from the novel at www.onserfdeel.be/en/a-beloved-student.

The authors of this article are currently translating the complete novel.

Passionately Aware of Past Civilisations
Poems by Benno Barnard

'Before we wrote, there was no humanity. / Before we read, there was no humanity. / Humans existed, but that's a different story.' So reflects sixty-year-old actress Coco, in the eponymous verse-drama which is her self-analytical monologue. Her lines give us an important truth about Benno Barnard himself (born in 1954). He is as passionately aware of past civilisations, of earlier testaments to the complications of being alive, as his felicitously ubiquitous mentor, T.S. Eliot. Sumerian myth, Homer, Talmudic Judaism, the whole corpus of Eliot's own work, Maximilian Schell's documentary about Marlene Dietrich, all unflaggingly suggest themes and images. But Barnard is also disturbingly aware that beneath literature, beneath all artefacts, whether from antiquity or our ontologically tortured present, lies Ur-consciousness, fed by the non-human, allied to all natural denizens and constituents of our planet. In one of his finest short poems - which make up the first section of this continuously thought-engaging volume - Barnard declares: 'The lake inside of me flows from another lake / that's down below.' Yet this poem ends not with primeval scenes but with a human affirmation: 'Your name, / written in water, is valid all the same.'

This is a gentle reminder that morally we have no alternative; whatever our feelings of existential confusion, we must attend to, even treasure, the fellow humans alongside whom we find ourselves, whether those present at our initial stage of life - Coco, even at sixty, is still emotionally mindful of Mama and Papa - or the serendipitous folk met during the seemingly random course of our social lives. The central poem sequence of this volume, 'The Castaway', whose affinity to *The Waste Land* is made explicit in its first eight lines: 'Madame Sosostris let a card / she'd kept for me since 1922 / slip through her jewel-encrusted fingers', proffers us a diversity of citizens past and present of a richly

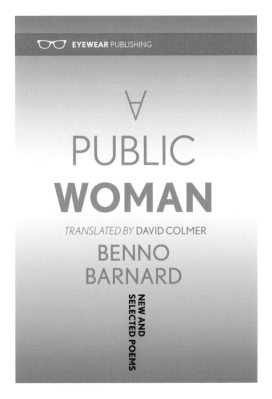

evoked Antwerp, but is also a tribute to an outsider, an outcast (its dedicatee, Eusebio G), a seaman from the Canaries, whom the poet honouring him never knew well, who came to live in Antwerp, spending his years 'from forty-six to sixty-four' (at which age he died) on its comparatively obscure Left Bank.

The short poems - which may, in their deliberately errant pursuit of a central metaphor, remind readers of Paul Celan, whose work Barnard has translated - are informed by the writer's personal difficulties in maintaining steadiness of relationship with the world outside himself, including cherished family members (mother, father, wife, son) with truth-seeking awareness of both death and chaos. In 'A Telephone Conversation with a Friend Who Has Cancer' each three-line stanza intensifies the agony of the title's situation until the poet protests: 'Death is an awkward solution for the riddle of time. / Death is a cack-handed remedy.' Even his own stoically practised art now appears doomed to failure, an attempt to 'hum postmodernism's / incoherent swan song'. Nevertheless in both of the two long poems the very process of artistic confrontation of existence becomes - no matter what exclamations of distress we hear - a kind of guarantee of telluric meaning, of some shape to life discernible, if only occasionally and then dimly.

For all the longevity of its traditions, the grace of its historic monuments and the liveliness of its current activities, the Antwerp that provides the context for Eusebio B contains much that is sombre - the proximity of Breendonk, the Nazi concentration camp with its horrors of the recent past, and the tawdriness of present-day mores: the red light district, fish and chip stands on a splendid river front, derelict lives in high-rise blocks. But somehow the feeling nature of so many even casual encounters, the constant going out of heart to heart succeeds in redeeming all these.

As for the monologue *A Public Woman*, it is at once a technical *tour de force* and a masterpiece of concentrated experience, surely surpassing many a contemporary novel in the vividness with which episodes and relationships are rendered, and the way the passing of time is conveyed. In Part One - for the retrospection of which the brilliantly rendered 'blank verse' (iambic pentameter) is the perfect vehicle - Coco gives us her early years of unsatisfactory parents (Mama self-absorbed, Papa happier with his stamp collection) and an education (Catholic, bourgeois) which never appealed to the whole of her personality, to that in her which would realise itself (but how completely?) in the classic dramatic roles, Medea, Jocasta, for which she earned fame. In Part Two - for which freer verse is employed - she takes us through her marriage to a conventional but admirable (and admiring) businessman husband, whom she (if not at the deepest level) betrays, and through her psychic identification with Marlene Dietrich. In Part Three Coco confronts death itself, as it visits both her parents, as it

must visit her. She has played so many archetypal roles, but 'I've never died in my life before.'

David Colmer worked with Benno Barnard, a kind of metric mentor for him, for many years before preparing this representative selection of his work. His empathy with the poet shows here in every supple line, whatever the particular verse form in which it appears. Coco's daughter is called Marina and we who, like Barnard, revere Eliot, recall the daughter in the most beautiful of his *Ariel Poems*, with its homage to what is 'more distant than stars and nearer than the eye'. It is a measure of Barnard and Colmer's achievement that we can without strain place *A Public Woman* in the company of Eliot's 'Marina'.

PAUL BINDING

A Public Woman, new and selected poems by Benno Barnard, translated from the Dutch by David Colmer, Eyewear Publishing, London, 2015.

A Sensational New Translation of Herman Gorter

The poet Herman Gorter (1864-1927) is still very much admired in Flanders and the Netherlands. Last century he was studied in great depth by Enno Endt and the biographer Herman de Liagre Böhl, and the "Vijftiger"[1] poets (including Lucebert) acknowledged their debt to his work. In the twenty-first century, interest is still being shown in Gorter in theses and studies. In 2010 his collection *Verzen* (translated by Paul Vincent in 2015 as *Poems of 1890*) was reprinted in the renowned *Perpetua* series of classics, while the writer, actor and performer Ramsey Nasr (born 1974) filmed Gorter's poem 'Ik was toen een arme jongen' (I was a poor boy then) and in 2014 Gorter's love letters to his muses and lovers Ada Prins and Jenne Clinge-Doorenbos were published.

But it has to be admitted that apart from Gorter's best-known epic poem, *Mei* (May, 1889), and his *Verzen* collection, much of his sizeable oeuvre (which also consists of socialist poems, essays, articles, booklets and letters) still goes unremarked. After 1897, when Gorter sought to associate himself first with socialism and then council communism, his oeuvre was given over entirely to the anticipated new era and it is precisely this part of his work that remains barely touched upon.

How different things are outside the Low Countries, where Herman Gorter is known more as a political activist than as one of the most gifted poets of his day. In his anthology of Herman Gorter's *Poems of 1890*, published in late 2015, the translator Paul Vincent tried pointedly to modify this image. In his introduction, which is both concise and outstanding, he situates Gorter's work emphatically in the developments taking place at the end of the nineteenth century, when the Netherlands 'became a more dynamic, outward-looking and forward-thinking place - an attitude that extended to culture'.

From his debut with *Mei*, Gorter, who as a classicist with a PhD earned his living giving private lessons, caused quite an upheaval among his contemporar-

Herman Gorter in 1923 © Letterkundig Museum, The Hague

ies and certainly among younger readers. 'This epic poem of some 4,000 lines, mostly in rhyming five-foot iambics', even developed into an iconic work for the Movement of Eighty:[2] 'A breath of fresh air in a literary culture dominated by plodding moralistic verse, often churned out by clergyman-poets'. Paul Vincent praises the poem for its 'vivid sensory images' and even calls it 'a celebration of the Dutch landscape'.

It is however a sign of Gorter's independence (an aspect of his life which, like his social awareness, can be traced back to his Mennonite upbringing) that he did not continue in this direction, but in his next collection wanted to do something different once again: 'the Poems of 1890 mark a radical new departure, not only in Dutch but in a European context'.

A year after *Mei*, Gorter once again published a stunning collection, called *Verzen*, much influenced by the writer Lodewijk van Deyssel (1864-

1952) and his ideas on 'sensitivisme'. Vincent extremely appositely describes this 'sensitivisme' as 'the recording of fleeting, fragmentary moments of experience of an almost mystical intensity'. Vincent in fact compares the artistic extremism of the collection with Arthur Rimbaud's *The Drunken Boat (Le Bateau ivre)* or *A Season in Hell (Une Saison en Enfer)*.

The *Verzen* collection comprises a hundred poems, some of only two lines, some several pages long, in which the feminine rhyme is immediately apparent. It was after all notable that even for such major poets of modernism as Martinus Nijhoff (1894-1953) and Gerrit Achterberg (1905-1962) rhyme remained important. Conversely, we also see 'irregular line lengths and syntax, a radical use of neologism, synaesthesia, surging eroticism, a haunting fragmentary musicality and occasional astonishingly simple and direct love poems'. In terms of its explosiveness, Paul Vincent comments that this form of expressionism can best be compared with that of Vincent van Gogh.

Up to now, only a few extracts from these *Verzen*, one of the glorious *tours de force* of the poetry of the Low Countries, have been available in English. In this anthology, Paul Vincent has translated approximately one third of the poems and has done this so sublimely well that I hope he will have the chance to continue the task. To give a small demonstration of his subtle brilliance, take the poem 'You see I love you, love'. This is one of the most oft-quoted love poems in Dutch literature and is so touching precisely because of its gentle, almost childlike simplicity. If you translate the first line literally, it comes out as 'You see I love you'. But Vincent has added the word 'love' to it again, and thereby accentuates both the tenderness of the verse and Gorter's musicality. In his afterword Vincent himself writes of this: 'I have sought not to reproduce that music, but to transpose it into a different form'. Vincent has of course rarely found a literal translation for the many neologisms that Gorter invented for this collection, but his fluid, often extremely musical translation does more than justice to the poet. Just read it:

> *The spring comes from afar, I hear it come hither*
> *and the trees hear too, the tall trees that shiver,*
> *and the tall skies, the heavenly skies*
> *the tingle-light skies, the blue-and-white skies,*
> *shiver skies.*

Vincent has already been honoured with the Vondel Dutch Translation Prize for his translation of *My Little War*, a novel by the Flemish author Louis Paul Boon (1912-1979). This should not prevent us from once again paying tribute to this virtuoso translator for the fact that has so matchlessly made Herman Gorter's delightful, sensitive world available to everyone outside the Low Countries.

ERNST BRUINSMA
Translated by Gregory Ball

Herman Gorter, *Poems of 1890. A Selection*, translated from the Dutch by Paul Vincent, UCL Press, London, 2015.

1   The *Vijftigers* formed a literary movement in the Netherlands language area in the late 1940s and the 1950s that turned firmly against existing views of art.
2   A movement for the renewal of Dutch literature that was active in the 1880s and the early 1890s.

'Das Magazin' and the Literary Journal in the Low Countries

Anyone looking to write a history of the literary journal in Flanders and the Netherlands will undoubtedly discover that 2011 was a pivotal year. That was the year when the Dutch State Secretary for Culture, the right-wing liberal Halbe Zijlstra, scrapped all subsidies for literary magazines as part of a general cost-cutting exercise. The reason given was the small target readership. At a time when austerity measures were being taken across the board, it was argued that giving public money to journals with so few readers could no longer be justified.

Unsurprisingly, there was a fierce reaction to this decision, which seemed to be driven more by the anti-cultural climate in Dutch politics than by any thoughts of making major savings. There were fears in cultural circles that this would mark the end of the literary journal, which some declared would simply be 'wiped from the face of the earth'.

Where are we today, five years later? Sadly, a number of journals have indeed disappeared due to lack of funds following the withdrawal of government support, including *Kort Verhaal* (Short Story) and *Parmentier*. At the same time, however, developments since 2011 have made clear that the literary journal, even in this age of dwindling readerships and digital media, is stronger than had been thought.

Even in that accursed year 2011, for example, several new journals were actually founded, including *Terras, Extaze* and *Das Magazin*. This last journal, in particular, has grown into a phenomenon within a short space of time. Not only does *Das Mag* (as it is generally known) have a circulation of 4,500 and the self-proclaimed accolade, according to its website, of being 'the biggest literary journal in the Netherlands', but it also attracts a striking amount of attention from literary circles, the media and even the academic world. It has received an important cultural award.

Das Mag has succeeded in positioning itself in the market as young, fresh and modern. That is immediately obvious when you pick up a copy. It is attractively designed, with colourful, stylised images and a different, hip 'house illustrator' for each edition, and so manages to remain far removed from the cliché of the dusty, old-fashioned literary journal. *Das Mag* is also very adept at using social media to promote itself, and also at raising its public profile with grandiose events, such as the *Das Mag Festivals*, which are declared to be the 'biggest reading club in the country'. Reading clubs are held at several locations within the same city, with an author and twenty-five readers. Afterwards there is a party that everyone can attend. The formula works. Heavily attended meetings in the magazine's home base of Amsterdam were followed by festivals in Ghent, Antwerp and London. Berlin is on the agenda for 2016.

In the autumn of 2015, *Das Mag* went a step further, setting up its own publishing house. On the one hand, that sounds logical - journals have traditionally provided a fertile pool of literary talent, in which publishers have been keen to fish. But at the same time it is remarkable, because it demonstrates a great deal of self-confidence in an ability to launch a publishing operation at a time when the book world mainly appears in the news as an economically downtrodden sector. But the people behind *Das Mag* are confident that they have the support of their readers. Just as when the journal was launched in 2011, the publishing operation was partly funded through crowdfunding among the journal's own readers - who are often, though by no means always, young people.

This underlines yet again what may be the most important factor in the success of *Das Mag*, its ability to engender reader loyalty. *Das Mag* creates a club feeling, a sense of belonging to a literary community. We have already talked about the design, the social media and the events, but the content of the journal also reflects that club feeling. *Das Mag* does not espouse a particular literary opinion, does not engage in polemics with other journals or generations, does not nurture any lofty ideas about the Art of Writing. As the author Kees 't Hart wrote: 'you don't need to do anything, you don't have to do anything, and you can take part if you feel like it. *Das Magazin* simply doesn't have an agenda, and makes that its agenda.' The only constant appears to be a positive, inclusive tone.

This lack of a clear profile is sometimes levelled against *Das Mag*, with critics arguing that the journal and its writers are too conformist, too little inclined to kick against the traces, lacking in virtually any ambition except to be liked. Overall, however, the story of *Das Mag* is above all one of hope. There are clearly still enough readers to support literary journals; it is simply a matter of reaching out to them and garnering their loyalty. Literature can only benefit from this.

And what about the polemic, the edginess, the debate? These will come as night follows day. The first book published by the *Das Mag* publishing house, for example, a collection of stories by Maartje Wortel, met with a very mixed response, and some writers - including a number who are counted in the *Das Mag* camp, such as Joost de Vries and Daan Heerma van Voss - are quick to say in interviews that they do not believe there is such a thing as a *Das Mag* club, and that they therefore do not belong to it.

And of course, there is also life outside *Das Mag*. A visitor browsing through the literary journals of the Low Countries will find an extremely diverse mix. The journal *Terras*, launched in the *annus horribilis* 2011, like *Das Mag*, not only focuses on international literature, but is also a multimedia phenomenon, with literary texts, blogs, essays, films, photos and compositions published on its website every week. The journal also projects itself as the

successor to and guardian of the treasures of the famed (in literary circles) but demised journal *Raster* (1967-2008). Old *Raster* articles are posted online, making them accessible once again.

The new journals also include young iconoclasts which are published exclusively online (*Samplekanon*), traditional paper-based literary vehicles (*Passage*) and 'a journal that reads like a newspaper but is stuffed full of literature' (*De Titaan*). There are journals which first closed but then started up again, either exclusively in digital format (www.armadawereldliteratuur.nl) or once more in a traditional paper version (*Kluger Hans*). But established veterans of the world of literary journals have also reinvented themselves or been given new impetus. The oldest literary journal in the Netherlands, *De Gids* (launched in 1837), has been taken under the wing of the opinion weekly *De Groene Amsterdammer*; a new editorial team at *De Revisor* (first published in 1974) has drastically changed course; and *Tirade* (first published in 1957) and *Hollands Maandblad* (launched in 1959) continue to dig up literary treasures.

In Flanders, a number of journals stand out for their willingness to experiment, not just with content, but also with form. *DW B* (launched in 1855) seeks out the confrontation of visual art and literature, and each edition of the journals *nY* (started in 2009) and *Deus Ex Machina* (1976) takes on a different appearance. Flemish journals are also pooling their strengths in the umbrella organisation Folio. This offers a platform where they can meet to learn from each other, to strengthen their position in negotiations for government grants and to find new readers. They are also increasingly turning their gaze towards the Netherlands, where they are finding an interested ear.

The conclusion? It is far too early to write off the literary journal, let alone to write it out of history.

PIETER COUPÉ
Translated by Julian Ross

Politics

Ideas, Ideals and Pressure for Change
Fifty Years of D66

Hans van Mierlo (1931-2010)

On the 14th October 1966 everything in the politics of the Netherlands changed. A band of 44 men, cut along more or less modern lines, and one woman, founded D66 - a party that intended to cock a snook at the political establishment which was still organized according to traditional blocks. Away with presorted electoral cohorts that ran their lives and welfare along Catholic, Protestant, Dutch Reformed, social democratic or liberal lines. In their place a party of ideas and ideals that wanted to kick hard and topple the house of cards that was vested interest.

The young party's first success was down to the leader. Hans van Mierlo (1931-2010) was a tall journalist with the stance of a statesman, a deep voice that inspired confidence, and a striking appearance. The images of the first election cartoon are iconic: Van Mierlo walking along the canals in Amsterdam, his long raincoat falling open, musing on how his party would shake up politics. Suddenly there was a party leader with the air of a new wave film star. Politics in the Netherlands leapt forward at least a quarter of a century with the visual metaphors of D66.

Van Mierlo and his lot were forerunners of the alternative thinkers who would shortly out themselves as Provos. D66 was also alternative, but in a more measured, consensus-seeking way. 'The reasonable alternative', that was to be the slogan for many years.

What did D66 really want? Government reform had been an important point for a long time. The rules of play of the democratic system needed to be changed, the (re)introduction of the district system, a directly elected prime minister who could choose the members of his own cabinet, mayoral elections, referenda - the complete package was referred to as the Crown Jewels of D66. Fifty years on not a single one of these things has got on to the Statute Book.

Among the originators were deserters from the liberal VVD and social democrats. For a long time these two spirits would continue to toss and turn in the breast of the party. In the early years the leftist forces were the stronger. Van Mierlo wanted close co-operation with the social democratic PvdA and other parties of the left, a merger if need be. In the social-economic area, the D66 of recent years is pre-eminently a liberal party which places great value on the independence of the individual and accords the government a modest role. 'Social liberal' is the term that has been coined to denote this position.

D66 is most influential in the area of ethics. The D66 ministers and members of parliament have made a strong contribution to donor registration and homosexual marriage, and they have left their mark on euthanasia legislation in the Netherlands.[1] On these topics the D66 politicians show themselves as true children of the breakdown of the traditional religious and socio-political 'pillars'.

Gradually the party has also presented itself as the party most favourably disposed to Europe. Where VVD, PvdA and the Christian democratic CDA still express some reservations from time to time, for D66 the gateway to heaven on earth is in Brussels. For D66ers closer European integration is a logical consequence of the demise of the nation state. Nationalism is an alien concept to the true follower of D66, who is prepared to hand over more power from The Hague to the European Union.

What has all of this meant for D66 in fifty years? The first post-war cabinet with no Christian party participation (1994-1998) would not have been possible but for D66. *Paars I* (Purple I), as this coalition of PvdA, VVD and D66 under the premiership of social democrat Wim Kok was called, introduced a fervour into politics in the Netherlands, in which much of D66's drive for change was recognizable. In *Paars II* the relationships seemed to have deteriorated too far for much more to be achieved.

In 2003 D66 stepped into government again, this time as junior partner in the Balkende II cabinet of CDA and VVD. It was a mixed blessing. D66 ministers lost credibility by supporting the hard right policy on immigration. The elected mayor perished in sight of the finish. The electorate was no longer interested either: in the 2006 opinion polls D66 were briefly down to 0 seats. Van Mierlo wondered aloud whether it wasn't 'enough after forty years'.

Under the present party leader, Alexander Pechtold, D66 has become a significant factor once more. Pechtold wants his party to behave responsibly, even if it's not in government. He doesn't vote against the plans of the Rutte government, and by negotiating with them ensures that D66 exerts influence on the policy. At the same time he is the fiercest opponent of the extreme right PVV leader Geert Wilders in the Second Chamber.

In the last municipal, European and provincial elections the party made gains overall. While all political parties in the Netherlands are experiencing a fall in membership numbers, D66 is on the rise. The party is led in a very professional manner, is involved in a number of local and provincial authorities, and has many representatives among the top civil servants. D66 has become part of the establishment - the only one of the new parties to do so. If that is what the founders had in mind in 1966, then their aim has been achieved.

ARIEJAN KORTEWEG
Translated by Sheila M. Dale

1 See *The Low Countries*, IX, 2001, pp. 296-298.

The Tong Tong Fair
The Biggest Eurasian Festival in the World

The Dutch word *Indisch* has nothing to do with India, but with the former Dutch colony of Indonesia. It was here that the Eurasian or *Indo* culture began, a mestizo culture with characteristics of East and West. Indonesian independence in 1949 sparked an exodus of the approximately 350,000 Dutch Indonesians, most of whom had a mixed Indo-European background (which could usually be traced back to a European man and a Javanese woman). The bloody war of independence and the nationalisation of foreign businesses made it impossible for them to remain in the young Indonesian Republic. These people were moreover Dutch citizens.

At the end of the 1950s, the Tong Tong movement began in the Dutch seat of government, The Hague. At its heart was the Eurasian journalist, writer and activist Tjalie Robinson (1911-1974), a pseudonym of Jan Boon. Robinson believed passionately that the Dutch public knew far too little about Indo-Dutch people and their culture. He argued that the Indo culture was an inseparable part of the Dutch cultural heritage, and in his magazine *Tong-Tong* (1958) he exhorted his readers to continue writing about it. In 1959 he founded the Indische Kunstkring Tong-Tong (IKK - Tong-Tong Eurasian Artistic Society) and a short time later, together with Mary Brückel-Beiten, he launched the Pasar Malam Tong-Tong fair as a fund-raising vehicle for the IKK.

The first Pasar Malam Tong-Tong (literally 'Tong-Tong evening market') was held in The Hague from 3-5 July 1959 and was an immediate hit. The event drew around three thousand visitors, most of them with an Indo-Dutch background. This was the first time since their lives in the Dutch East Indies that so many Indos had gathered together in one place. This gave the event an emotional charge which left an indelible impression that lasts to the present day.

The Pasar Malam Tong-Tong has changed its name twice: in the 1970s it became the Pasar

Malam Besar (literally 'great evening market'), and in 2008 it was renamed the Tong Tong Fair. By including a reference to the Tong-Tong movement, the organisers were seeking to make their ambitions clear, although the Tong Tong Fair is known above all as an exotic shopping spectacle (with large numbers of merchants from Southeast Asia) and as an enormous culinary festival, it also serves as a sort of directory of Indo-European *culture*. The present organisers, who include Tjalie Robinson's grandchildren, have continued to devote unwavering attention to that culture, which has continued to develop even without the existence of the Dutch East Indies. That culture can be seen in the themed theatres that have been added to the commercial and culinary activities of the Fair, where a varied cultural and educational programme unfolds each year.

The Tong Tong Fair, which still takes place in The Hague, has acquired an educational function because of these cultural programmes. The Dutch education system almost totally ignores the colonial past of the Netherlands, but anyone wanting to know about Indo-European cultural history will find it at the Tong Tong Fair in the form of lectures, debates, exhibitions and musical, dance, theatrical and literary performances.

In addition, the fair continues to fulfil a social function. It is a setting where Eurasians can be themselves, they do not have to choose between East or West, but can simply be Indos. Its combination of social, cultural and commercial functions gives the Tong Tong Fair the air of a small town.

Over the course of more than half a century, modern Indonesia has also found a place at the Tong Tong Fair. In the 1960s, relations between the Netherlands and Indonesia were still strained, and the bloody war of independence and forced exodus had wounded (Indo-) Dutch people (too) deeply. This began to change slowly in the 1970s, and today the Tong Tong Fair is filled with music and dance from modern-day Indonesia, with the organisers constantly seeking out new combinations of art and culture from East and West. By never losing sight of its own mixed roots, the Tong Tong Fair has even become an important podium for world music and dance. The British music journal *Songlines* and *The Rough Guide to World Music*, both internationally recognised as the most authoritative publications on world music, have written about the role of the Tong Tong Fair as a European world music podium that fuses East and West.

There was a certain inevitability about it when this Grand Old Lady of multicultural festivals, and the biggest Eurasian festival in the world, received an award. In 2007 the Fair was awarded the National Events Grand Prix, the Dutch events 'Oscar'. The Fair was twice opened by the former Queen Beatrix.

FLORINE KONING
Translated by Julian Ross

The next Tong Tong Fair will take place in The Hague from 28 May to 5 June 2016 inclusive (see tongtongfair.nl).

Theatre

Shaking the Audience Awake
Johan Simons's Personal Style and Mission

'I could wallpaper my whole house twice over, once with positive reviews and once with negative ones', said the Dutch theatre director Johan Simons (born in 1946) in 2014 in a passionate plea for subsidised arts. He had just been inducted as a member of the Dutch Academy of Arts. 'National excellence? International renown? It takes years of trying and having the chance to fail.' Simons should know. He was offered and seized his chances. And in the meantime he has become an internationally acclaimed theatre director who has won many awards, including the prestigious Prins Bernhard Cultuurfonds Prize (2014) for his whole oeuvre.

Yet Simons was a late bloomer, he was thirty-eight when he directed his first piece of theatre. He had a long way to go, after all. He likes to mention his simple background as a baker and farmer's son in Heerjansdam, a village just under Rotterdam where, in his own words, 'in the worst case you became a farm labourer and in the best an accountant'. As a boy he wanted to be a missionary and delivered entire sermons on the school playground, using wonderful imagery even then. But he lost his faith and went off to the Rotterdam Dance Academy. He danced in musicals like *Jesus Christ Superstar* and *Hair*, but wasn't good enough for ballet and ended up in the theatre.

In 1985 Simons set up the Hollandia theatre company with Paul Kloek. Hollandia produced theatre projects on location: Greek tragedies and farming dramas in a breaker's yard, pigsty or greenhouse. His ambition was to make musical theatre for people who would never set foot inside the theatre otherwise. Simons was only sporadically successful in this. Hollandia mainly attracted a highly-educated audience from Amsterdam, people who had to drive an hour to attend a performance. The company made raw, exciting, poetic theatre. Theatre in the shit. It was different, new. Its place in the Dutch theatre establishment was assured.

At Hollandia Simons built a tight-knit group of actors with whom he would continue to work, including his wife Elsie de Brauw. He developed his own style, a 'sculpted theatre' focussing heavily on rhythm, voice and movement. His background as a dancer and his dyslexia influenced his expressive and spatial way of working. In 2000 Simons made the switch to a larger public, when Hollandia merged with Zuidelijk Toneel to form ZT Hollandia, with Eindhoven as its home base. He made no secret of the fact that he wanted to become one of the most important theatre makers in Europe. His international rise began in 2001, during the Salzburg Festival, when ZT Hollandia was the first Dutch company ever to perform there. Simons was also the first Dutch director at the Avignon Festival, in 2004. He was invited to stage pieces in major German theatres and directed operas in Paris, and in 2005 he became the artistic director of NTGent.

In 2010 he was appointed artistic director of the Müncher Kammerspiele. Suddenly he had a good thirty million euros in subsidies at his disposal. He took some Dutch and Flemish actors with him to Germany and gave them major roles, whether or not their German was perfect. In Munich his 'Dutch levity' was much appreciated. Where a German director would not dare interfere with the texts of Goethe, Schiller or Brecht, Simons did not hesitate to adapt them. Simons felt at home there, 'In Germany, and certainly in Munich and in the city theatre system that I work in, art and artistic autonomy are fiercely protected. That means I can work in a rather luxurious but at the same time very radical way.' In his opinion, it was hard to find politicians in the Netherlands who would automatically defend the arts. When Dutch cultural subsidies were cut by up to 40%, in 2011, Simons was incensed. 'Actually', he said at the time, 'the Queen should abdicate now. She should say, "I don't want to reign in a country like this"'. He pleaded for a layered society, in which there is room for entertainment but also for elite art. 'It's important to oppose the

Johan Simons

Falling Down, Getting Up and Carrying On
Ann Van den Broek's Choreography

Confrontational, intriguing, daring and temperamental; these are just a few of the adjectives used to describe Ann Van den Broek's dance oeuvre. This choreographer (born 1970) finds the inspiration for her language of movement very close to herself. She unravels her emotions and then tests them against other people and the spirit of the age. The result of the impressions she acquires is a merciless analysis of universal themes such as compulsive behaviour, lust, solitude and vanity. Van den Broek looks for answers to such questions as: What sort of rhythmicality goes with fear? What are the different variations of restlessness? How do you translate sexual urges into movements?

The dance language that emerges from this is a compelling portrait of recognisable behaviour patterns. Don't expect a strict interpretation of the subject, but rather freedom of interpretation for the audience and the choreographer. And this is precisely the intention, because Van den Broek wants to communicate continuously with the audience so that they confront their own desires and impulses. The fact that the audience is important is also reflected in the name of her company - WArd/waRD - which is based in Antwerp. The word 'ward' is mirrored in an attempt to symbolise the mutual relationship between the dancers themselves and between them and the audience.

Van den Broek set up the company in 2000 to carry on her work under a single name. In the Netherlands she initially worked through the Korzo production company in The Hague, but in 2008 she decided to set up a WArd/waRD organisation in The Hague too. Working from bases in two countries has its advantages: she can develop a unique dance language without the restrictions of a single country. And WArd/waRD not only produces Van den Broek's work, but also engages in co-productions. Yet her unmistakable DNA always runs through all the productions.

discourse of art-haters who say that art is a leftist hobby, that art is elitist and should therefore be written off. A society needs its elite.'

Simon's social and political engagement is obvious from his work. In 2015 he returned to NTGent, where he put the world on the stage with unemployment, illegal employment and the influx of refugees. He wants to shock his audience and shake them awake, to force them to engage in debate and to ask questions. As a consummate multitasker, Simons continues to achieve these ambitions in Germany, as well, as the artistic director of the Ruhrtriënnale (till 2017) and of the Schauspielhaus Bochum (from 2018). As of 2017, he will do so again in the Netherlands, where he will be associated with Theater Rotterdam, a new theatre to be modelled along German lines. It is the perfect job for him. Because Simons is a man with a mission: to give art the place it deserves in society.

MARLEEN BROCK
Translated by Lindsay Edwards

Before Van den Broek became a choreographer herself, she explored the limits of her body by dancing with several companies. When she launched into her solo career in 2000, her focus was chiefly on body language, but live video, live sound and sign language gradually gained in importance. Ann Van den Broek's stage sets are always modest. It is mainly the patterns of movement that make it appear they are set in real-life surroundings.

Van den Broek danced her first solo as early as 1995. It was called *Skótoseme*, and in it she examined the limits of her inner motivations. In 2000 and 2001 this was followed by two solos: *Annexe and Hurry up Please, It's Time*. After these solos, Van den Broek was ready for her first group piece with Dansgroep Krisztina de Châtel, FF+Rew. This work was about the repercussions of an emotional blow, made intensely palpable by a repetition of movements. Because repetition allows emotions to be explored and refined. Falling down, getting up and carrying on. The title refers to the rewind and fast forward buttons on a cassette recorder.

Falling down, getting up and carrying on are movements that Van den Broek has already experienced often in her life. Her dance language is hard to understand without an insight into her personal story. She grew up in a family where life was not easy and her oeuvre is mainly influenced by Thomas, her brother, who suffered from psychoses for ten years. In *The Lady in Black* (2015), Van den Broek says: 'My brother set the tone of a lot of my work, because my pieces are always about the way the outside world deals with people who do not follow the normal path through life'.

The Lady in Black, a documentary by the director Lisa Boerstra, shows how the life and work of the choreographer, who always wears black, are interwoven. The viewer gets to know Van den Broek as an extremely dedicated and intractable choreographer who pushes her dancers' bodies to extremes. One of these dancers compares Van den Broek to a pit bull terrier that bites, chews and only lets go when it has got what it wants. And what she wants is to show humans of flesh and blood. The technical aspect of dance is of less importance.

In a substantial number of Van den Broek's pieces the stage is given over to women. In *Quartet with One* (2002), for example, she shares the stage with the dancer Sophie Janssens and in 2003 she also performed a pas de deux in *Rest Room*, this time with the dancer Einat Tuchman. But the woman's perspective is only expressed fully in the piece *Co(te)lette* (2008). This work, which flirts with wordplay, as is often the case in Van den Broek's oeuvre, is a reference both to the name of the French writer and to a meat chop. *Co(te)lette* is a confrontational and disturbing portrait of female sexuality in which three women dancers move vehemently, feel themselves and repeat sexual positions. It makes one reflect on women's experience of sex.

Ann Van den Broek - WArd/waRD, *The Black Piece*, 2014
© M. Vanden Abeele

Ann Van den Broek - WArd/waRD, *The Red Piece*, 2013
© M. Vanden Abeele

In 2008 Van den Broek also staged an auto-biographical work. In *I Solo Ment* a mentally isolated man is set opposite a woman who wants to get through to him. This piece is dedicated to her brother Thomas, whom she has in vain tried to help during his psychoses.

There is no question that Van den Broek is a dedicated choreographer. Having no longer danced in her pieces for ten years, she once again appeared on stage in *Ohm* (2010) and *The Red Piece* (2013). She does not want to lose the feel for dance itself. In *Ohm* she pumps up the rhythm by stamping on a sheet of metal. And in *The Red Piece* it is her heels that drive the tempo. *The Red Piece* follows the pulsing rhythm of a heart: impassioned, controlled and structured. In *The Black Piece* (2014) it is the rhythm itself that sets the tone. The performance is varied with highs, lows and interruptions.

In 2015 it was fifteen years since Van den Broek had set up her dance company. Her latest piece, *Pushing the Wheel* (2015), in which a retrospective section is linked to a look ahead to the future, was made on the occasion of the fifteenth anniversary of WArd/waRD. By means of flash-forwards, this performance gives the spectator an idea of the undoubtedly powerful future work of this talented choreographer.

LIZA NOTERIS
Translated by Gregory Ball

www.wardward.be

Marcelle Schots, *Protect / Perform, On the work of / over het werk van Ann Van den Broek - WArd/waRD*, WArd/waRD, Antwerp, 2015.

Visual Arts

An Echoless Organ Grinder
The Life Story of Felix Nussbaum

I am easily tempted. At the end of the millennium a couple of sentences in a biography of Stefan Zweig were enough to inspire me to write a book. Biographer Serge Niémetz quoted the young German author Irmgard Keun, elegantly describing a meeting between several important literary figures at a café in Ostend. The scene took place in the summer of 1936 and, besides Stefan Zweig, those present were a good-humoured Egon Erwin Kisch and an inebriated Joseph Roth.

It turns out that a large number of German writers stayed in Ostend in the summer of '36, most of them people of Jewish background. I wrote up this small but well-documented chapter of exile history in Ostend: Stefan Zweig, Joseph Roth, and the Summer Before the Dark (OT: *Oostende, de zomer van 1936*).[1] The cover showed the well-known photo of Roth and Zweig on the Belgian coast.

Shortly after the book was published in 2001 I saw a painting I would have preferred to have had on the cover, because it so perfectly captured the atmosphere of Ostend harbour during the interbellum as I had experienced it in much of the writing of 'my' exiles. The canvas presented Ostend Fish Market in 1936, its painter Felix Nussbaum. I was previously unaware that this Jewish artist had come to Ostend fleeing Nazism and I immediately wanted to know everything there was to know about Nussbaum. As I mentioned, I am easily tempted into a new book. Certainly in this case, as Nussbaum's life story, the way he completely disappeared under the radar after his death at Auschwitz and resurfaced decades later, seemed amazingly exciting, and the work he left behind intriguingly clever.

Although Felix Nussbaum lived with his wife Felka Platek in Belgium from 1935 to 1944, it soon became clear to me that he barely enjoyed any fame there. In Germany it was different. In 1970 more than 100 of his paintings, which had been rotting in a cellar in Brussels until then, turned up in the city of his birth, Osnabrück, where he grew up in a

Felix Nussbaum, *Triumph des Todes* (Triumph of Death), 1944
© Felix-Nussbaum-Haus, Osnabrück

small Jewish community, subsequently destroyed under the Third Reich. In a form of Wiedergutmachung in Osnabrück a long-term project started up to restore the life's work of this former citizen. In 1998 Nussbaum was even given a dedicated museum, designed by famous architect Daniel Libeskind.

The fact that Nussbaum, whose name and work had been completely erased by Hitler, was suddenly a well-known figure in Osnabrück, was not enough to discourage me from writing a biographical work about him. On the contrary, this made it possible. The research I had already carried out in Osnabrück not least the online catalogue of Nussbaum's work set up by the Nussbaum museum, was a firm foundation for the task I faced, a book zooming in on Felix Nussbaum's exile years in Belgium. A meeting with Nussbaum's first biographers, Peter Junk and Wendelin Zimmer, and their support were a nudge in the right direction.

When my search began there was hardly anyone left who had known Nussbaum personally. A memorable exception was a lady I tracked down in America who had provided him with some painting materials at the Mechelen Dossin transit camp, while he awaited transport to Auschwitz. None of Nussbaum's most intimate circle - his wife, parents or brother - survived the camps. Besides hundreds of paintings and drawings, Nussbaum only left behind a few dozen letters. After searching archives in Belgium and abroad I was able to add a handful more. I was more successful in finding traces of his existence in the press and in the memoires of those who had crossed his path. Information was still scarce, though, when it came to the many phases of Nussbaum's short life - his arrest and experiences in a French camp at the start of the war, his life in hiding when the Jews were being hunted down in Brussels, his stay at the Dossin barracks and deportation to Auschwitz. I was able to circumvent such gaps with the help of accounts by others in the many archives on World War II and the persecution of the Jews. The largest archive of all, the World Wide Web, also proved an inexhaustible treasure trove, supplying Nussbaum's story with the broad context I wanted. Particularly when

Felix Nussbaum, *Orgelmann* (Organ Grinder), 1943
© Felix-Nussbaum-Haus, Osnabrück

it comes to areas such as the history of the Jews, exile, and local details of Ostend and Brussels, the internet is an infinite archive.

Felix Nussbaum liked to portray himself as an organ grinder. His tragedy was that he lived in a period which deprived him of any echo. In the end I spent more time looking for a way to tell this story than searching for traces of Nussbaum's existence in the first place: how could I best reinforce the echo his work had achieved by its own strength?

MARK SCHAEVERS
Translated by Anna Asbury

Mark Schaevers, *Orgelman. Felix Nussbaum, een schildersleven* (Organ Grinder. Felix Nussbaum, the Life of an Artist), De Bezige Bij, Amsterdam, 2014.

The German translation, *Orgelmann*, is to be published at the end of 2016 by Galiani Verlag Berlin.

1   Published by Uitgeverij Atlas, Amsterdam.

'The Way of All Flesh'
The Graffiti Artist ROA

Zoom in - come on, even closer - and you will see an undercoat of white latex paint applied with a roller, decorated with short black marks from a spray can. A double monochrome on a crumbling brick wall, dead wood or bleak concrete.

Zoom right out and you find yourself face to face with an animal. It remains sitting there motionlessly, but if you look at it long enough you could swear that little shudders passed through its huge body, or that in an unguarded moment it took a quick breath. You imagine that as soon as you turn your back it gives a sigh of relief and relaxes, as if it had been holding this immobile pose just for you.

These amazingly anatomically correct depictions of massively outsized animals in stylish black & white are the trade mark of the anonymous graffiti artist ROA, the only Belgian street artist to be included in *Art in the Streets*, the prestigious 2011 survey exhibition by the curator Jeffrey Deitch at the Museum of Contemporary Art in Los Angeles. This provided him with gilt-edged artistic credentials, since his work hung alongside that of such pioneers as Keith Haring, Shepard Fairey and Banksy. No other Belgian artist has worked abroad as much as ROA in recent years; usually out in the streets, but occasionally in the sheltered cocoon of galleries in London, Brussels and New York. The street is his natural biotope, it is here that he does drawings on walls several metres high, often from a hydraulic platform, armed with a paint roller and spray can.

ROA learned his craft on the street too, as a young graffitist working at night in Ghent in the late 1980s. There are hardly any traces left of his earliest work, which the man in the street and municipal officials invariably classified as 'vandalism'. Graffiti exists exclusively in the here and now, and what is created today may tomorrow already be removed by a cleaning team or overpainted by an unscrupulous rival. Later, a half-ruined overgrown factory in the Ghent area served as his studio. While he luxuriated in its almost hallowed silence, interrupted only by the hissing of spray cans and the chirruping of sparrows, he refined his style by decorating the walls with all manner of running, crawling, swimming and flying creatures. But the street remains his preferred canvas, because there his work becomes a part of the lives of local residents, and attracts the attention of chance passers-by. As he tells us: 'They are first surprised, shocked or charmed, but gradually they start to relate to it'.

ROA does not choose his subjects at random, he researches the indigenous species of the country he is travelling to, although he never knows in advance exactly what he will be painting - it depends on the location, the local people, and the inspiration of the moment. An iguana in Puerto Rico, an anteater in Jamaica, elephants and rhinoceroses in Johannesburg, seals in San Francisco, crocodiles and tortoises in Australia, magpies, beavers and rabbits in the moribund village of Doel in the Antwerp polder, a slender kid with an arrogant look in its eye in the Walloon village of Tourinnes-la-Grosse. And elsewhere rats, wild boar, bulls and beetles. Sometimes all that's left on their bones is rotting flesh, sometimes none at all, and then this creature of three metres by eight turns into an imposing ode to mortality. 'The way of all flesh' would make a good tag line to accompany his steadily expanding oeuvre.

ROA's work sometimes inflames local feelings. A civil servant in the London borough of Hackney wanted to have the rabbit that ROA had planted on the side of a café removed (paint is paint after all), but a petition signed by the locals put a stop to it. In the American city of Rochester, a number of sick minds saw a pornographic posture in the cuddly pose adopted by two sleeping bears, which led to some furious argument. Once in a while he makes a statement in paint. In 2013 the Norwegian city of Stavanger, home of the annual Nuart Festival, was treated to a whale chopped up into slices - an artistic harpoon through the host country's heart. That year Norway had caught a record number of whales. In 2014 he painted a three-storey-high

London © ROA.

Rome © ROA

bear cub in Rome, with a stun dart in its paw, a reference to the death of the wild brown bear called Daniza, which was killed after it had attacked a mushroom-picker (the bear had just wanted to protect her cubs).

'I don't make the world any better, at most I make it a little more interesting', as ROA once said, 'It's nice when people take my work seriously, because I take it extremely seriously myself, but on the other hand it's no more than paint on a wall'. But it's paint which - when you zoom right out - amuses, makes you reflect, and even moves you.

KRISTOFF TILKIN
Translated by Gregory Ball

Adriaen de Vries
'The Most Famous Modeller-Artist of All'

'A sculptor has come from Florence, with whom we have negotiated for months and who is now working very contentedly... He is a Dutchman of thirty years old. ... Please God he shall meet our expectations.' The sculptor spoken of with such great anticipation in this 1586 letter is Adriaen de Vries (1556-1626). At the time he had been in the service of Pompeo Leoni in Milan for just one week. Leoni ran one of the largest sculpture workshops in Europe. He had engaged De Vries to work on one of the most prestigious sculpture projects of the era: the high altar for the Escorial, King Philip II's palace near Madrid. De Vries made three of the fifteen life-sized bronze statues that adorn the high altar. At that time he had already been in Italy for five years or so. In about 1580 we find him in Florence, where he gained his first experience of work in the service of Giambologna (Jean de Boulogne), who originated from what is now French Flanders and was a celebrated sculptor to the Medici. The work of Giambologna and Leoni played a decisive role in the successful career De Vries could look forward to.

Adriaen de Vries, *Bacchus Discovering Ariadne on Naxos*, Prague, c. 1611, bronze © Rijksmuseum, Amsterdam.

Adriaen de Vries was born in The Hague, the son of a prosperous pharmacist. He must have left his native country for Italy sometime around 1575-1580. For an ambitious artist it was of great importance to spend time studying in the birthplace of the Renaissance: it considerably improved his career prospects and provided opportunities to join the service of a foreign ruler. In the sixteenth century, a conspicuously large number of artists from the Netherlands expressed this ambition; in Italy these 'northern foreigners' were for convenience's sake called *fiamminghi* (Flemings), a collective name for everyone from the Low Countries. This nickname was also applied to De Vries, even though he signed his name proudly with the Latin appendage *Hagiensis Batavus* (Hollander from The Hague).

De Vries's great talent did not go unnoticed. Via Turin, where he obtained his first independent post

as court sculptor to Duke Carlo Emanuele I of Savoy, he ended up at the court of Emperor Rudolf II in Prague in 1589. The Prague court was the absolute cultural hotspot north of the Alps at that time and the eccentric emperor was the most important Maecenas of his day. Rudolf had brought many leading artists together there, often originating from the Netherlands, but he had so far lacked a first-rate sculptor at his court. De Vries immediately handed over his visiting card in the form of two finely-crafted monumental statues with which he entirely lived up to his reputation as a prominent sculptor of bronze. With his *Mercury Abducting Psyche* (1593), which is now in the Louvre in Paris, he demonstrated that he could make two figures 'float in the air' and offer a fine outline from every angle.

Apart from an interval of several years in Rome and Augsburg (1594-1601) - where he made two fountains which can still be seen there - Adriaen de

Vries spent the rest of his life in Prague. The fountains in Augsburg made a substantial contribution to his fame: they led the Danish King Christian IV to commission a fountain too, in 1613, for the forecourt of his Frederiksborg Castle. However, the bronze sculptures of this watery monument dedicated to Neptune, the god of the sea, were plundered by the Swedes as early as 1659. One of them, a *Triton* that originally spouted water from the edge of the basin, is now in the Rijksmuseum in Amsterdam. After this intermezzo in Augsburg, De Vries returned to Prague. From then on he produced a lot of work for Rudolf's collections - partly to glorify imperial power, partly as works of art in their own right: portraits and allegories, and also works of an erotic-mythological nature. The relief entitled *Bacchus Discovering Ariadne on Naxos*, which must have been made for the emperor in about 1611, is typical of this sensually stimulating 'Rudolfian' art. We see the athletic Bacchus dashing at full speed into the bedroom of the gracefully slumbering Ariadne under the watchful eye of a small Amor. It is not hard to guess what follows...

After the death of Rudolf II in 1612, Prague soon lost its status as the capital of European culture, but this did no harm to De Vries's career. On the contrary, the last ten years of his life saw the creation of some of his most radical works; they are characterised by an increasingly sketchy and virtuoso style of modelling and by extremely dynamic compositions. The best illustration of this is the 1626 *Bacchant* - De Vries's last work - recently acquired by the Rijksmuseum. This bronze is the masterly conclusion to a majestic oeuvre and confirms Adriaen de Vries's reputation as 'the most famous modeller-artist of all', as he was justifiably labelled in 1620.

FRITS SCHOLTEN
Translated by Gregory Ball

Adriaen de Vries, *Triton*, Prague, c. 1615-1618, bronze
© Rijksmuseum, Amsterdam (given on loan by the National-museum, Stockholm)

Contributors

Eline Van Assche
Editor
eline_vanassche@yahoo.com

Abdelkader Benali
Writer
abenali@xs4all.nl

Paul Binding
Writer and Critic
paulbinding@yahoo.co.uk

Derek Blyth
Journalist
derekblyth@lycos.com

Kurt De Boodt
Poet and critic
kurt.de.boodt@telenet.be

Marleen Brock
Historian
mmjbrock@gmail.com

Ernst Bruinsma
Editor
e.bruinsma@afuk.nl

R.C. Van Caenegem
Em. Professor of History
roger.van.wynsberge@telenet.be

Dorothee Cappelle
Administrative Secretary Ons Erfdeel vzw
adm2@onserfdeel.be

Pieter Coupé
Secretary Ons Erfdeel. Vlaams-
Nederlands cultureel tijdschrift
onserfdeel@onserfdeel.be

Kris Deschouwer
Professor in Political Science
Kris.Deschouwer@vub.ac.be

Luc Devoldere
Chief Editor Ons Erfdeel vzw
luc.devoldere@onserfdeel.be

Lindsay Edwards
Translator
LindsayEdwards@gmx.net

Piet Gerbrandy
Poet and Critic
psgerb@xs4all.nl

Toon Horsten
Critic
Toon.Horsten@stripgids.org

Jan Van Hove
Art Critic
Jan.van.hove@standaard.be

Jaap Huisman
Architecture Critic
huismanjaap22@gmail.com

Frederike Huygen
Critic
f.huygen@xs4all.nl

Florine Koning
Communication Advisor
info@scripteq.nl

Ruud Koole
Professor in Political Science
Koole@fsw.leidenuniv.nl

Ariejan Korteweg
Journalist
a.korteweg@volkskrant.nl

Christiane Kuby
Translator
christiane.kuby@planet.nl

Tom Lanoye
Writer
tom@lanoye.be

Philippe Noble
Translator
noblephilippe@gmail.com

Mirjam Noorduijn
Critic
mirjamnoorduijn@planet.nl

Liza Noteris
Critic
liza.noteris@gmail.com

Cyrille Offermans
Writer and Critic
cyrilleoffermans@home.nl

Ewald Pironet
Journalist
ewald.pironet@gmail.com

Tineke Reijnders
Critic
tineker@xs4all.nl

Richtje Reinsma
Critic
richtje.reinsma@gmail.com

Matthijs de Ridder
Writer and Critic
matthderidder@gmail.com

Reinier Salverda
Honorary Professor of Dutch
reiniersalverda@yahoo.co.uk

Mark Schaevers
Writer and Journalist
mark.schaevers@telenet.be

Frits Scholten

Art Historian

f.scholten@rijksmuseum.nl

Jelle Schot

Film Critic

jelleschot@hotmail.com

Gary Schwartz

Art Historian

Gary.Schwartz@xs4all.nl

Manfred Sellink

General director and head curator, Royal
Museum of Fine Arts, Antwerp

manfred.sellink@kmska.be

Dirk Steenhaut

Journalist

dirk_steenhaut@hotmail.com

Bart Tijskens

Music Critic

bart.tijskens@vrt.be

Kristoff Tilkin

Journalist and Critic

kristoff.tilkin@humo.be

Paul Vincent

Translator

paulfrankvincent@gmail.com

Hendrik Vos

Professor of European Studies

hendrik.vos@Ugent.be

Jeroen Vullings

Critic

jeroen.vullings@me.com

Bonny Wassing

Lector Dutch

bonny@xs4all.nl

Translators

Anna Asbury
Gregory Ball
Pleuke Boyce
Sheila M. Dale
Lindsay Edwards
Yvette Mead
Zoe Perot
Jonathan Reeder
Julian Ross
Paul Vincent

Advisors on English usage
Lindsay Edwards (Belgium)
Elisabeth Salverda (United Kingdom)

Colophon

Institution

This twenty-fourth yearbook is pub-lished by the Flemish-Dutch cultural institution 'Ons Erfdeel vzw', with the support of the Dutch Ministry of Education, Culture and Science (The Hague), the Flemish Authorities (Brussels) and the Provinces of West and East Flanders.

In association with

'Ons Erfdeel vzw' also publishes the Dutch-language periodical *Ons Erfdeel* and the French-language periodical *Septentrion. Arts, lettres et culture de Flandre et des Pays-Bas,* the bilingual yearbook *De Franse Neder-landen – Les Pays-Bas Français* and a series of books in several languages covering various aspects of the culture of the Low Countries.

The Board of Directors of 'Ons Erfdeel vzw'

President:
Herman Balthazar

Managing Director:
Luc Devoldere

Directors:
Bert De Graeve
Patrick Kindt
Hilde Laga
Mark Leysen
Marita Mathijsen
Frits van Oostrom
Danny De Raymaeker
Paul Schnabel
Adriaan van der Staay
Ludo Verhoeven

Honorary President:
Philip Houben

Address of the Editorial Board and the Administration

'Ons Erfdeel vzw', Murissonstraat 260,
8930 Rekkem, Flanders, Belgium
T +32 56 41 12 01, F +32 56 41 47 07
www.onserfdeel.be, www.onserfdeel.nl
thelowcountriesblog.onserfdeel.be
VAT BE 0410.723.635

Philippe Vanwalleghem *Head of Administration*
Dorothee Cappelle *Administrative Secretary*

Aims

With *The Low Countries,* a yearbook founded by Jozef Deleu (Chief Editor from 1993 until 2002), the editors and publisher aim to present to the world the culture and society of the Dutch-speaking area which embraces both the Netherlands and Flanders, the northern part of Belgium.

The articles in this yearbook survey the living, contemporary culture of the Low Countries as well as their cultural heritage. In its words and pictures *The Low Countries* provides informa-tion about literature and the arts, but also about broad social and historical developments in Flanders and the Netherlands.

The culture of Flanders and the Netherlands is not an isolated phenomenon; its development over the centuries has been one of continuous interaction with the outside world. In conse-quence the yearbook also pays due attention to the centuries-old continuing cultural interplay between the Low Countries and the world beyond their borders.

By drawing attention to the diversity, vitality and international dimension of the culture of Flanders and the Netherlands, *The Low Countries* hopes to contribute to a lively dialogue between them and other cultures.

ISSN 0779-5815
ISBN 978-90-79705-245
Statutory deposit no. D/2016/3006/1
NUR 612

Copyright © 2016 'Ons Erfdeel vzw' and SABAM Belgium 2016
Printed by die Keure, Bruges, Flanders, Belgium
Design by Stelvio D'Houst (die Keure)

Prices for the yearbook 2016, no. 24

Belgium € 37, The Netherlands € 39, Europe € 39

Other Countries: € 45
All prices inclusive of shipping costs

You can order this book from our webshop at www.onserfdeel.be and pay by credit card

As well as the yearbook
The Low Countries,
the Flemish Netherlands
Institution 'Ons Erfdeel vzw'
publishes a number of books
covering various aspects of
the culture of Flanders and
the Netherlands.

Wim Daniëls
Talking Dutch.
Illustrated; 80 pp.

J.A. Kossmann-Putto &
E.H. Kossmann
The Low Countries.
History of the Northern
and Southern Netherlands.
Illustrated; 64 pp.

Isabella Lanz &
Katie Verstockt,
Contemporary Dance
in the Low Countries.
Illustrated; 128 pp.

Mark Delaere &
Emile Wennekes,
Contemporary Music in
the Low Countries.
Illustrated; 128 pp.

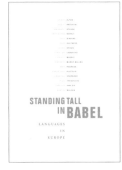

Standing Tall in Babel.
Languages in Europe.
Sixteen European writers
about their mother tongues.
Hardcover; 144 pp.

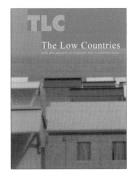

Between 1993 and 2015
twenty-three issues of the
yearbook *The Low Countries*
have been published.

EUROPE

NORTH
SEA

GRONINGEN
•Groningen
Leeuwarden
FRIESLAND
Assen
DRENTHE
NORTH
HOLLAND
FLEVOLAND
Lelystad
•Zwolle
Haarlem
OVERIJSSEL
•AMSTERDAM
The Hague
Utrecht
SOUTH
HOLLAND
UTRECHT
GELDERLAND
Arnhem
ZEELAND
Middelburg
's-Hertogenbosch
NORTH BRABANT
LIMBURG
Antwerp
ANTWERP
LIMBURG
Bruges•
EAST
WEST
Ghent
Hasselt
FLANDERS
FLANDERS
FLEMISH BRABANT
Maastricht
GERMANY
BRUSSELS
•Leuven
•Wavre
WALLOON BRABANT
Liège
HAINAUT
LIÈGE
FRANCE
Mons
Namur
NAMUR
LUXEMBOURG
LUX.
Arlon

0   km   50

© Carto

	Dutch language area
	French language area in Belgium
	Brussels bilingual area: Dutch and French
	German language area in Belgium
	Bilingual area : Dutch and Frisian
◉	Capital city
•	Provincial capital
—	National frontier
······	Provincial Boundary